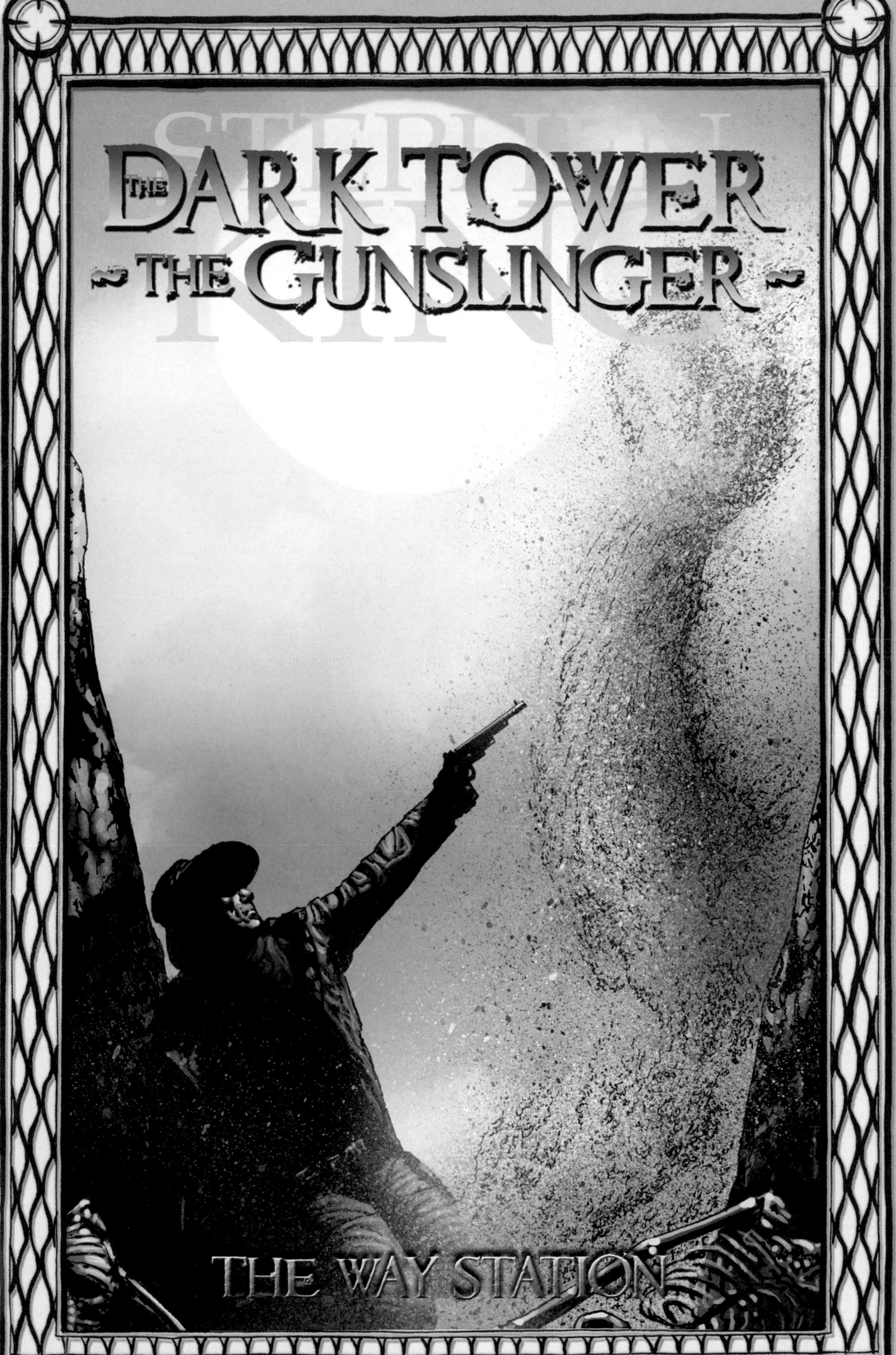
THE DARK TOWER
THE GUNSLINGER
THE WAY STATION

THE DARK TOWER
~THE GUNSLINGER~

THE WAY STATION

CREATIVE DIRECTOR AND EXECUTIVE DIRECTOR
STEPHEN KING

PLOTTING AND CONSULTATION
ROBIN FURTH

SCRIPT
PETER DAVID

ARTIST
LAURENCE CAMPBELL

COLOR ART
RICHARD ISANOVE

LETTERING
VC'S JOE SABINO

PRODUCTION
MAYELA GUTIERREZ

COVER ART
LAURENCE CAMPBELL & RICHARD ISANOVE

DARK TOWER: THE GUNSLINGER — THE WAY STATION. Contains material originally published in magazine form as DARK TOWER: THE GUNSLINGER — THE WAY STATION #1-5. First printing 2012. ISBN# 978-0-7851-4935-4. Published by MARVEL WORLDWIDE, INC., a subsidiary of MARVEL ENTERTAINMENT, LLC. OFFICE OF PUBLICATION: 135 West 50th Street, New York, NY 10020. Copyright © 2011 and 2012 Stephen King. All rights reserved. $24.99 per copy in the U.S. and $27.99 in Canada (GST #R127032852); Canadian Agreement #40668537. All characters featured in this issue and the distinctive names and likenesses thereof, and all related indicia are trademarks of Stephen King. No similarity between any of the names, characters, persons, and/or institutions in this magazine with those of any living or dead person or institution is intended, and any such similarity which may exist is purely coincidental. Marvel and its logos are TM & © Marvel Characters, Inc. **Printed in the U.S.A.** ALAN FINE, EVP - Office of the President, Marvel Worldwide, Inc. and EVP & CMO Marvel Characters B.V.; DAN BUCKLEY, Publisher & President - Print, Animation & Digital Divisions; JOE QUESADA, Chief Creative Officer; TOM BREVOORT, SVP of Publishing; DAVID BOGART, SVP of Operations & Procurement, Publishing; RUWAN JAYATILLEKE, SVP & Associate Publisher, Publishing; C.B. CEBULSKI, SVP of Creator & Content Development; DAVID GABRIEL, SVP of Publishing Sales & Circulation; MICHAEL PASCIULLO, SVP of Brand Planning & Communications; JIM O'KEEFE, VP of Operations & Logistics; DAN CARR, Executive Director of Publishing Technology; SUSAN CRESPI, Editorial Operations Manager; ALEX MORALES, Publishing Operations Manager; STAN LEE, Chairman Emeritus. For information regarding advertising in Marvel Comics or on Marvel.com, please contact John Dokes, SVP Integrated Sales and Marketing, at jdokes@marvel.com. For Marvel subscription inquiries, please call 800-217-9158. **Manufactured between 4/30/2012 and 5/28/2012 by R.R. DONNELLEY, INC., SALEM, VA, USA.**

10 9 8 7 6 5 4 3 2 1

ASSISTANT EDITORS
RACHEL PINNELAS & JON MOISAN

CONSULTING EDITOR
RALPH MACCHIO

EDITOR
SANA AMANAT

COLLECTION EDITOR
MARK D. BEAZLEY

ASSISTANT EDITORS
NELSON RIBEIRO & ALEX STARBUCK

EDITOR, SPECIAL PROJECTS
JENNIFER GRÜNWALD

SENIOR EDITOR, SPECIAL PROJECTS
JEFF YOUNGQUIST

SENIOR VICE PRESIDENT OF SALES
DAVID GABRIEL

SVP OF BRAND PLANNING & COMMUNICATIONS
MICHAEL PASCIULLO

ASSOCIATE PUBLISHER & SVP, PRINT, ANIMATION and Digital Media
RUWAN JAYATILLEKE

BOOK DESIGN
PATRICK MCGRATH

EDITOR IN CHIEF
AXEL ALONSO

CHIEF CREATIVE OFFICER
JOE QUESADA

PUBLISHER
DAN BUCKLEY

SPECIAL THANKS TO
CHUCK VERRILL, MARSHA DEFILIPPO, BARBARA ANN MCINTYRE, BRIAN STARK,
JIM NAUSEDAS, JIM MCCANN, ARUNE SINGH, JEFF SUTER, JOHN BARBER, LAUREN
SANKOVITCH, MIKE HORWITZ, CHARLIE BECKERMAN & CHRIS ELIOPOULOS

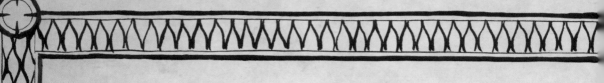

Dear Fellow Constant Readers,

Welcome to *The Way Station*. Like *The Journey Begins* and *The Battle of Tull*, this arc is an adaptation of an early section of *The Gunslinger*. For those of you who are interested in literary history, both of the chapters adapted here were originally published as short stories in *The Magazine of Fantasy and Science Fiction* during the 1980s. "The Way Station" was published in 1980, and "The Oracle of the Mountains" appeared in 1981. Sounds like a long time ago? Well, I suppose it was. But then again, we all know that our wandering gunslinger transcends time!

As fans of the original novel will recognize, our present tale is much longer than the corresponding section found in *The Gunslinger*. The first issue you now hold in your hands spans more than twenty pages, whereas the original is only four and a half pages long. How in the world did we manage to expand our tale so much? Well, that has to do with the art of transforming words into images.

First of all, let's take a look at the original section, written by the King himself. "The Way Station," which is Chapter 2 of *The Gunslinger*, begins as follows:

A nursery rhyme had been playing itself through his mind all day, the maddening kind of thing that will not let go, that mockingly ignores all commands of the conscious mind to cease and desist. The rhyme was:

The rain in Spain falls on the plain.

He . . . knew why the rhyme had occurred to him in the first place. There had been the recurring dream of his room in the castle and of his mother, who had sung it to him as he lay solemnly in the tiny bed by the window of many colors . . . she sang to him at naptimes and he could remember the heavy gray rainlight that shivered into rainbows on the counterpane; he could feel the coolness of the room and the heavy warmth of blankets, love for his mother and her red lips, the haunting melody of the little nonsense lyric, and her voice.

Now it came back maddeningly, like a dog chasing its own tail . . . All his water was gone, and he knew he was very likely a dead man . . . Since noon he had been watching his feet rather than the way ahead. Out here even the devil-grass had grown stunted and yellow. The hardpan had disintegrated in places to mere rubble. The mountains were not noticeably clearer, although sixteen days had passed since he had left the hut of the last homesteader, a loony-sane young man on the edge of the desert . . .

The beauty of this passage comes from its immediacy. It is almost as if we, as readers, are sitting inside Roland's mind, listening to his thoughts. We hear the nursery rhyme, and then we have a brief but vivid flash of Roland's childhood bedroom, and of his mother, singing to him. Suddenly, we cut to the present. Roland is staring at the stunted devil grass growing all around him, and the rubble-strewn hardpan. We learn that he has been traveling for sixteen days, and that the last person he saw was a desert dweller named Brown. As the section progresses, we watch Roland stagger, fall, and get up again. He is too proud to die on his knees. All gunslingers know pride — the invisible bone that keeps the neck stiff. The importance of pride was drilled into Roland by his father, and was beaten into him by his scarred old teacher, Cort.

Until the very end of these four and a half pages, when Roland comes upon the Way Station and the strange, ghostly figure he sees there, our gunslinger is trudging forward in a landscape that is dry and monotonous. Very little actually happens around him, save for his slow but steady progress across the hardpan. What keeps us glued to the page is Roland's powerful internal monologue — a monologue punctuated by brief, hallucinatory memories and a driving, desperate thirst. Yet how do we, as comic book writers, transform internal monologue into vivid action?

When I began this adaptation, I had a long debate with myself. What would be the best way to transform Roland's opening internal monologue into a dynamic visual story? How could I get across the power of the original, while also weaving in the subtle nuances that come from a chapter being part of a longer tale? It seemed to me that I had a very clear decision to make. I could either cut the scene down to its bare bones and begin with Roland trudging across the desert, or I could try a riskier approach, one that attempted to bring Roland's internal monologue to life while simultaneously playing on the original novel's use of flashback, doubling back, and déjà vu. As I said, the latter was a riskier approach, but I thought that if I could carry it off, then Peter, Laurence, and Richard would have a lot more room to fly and we'd do more justice to the scope of Stephen King's work. In the end, I chose risky over safe.

As with all tales, risky or not, I had to begin somewhere. So, I decided to begin at the beginning. Unfortunately I couldn't start with that iconic line, "The man in black fled across the desert, and the gunslinger followed." We had used that already, and on several occasions. However I felt I could play on the next major event of The Gunslinger, namely Roland's meeting with the desert dweller named Brown. As my fellow Constant Readers know, I had also used that scene once already (namely at the outset of The Journey Begins), but I did think there was room for me to play with it just once more. After all, such a doubling back would work very well with the themes that Stephen King wove into his 2003 rewrite of the novel.

As those of you who have read the revised edition of *The Gunslinger* know, Stephen King inserted three new front pages into the novel. On the first page is a quote from the novel *Look Homeward, Angel;* on the second is the lone number 19; and on the third is the single word RESUMPTION. In his brief introduction to *Wolves of the Calla*, Steve King tells us that RESUMPTION is the Gunslinger's new subtitle. In addition to this new subtitle of Resumption, Stephen King added an eerie sense of déjà vu to his tale. On several occasions in the 2003 rewrite, Roland experiences an uncanny feeling of familiarity with situations that are actually new to him, almost as if he has lived them before. At other times, he feels like the world around him is ephemeral or unreal, almost as if he cannot experience reality, or time, as other people do. In fact, in the revised opening sequence, Roland feels as if the world yawns open, becoming momentarily transparent. A few pages later, he articulates his sense that he is somehow untethered from reality—as if the rules that govern time and life for ordinary men do not apply to him.

We all know that Roland is not like ordinary men and women, but I thought that we, as a comic book team, could push our comics in the direction that Stephen King intended in his rewrite. If we could combine a sense of déjà vu with a sense of Roland being somehow exempt from the normal laws of time and space, we could recreate the scene in Brown's hut but also make it new. Not only would we be echoing the themes that Stephen King wove into his rewrite, but this scene would also allow us to recap our story so far, and to subtly inform new readers about the important concepts found in Mid-World—namely the cyclical nature of time and *ka*.

After the brief scene that takes place in Brown's hut, we move on to the bulk of the narrative, which takes place during Roland's trek across the desert. In the novel we're told that sixteen days pass between Roland leaving Brown's hut and Roland stumbling across the Way Station, so I couldn't help but wonder what happened during those lost days. If the sun and wind of the Mohaine were as unrelenting as they seemed, then Roland must have found water *somewhere* during that period, but where? Here's the note I inserted after Scene 1 (Roland Wakes up in Brown's Hut--Again), and before Scene 2 (The Desert):

NOTE: After leaving Brown's hut, Roland traveled for 16 days through the desert. Since in such hot, dry, and possibly windy conditions a man needs up to a gallon of water a day to stay healthy, there's no way that Roland could carry enough water with him to continue his journey. Hence, he needs to find water along the way. The first section of this story plays off of this need for water. Since Roland could only survive 3-5 days (at most) without anything to drink, I thought it would be interesting if we showed him finding water, and then slowly dehydrating and hallucinating . . .

The scene where Roland takes water from a dead man in the desert is actually adapted from Ingmar Bergman's fantastic film *The Seventh Seal*. In that tale, a wandering knight (who is a little bit like Roland) travels across a desolate landscape while playing a game of castles with his own man in black. The Dogan that Roland briefly visits (and where he is attacked by dogs) is based on a Dogan that he sees in the final book of the series. And by the way, Roland's dog meat feast is a joke for diehard fans of *The Wastelands*. Who can forget Roland stating that eating billy-bumbler meat is even worse than eating dog? And yes, our gunslinger admits that he HAS dined on pooch, so I thought it would be good to show when, and how! (Many thanks to Peter David for pointing out that our gunslinger really couldn't eat a dog that was possibly tainted with rabies, and for saving our bacon by finding a way to script through the dilemma!)

My favorite part of plotting the first issue was writing about Roland's hallucinations. Two brief sentences in the original novel sparked a whole scene in my mind. To me, there was a parallel between the burning sun and the window of many colors in Roland's childhood bedroom. Showing Gabrielle singing to her young son was a perfect way to recap Roland's matricide, and his guilt over his accidental murder of the woman who gave birth to him. And of course, this vision of Roland's mother had to turn deadly. The woman who betrayed the gunslingers to John Farson just *had* to become a symbol of the deadly desert—a living dust devil.

And so my dear friends, thanks again for traveling with us. Until next time, long days and pleasant nights!

All the best,
Robin Furth

This is your sigul, whispered the fading voice.
This is your promise that things may be different,
Roland — that there may yet be rest. Even salvation...
if you stand. If you are true.

STEPHEN KING

THE DARK TOWER
~ THE GUNSLINGER ~

THE WAY STATION

CHAPTER ONE

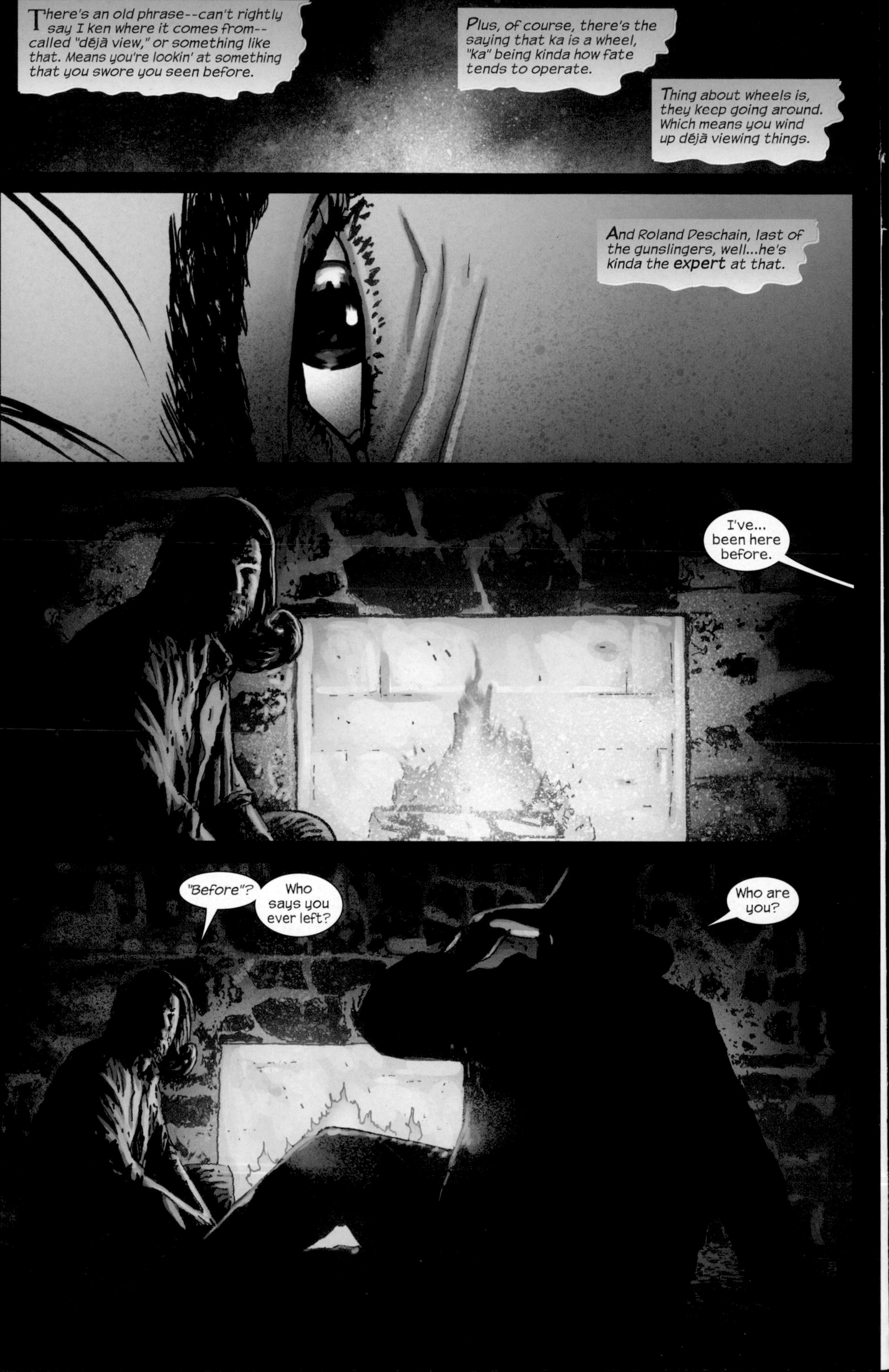
There's an old phrase--can't rightly say I ken where it comes from--called "dējā view," or something like that. Means you're lookin' at something that you swore you seen before.
Plus, of course, there's the saying that ka is a wheel, "ka" being kinda how fate tends to operate.
Thing about wheels is, they keep going around. Which means you wind up dējā viewing things.
And Roland Deschain, last of the gunslingers, well...he's kinda the **expert** at that.
I've... been here before.
"Before"?
Who says you ever left?
Who are you?

Brown. Same as I was yesterday, and will be tomorrow, most like.
This here's Zoltan, and he's likewise staying that way.
And... how came I here?
Usual way, I reckon. Then you told me a story, and then you fell asleep.
Which shouldn't be taken as a comment on the story's quality. Quite a yarn it was. *We* stayed awake.
It's...starting to come back to me. But I *left* this place.
Ages ago.
It's almost like...
Sorcery.
And I've known a sorcerer or two.

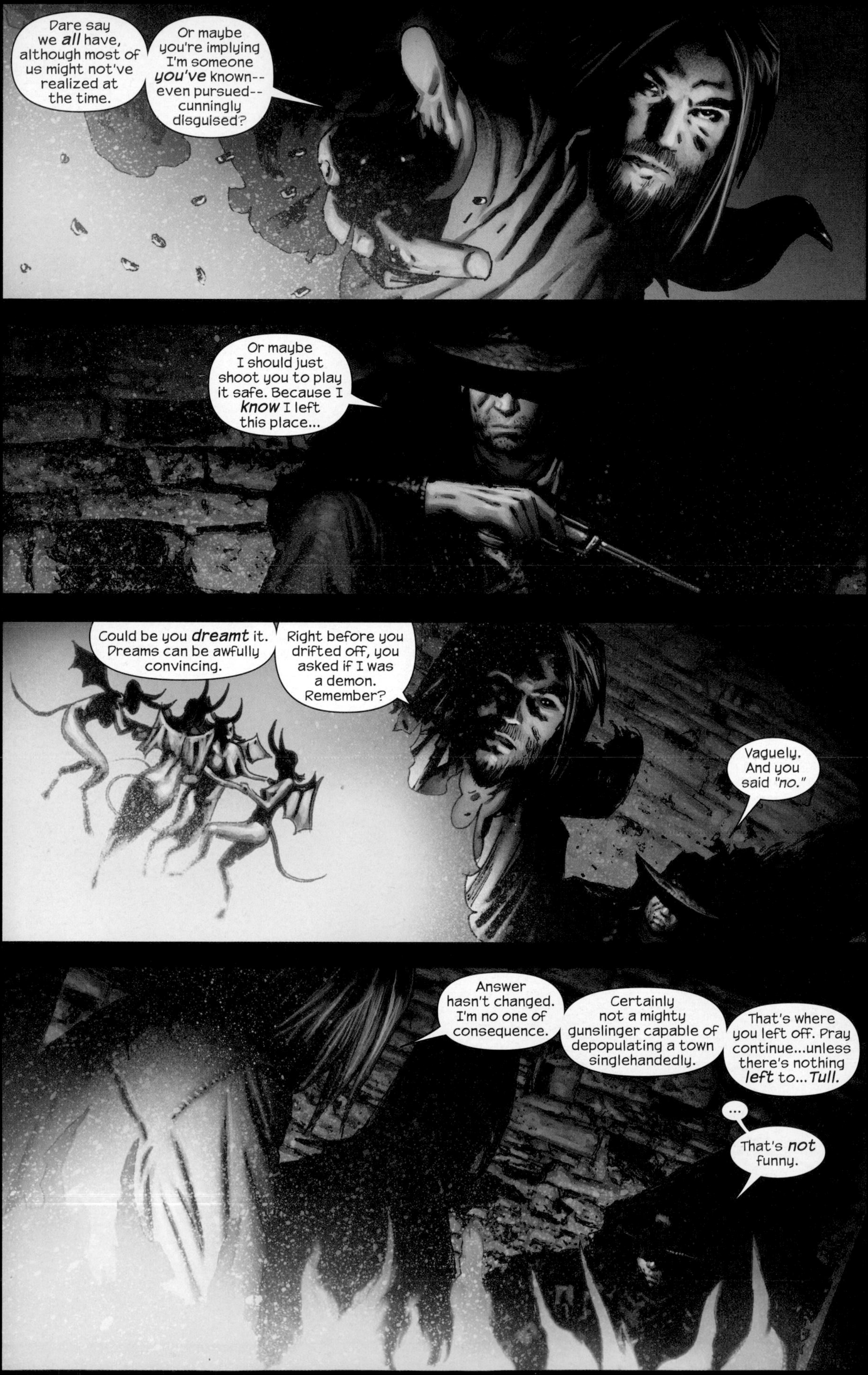
Dare say we *all* have, although most of us might not've realized at the time.
Or maybe you're implying I'm someone *you've* known--even pursued--cunningly disguised?
Or maybe I should just shoot you to play it safe. Because I *know* I left this place...
Could be you *dreamt* it. Dreams can be awfully convincing.
Right before you drifted off, you asked if I was a demon. Remember?
Vaguely. And you said "*no*."
Answer hasn't changed. I'm no one of consequence.
Certainly not a mighty gunslinger capable of depopulating a town singlehandedly.
That's where you left off. Pray continue...unless there's nothing *left* to... *Tull*.
...
That's *not* funny.

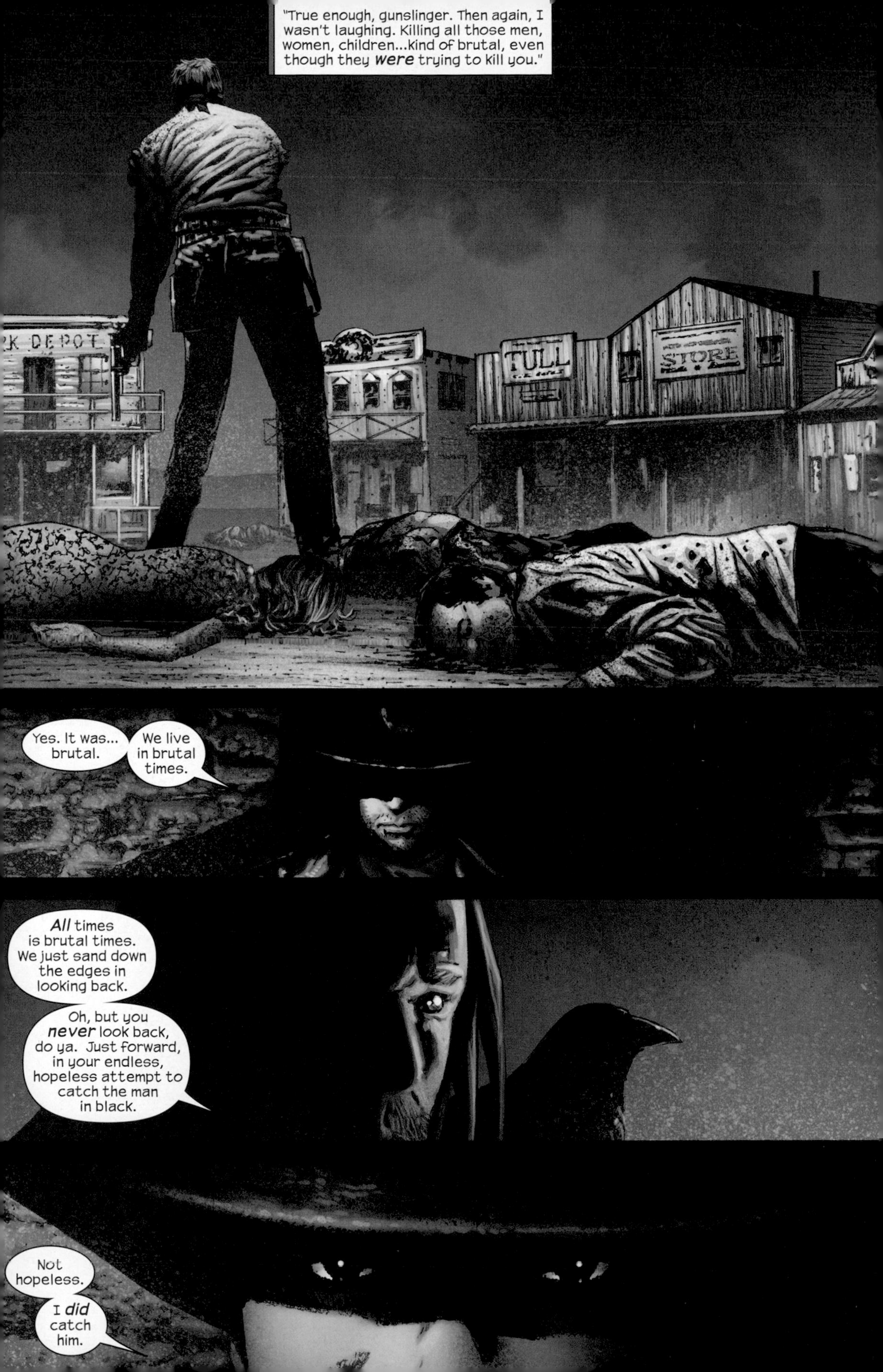
"True enough, gunslinger. Then again, I wasn't laughing. Killing all those men, women, children...kind of brutal, even though they *were* trying to kill you."
DEPOT
TULL
STORE
Yes. It was... brutal.
We live in brutal times.
All times is brutal times. We just sand down the edges in looking back.
Oh, but you *never* look back, do ya. Just forward, in your endless, hopeless attempt to catch the man in black.
Not hopeless.
I *did* catch him.

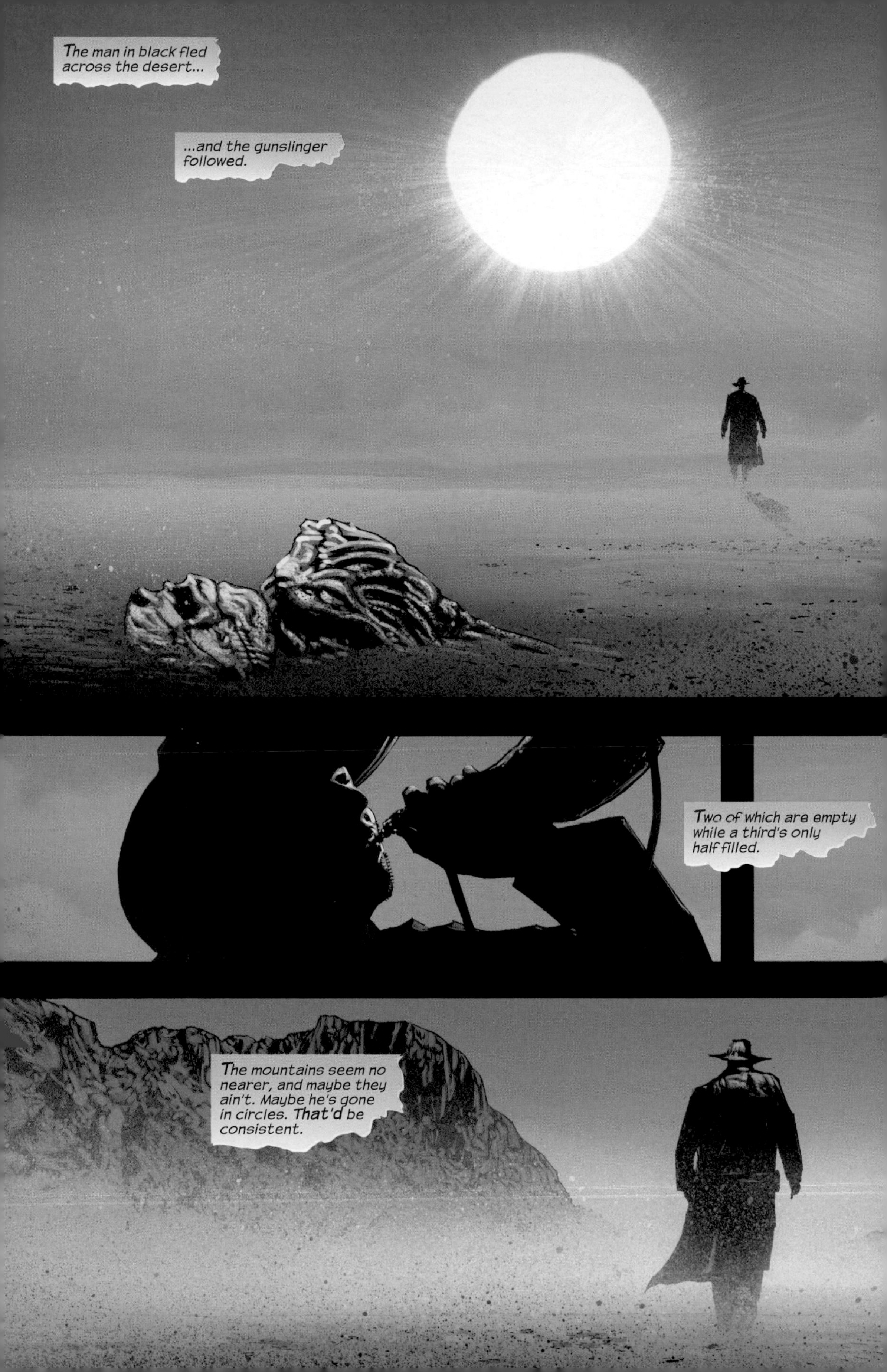
The man in black fled across the desert...
...and the gunslinger followed.
Two of which are empty while a third's only half filled.
The mountains seem no nearer, and maybe they ain't. Maybe he's gone in circles. That'd be consistent.

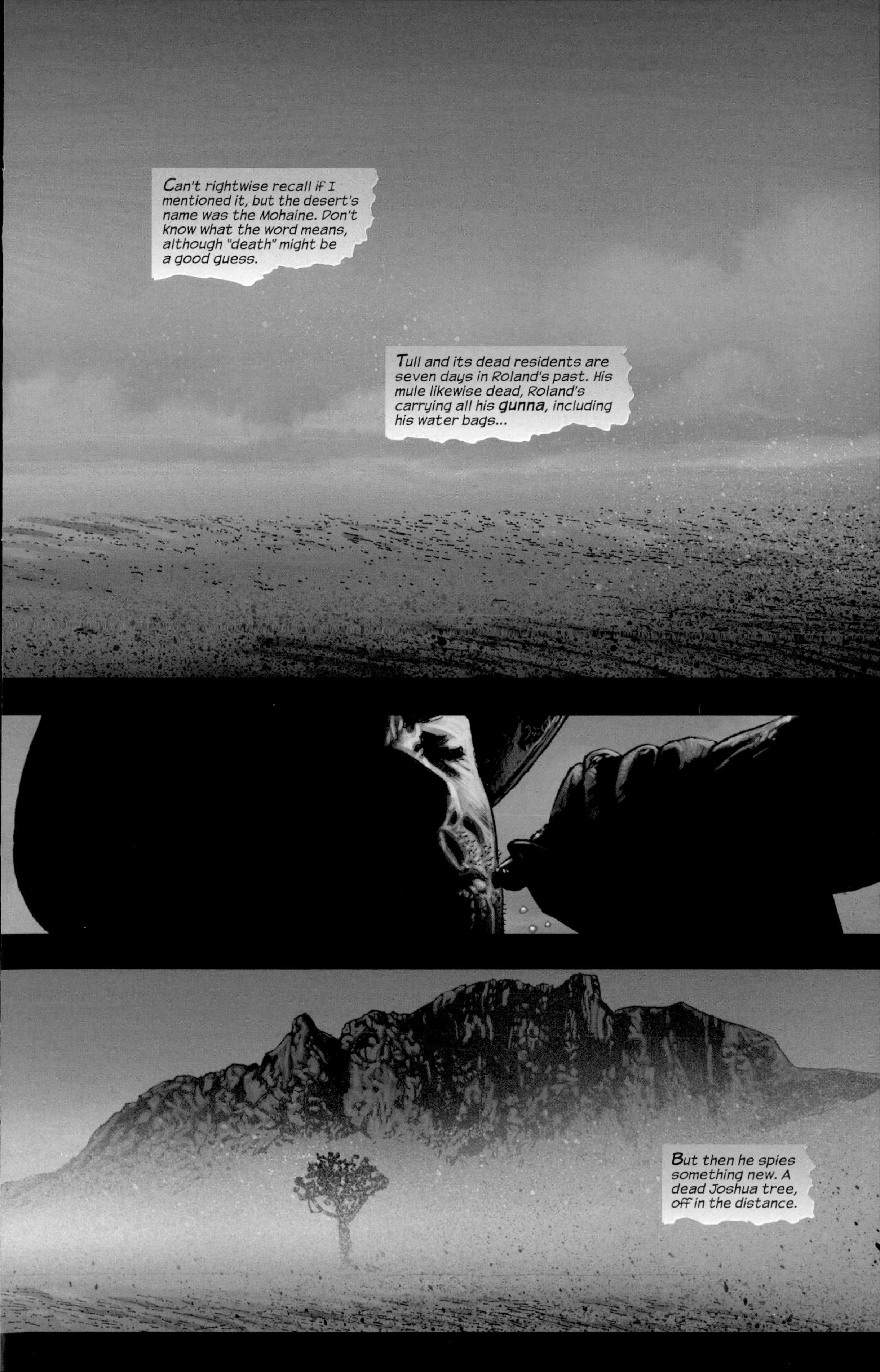
Can't rightwise recall if I mentioned it, but the desert's name was the Mohaine. Don't know what the word means, although "death" might be a good guess.
Tull and its dead residents are seven days in Roland's past. His mule likewise dead, Roland's carrying all his gunna, including his water bags...
But then he spies something new. A dead Joshua tree, off in the distance.

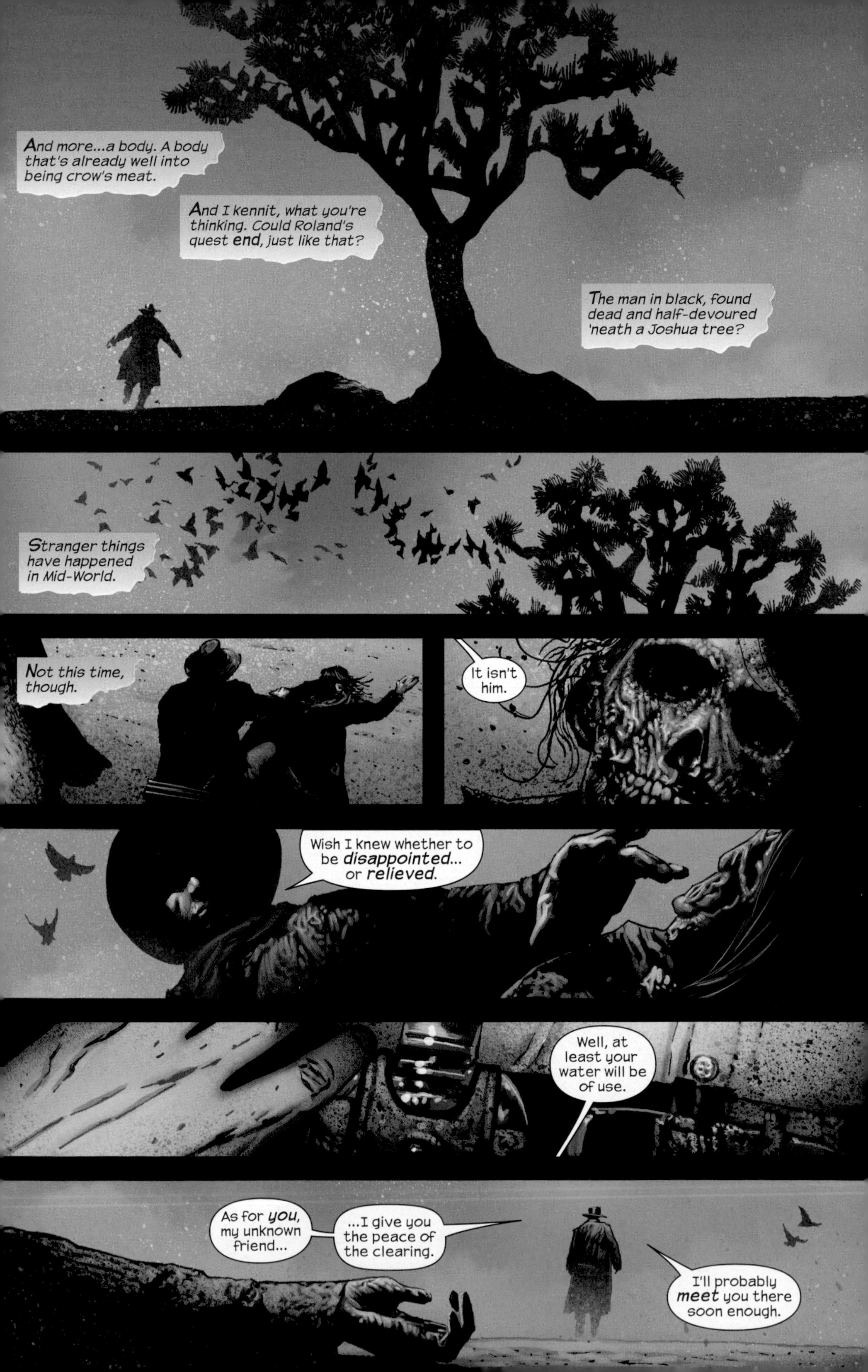
And more...a body. A body that's already well into being crow's meat.
And I kennit, what you're thinking. Could Roland's quest end, just like that?
The man in black, found dead and half-devoured 'neath a Joshua tree?
Stranger things have happened in Mid-World.
Not this time, though.
It isn't him.
Wish I knew whether to be disappointed... or relieved.
Well, at least your water will be of use.
As for you, my unknown friend...
...I give you the peace of the clearing.
I'll probably meet you there soon enough.

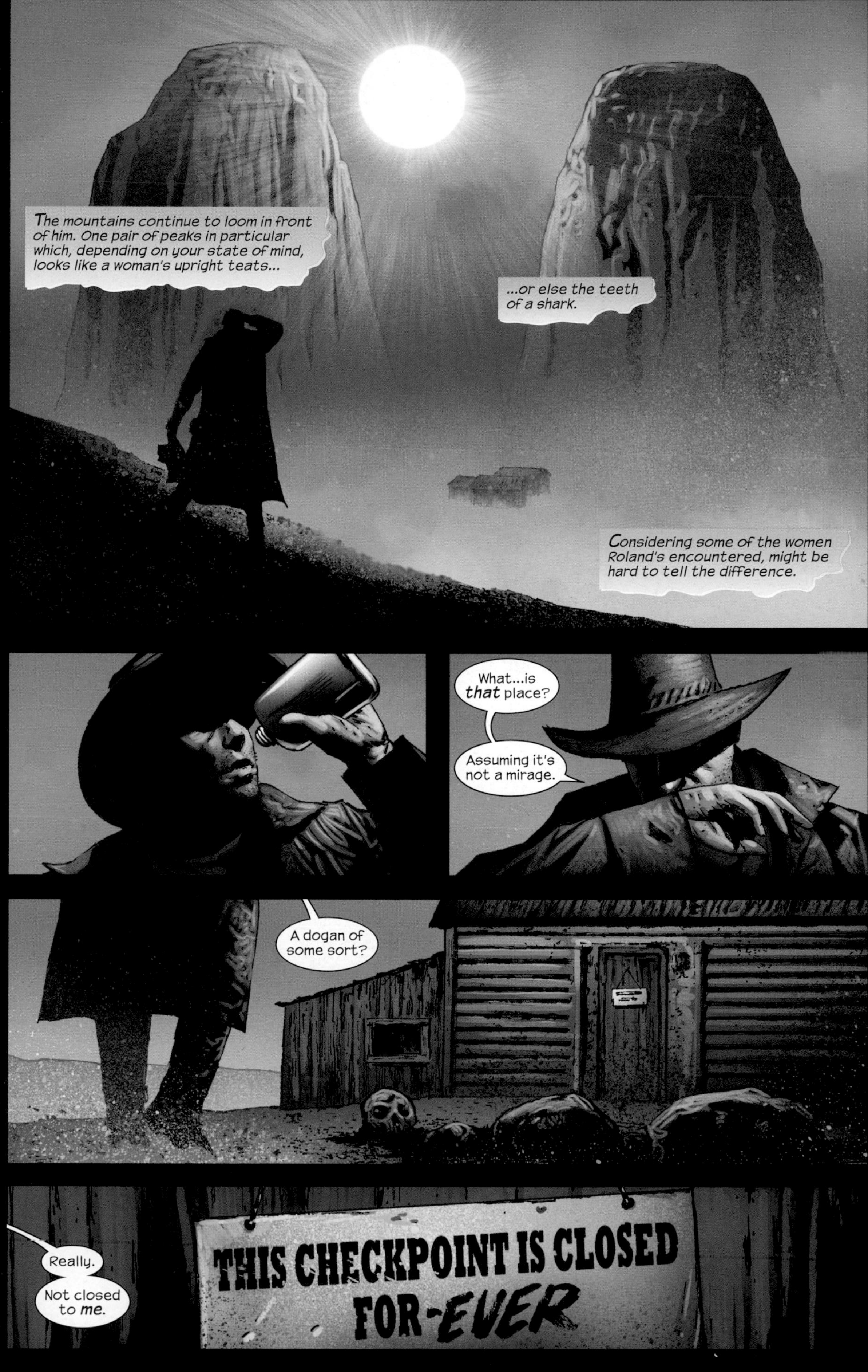

The mountains continue to loom in front of him. One pair of peaks in particular which, depending on your state of mind, looks like a woman's upright teats...
...or else the teeth of a shark.
Considering some of the women Roland's encountered, might be hard to tell the difference.
What...is *that* place?
Assuming it's not a mirage.
A dogan of some sort?
Really.
Not closed to *me*.
THIS CHECKPOINT IS CLOSED FOR-EVER

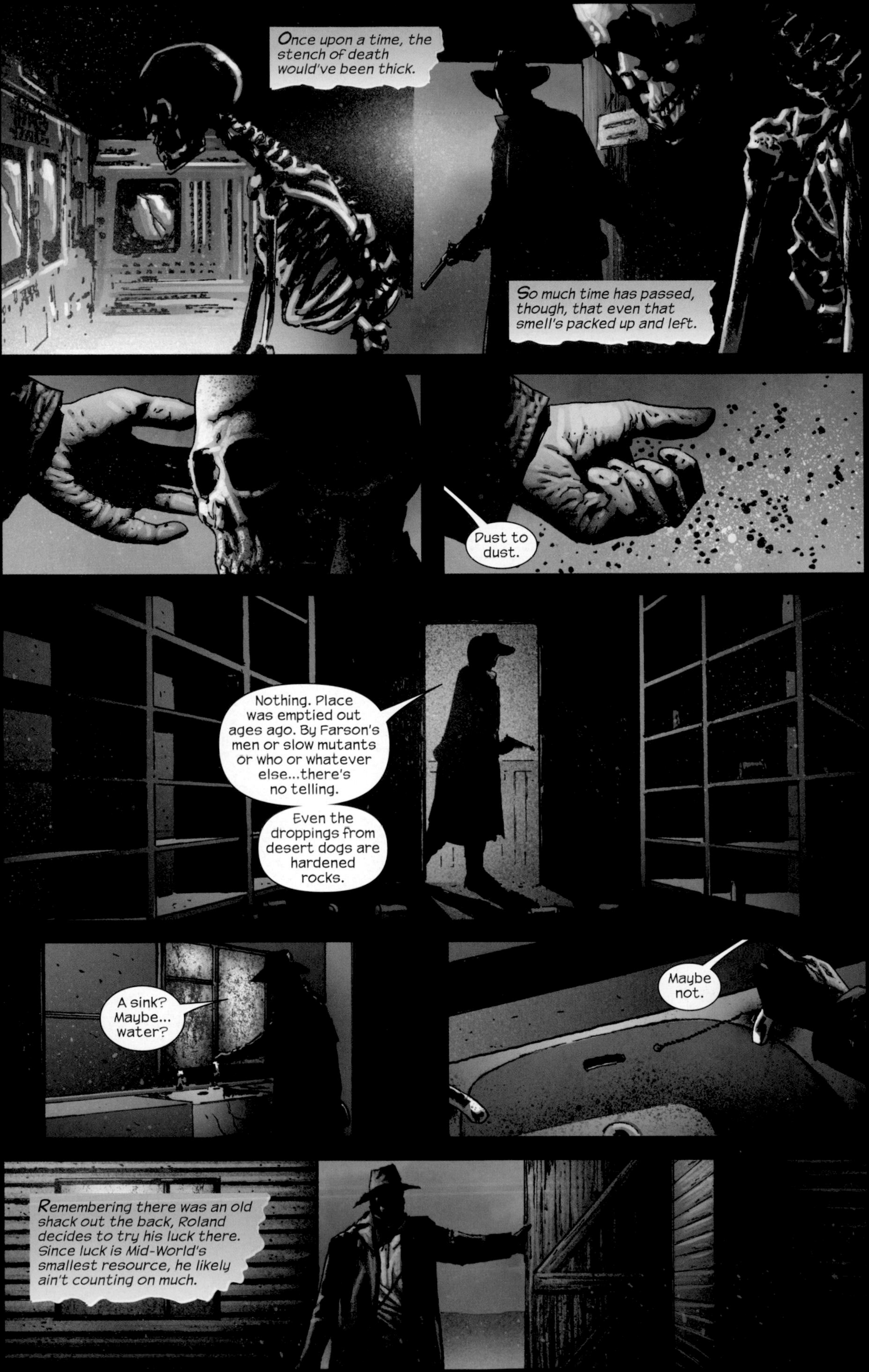
Once upon a time, the stench of death would've been thick.
So much time has passed, though, that even that smell's packed up and left.
Dust to dust.
Nothing. Place was emptied out ages ago. By Farson's men or slow mutants or who or whatever else...there's no telling.
Even the droppings from desert dogs are hardened rocks.
A sink? Maybe... water?
Maybe not.
Remembering there was an old shack out the back, Roland decides to try his luck there. Since luck is Mid-World's smallest resource, he likely ain't counting on much.

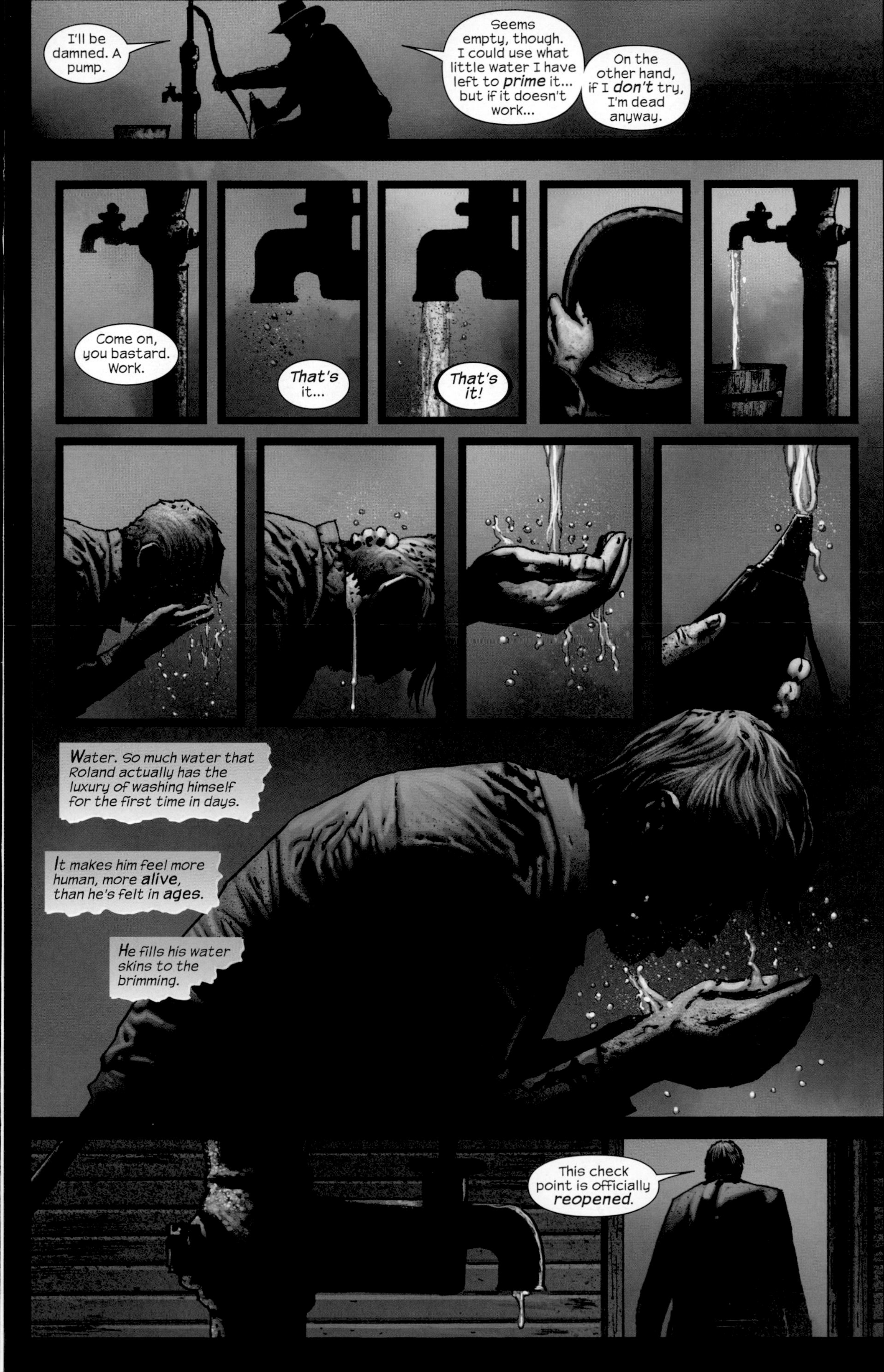
I'll be damned. A pump.
Seems empty, though. I could use what little water I have left to *prime* it... but if it doesn't work...
On the other hand, if I *don't* try, I'm dead anyway.
Come on, you bastard. Work.
That's it...
That's it!
Water. So much water that Roland actually has the luxury of washing himself for the first time in days.
It makes him feel more human, more ***alive****, than he's felt in* ***ages****.*
He fills his water skins to the brimming.
This check point is officially ***reopened***.

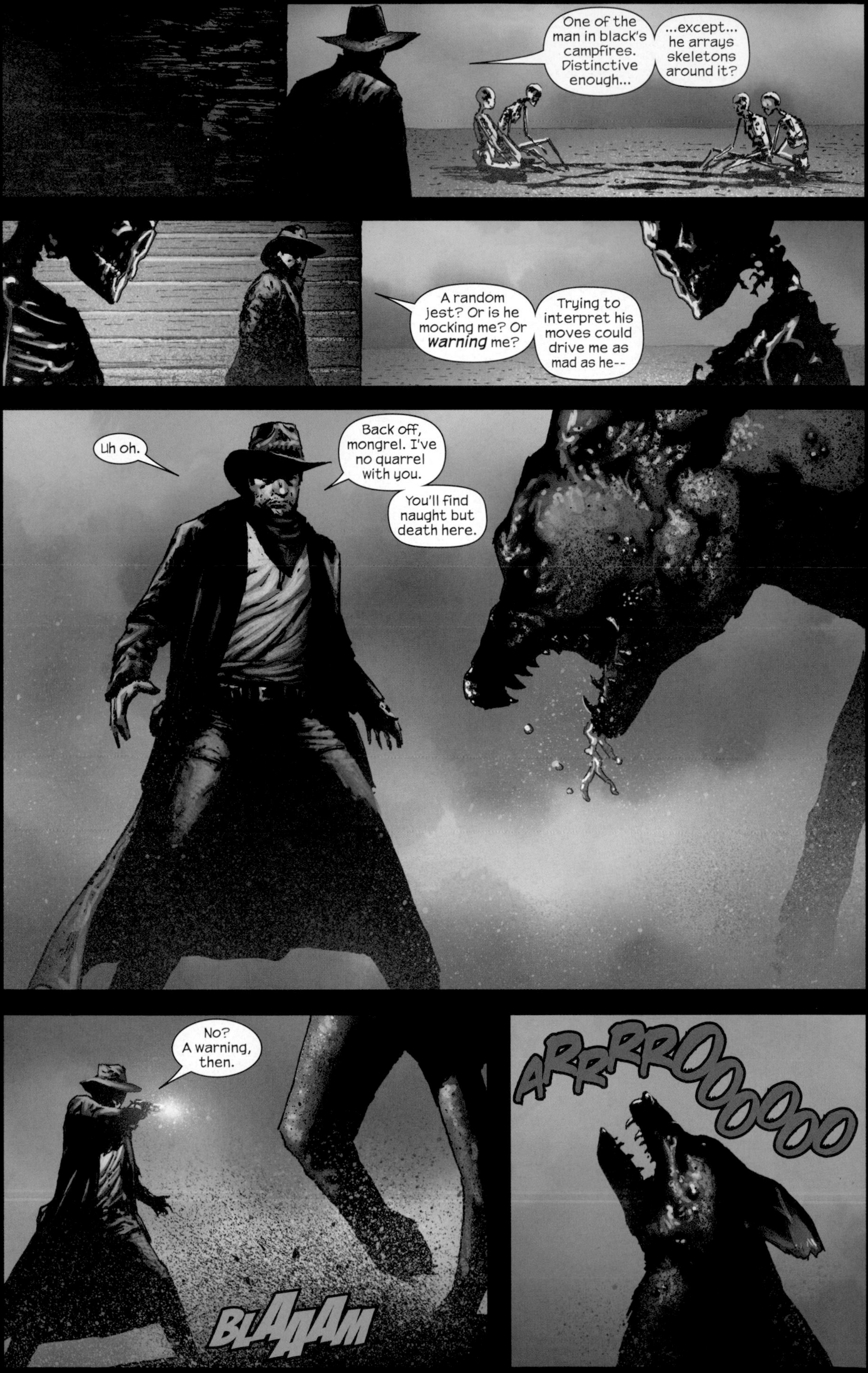
One of the man in black's campfires. Distinctive enough...
...except... he arrays skeletons around it?
A random jest? Or is he mocking me? Or *warning* me?
Trying to interpret his moves could drive me as mad as he--
Uh oh.
Back off, mongrel. I've no quarrel with you.
You'll find naught but death here.
No? A warning, then.
BLAAAM
ARRRROOOOOO

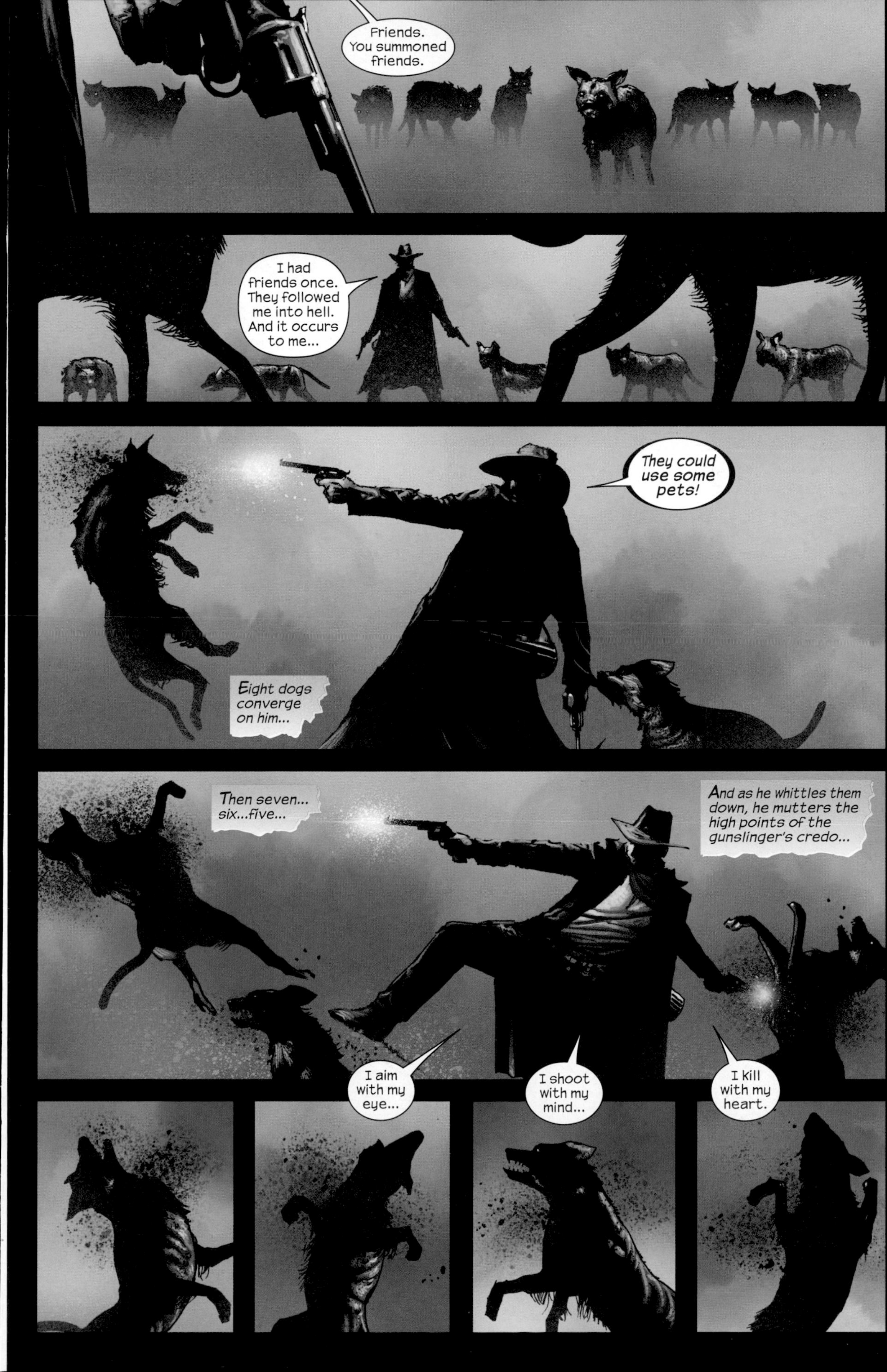
Friends. You summoned friends.
I had friends once. They followed me into hell. And it occurs to me...
They could use some pets!
Eight dogs converge on him...
Then seven... six...five...
And as he whittles them down, he mutters the high points of the gunslinger's credo...
I aim with my eye...
I shoot with my mind...
I kill with my heart.

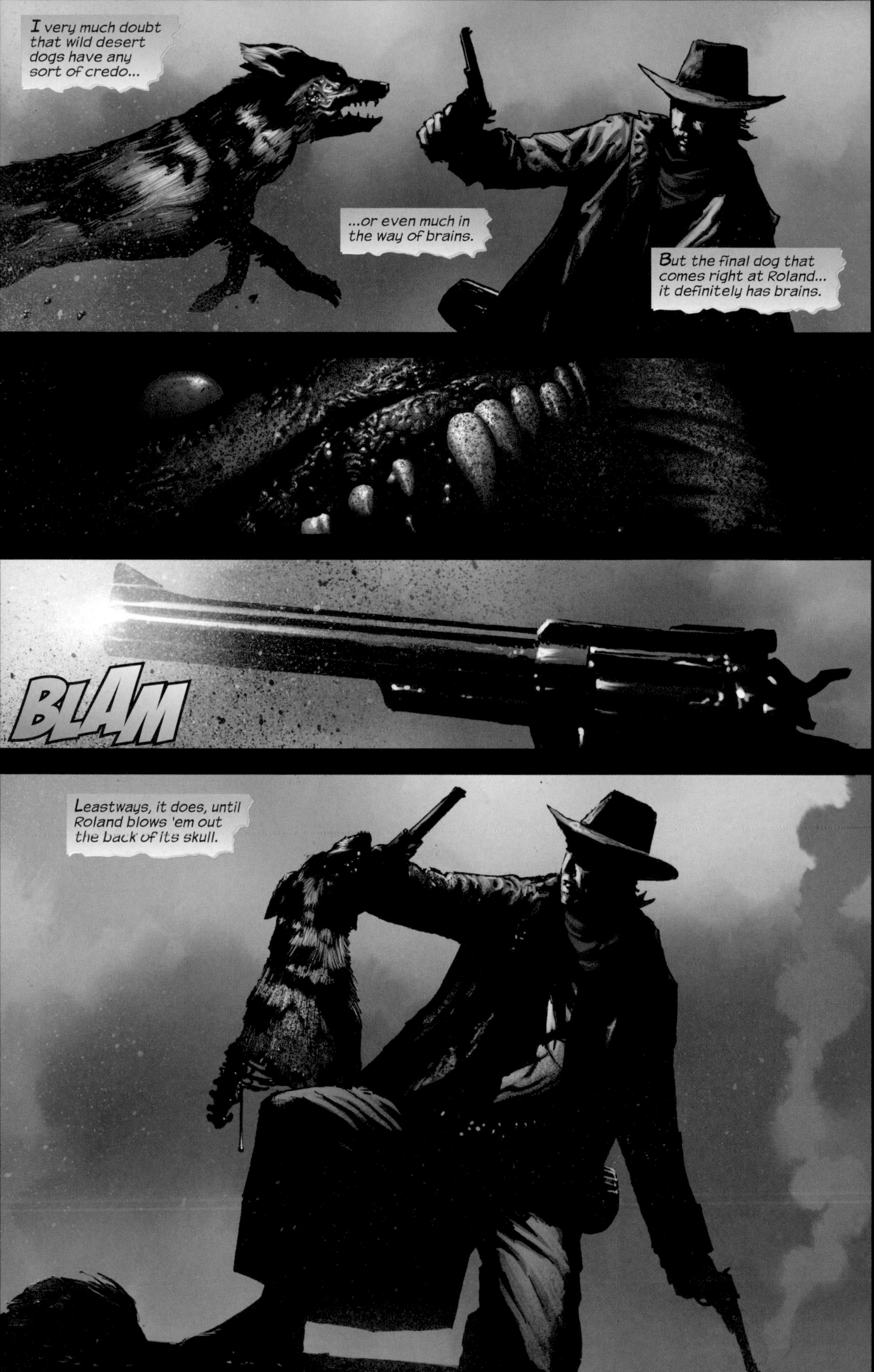
I very much doubt that wild desert dogs have any sort of credo...
...or even much in the way of brains.
But the final dog that comes right at Roland... it definitely has brains.
BLAM
Leastways, it does, until Roland blows 'em out the back of its skull.

Son of a bitch. Even in death, the thing plagues me.

Let's hope its plague doesn't continue after its death. If it was *diseased*...

Well, all I can do is cleanse it best I can, bandage it, and let time tell.

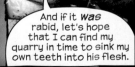

And if it *was* rabid, let's hope that I can find my quarry in time to sink my own teeth into his flesh.

If I'm to die of the frothing illness, God grant me the opportunity to take the man in black with me.

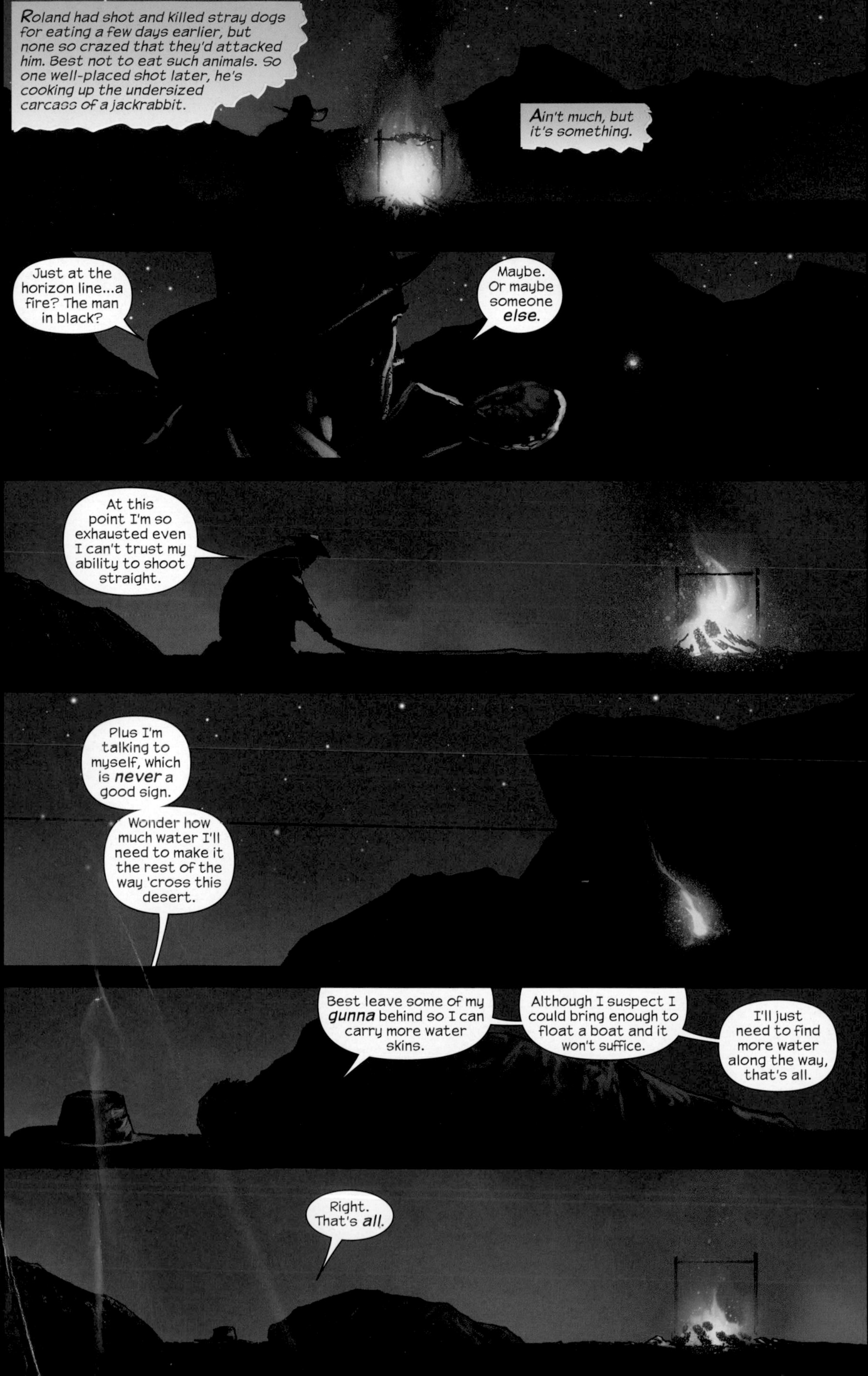
Roland had shot and killed stray dogs for eating a few days earlier, but none so crazed that they'd attacked him. Best not to eat such animals. So one well-placed shot later, he's cooking up the undersized carcass of a jackrabbit.
Ain't much, but it's something.
Just at the horizon line...a fire? The man in black?
Maybe. Or maybe someone *else*.
At this point I'm so exhausted even I can't trust my ability to shoot straight.
Plus I'm talking to myself, which is *never* a good sign.
Wonder how much water I'll need to make it the rest of the way 'cross this desert.
Best leave some of my *gunna* behind so I can carry more water skins.
Although I suspect I could bring enough to float a boat and it won't suffice.
I'll just need to find more water along the way, that's all.
Right. That's *all*.

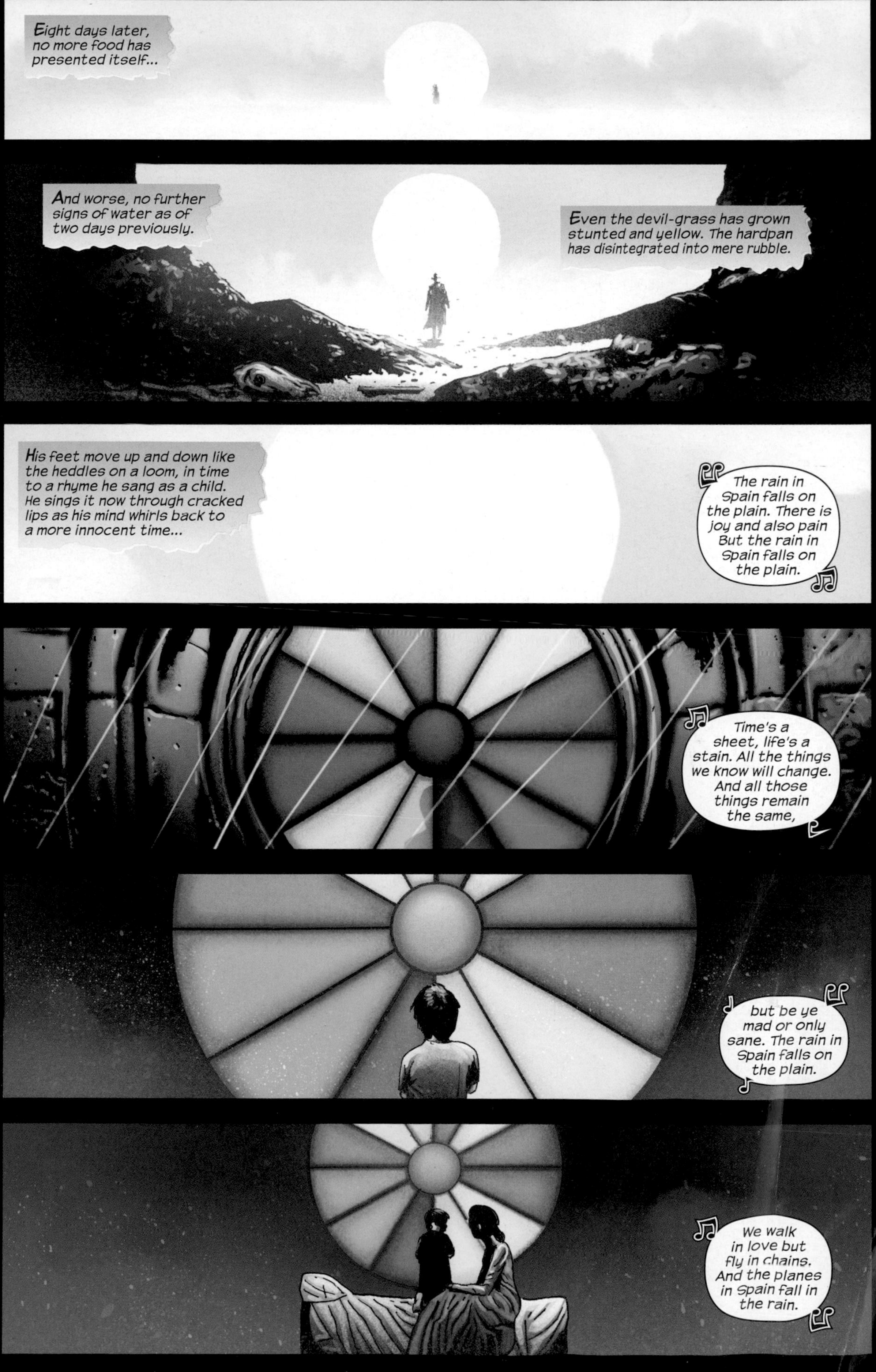
Eight days later, no more food has presented itself...
And worse, no further signs of water as of two days previously.
Even the devil-grass has grown stunted and yellow. The hardpan has disintegrated into mere rubble.
His feet move up and down like the heddles on a loom, in time to a rhyme he sang as a child. He sings it now through cracked lips as his mind whirls back to a more innocent time...
The rain in Spain falls on the plain. There is joy and also pain But the rain in Spain falls on the plain.
Time's a sheet, life's a stain. All the things we know will change. And all those things remain the same,
but be ye mad or only sane. The rain in Spain falls on the plain.
We walk in love but fly in chains. And the planes in Spain fall in the rain.

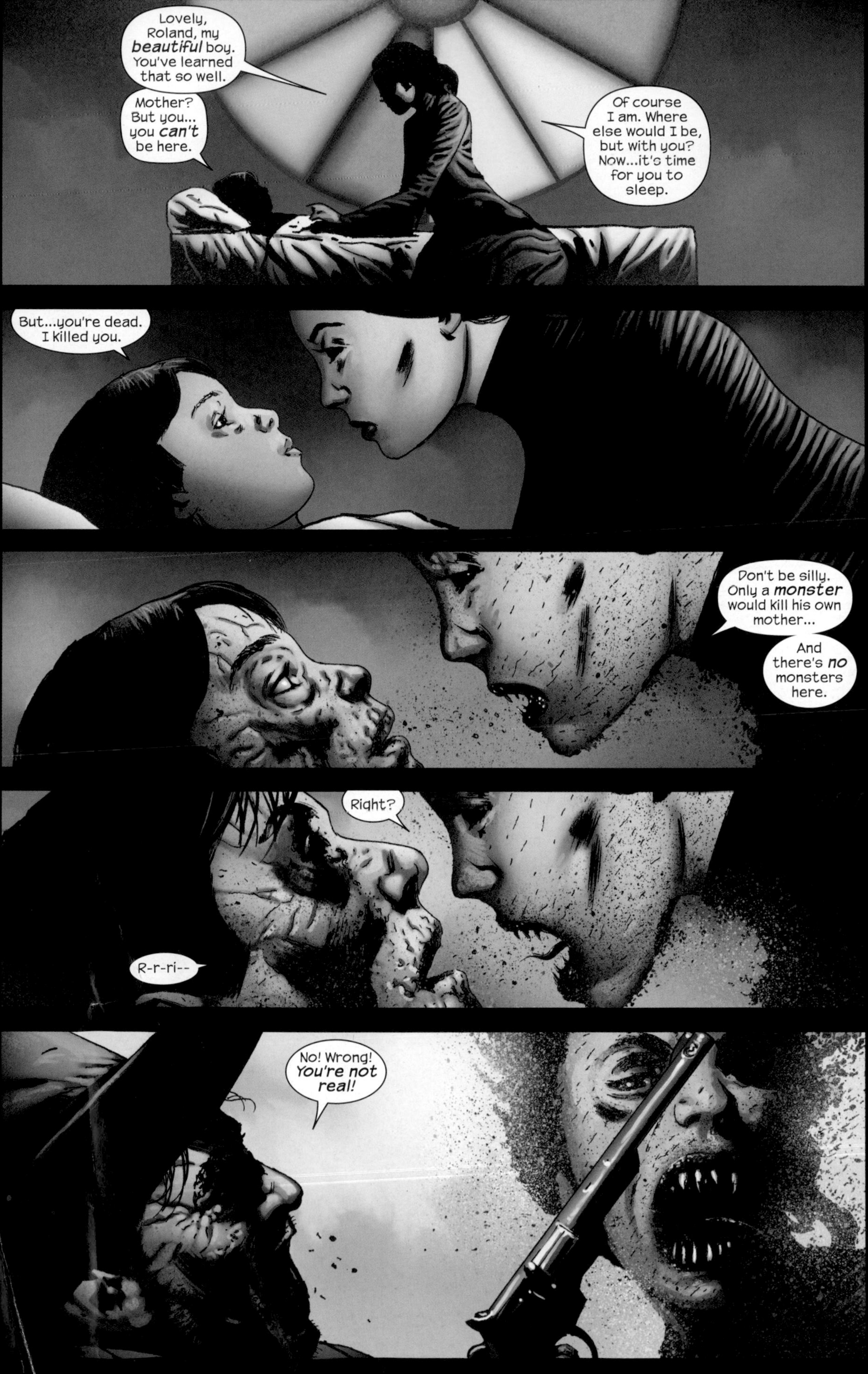
Lovely, Roland, my *beautiful* boy. You've learned that so well.
Mother? But you... you *can't* be here.
Of course I am. Where else would I be, but with you? Now...it's time for you to sleep.
But...you're dead. I killed you.
Don't be silly. Only a *monster* would kill his own mother...
And there's *no* monsters here.
Right?
R-r-ri--
No! Wrong! *You're not real!*

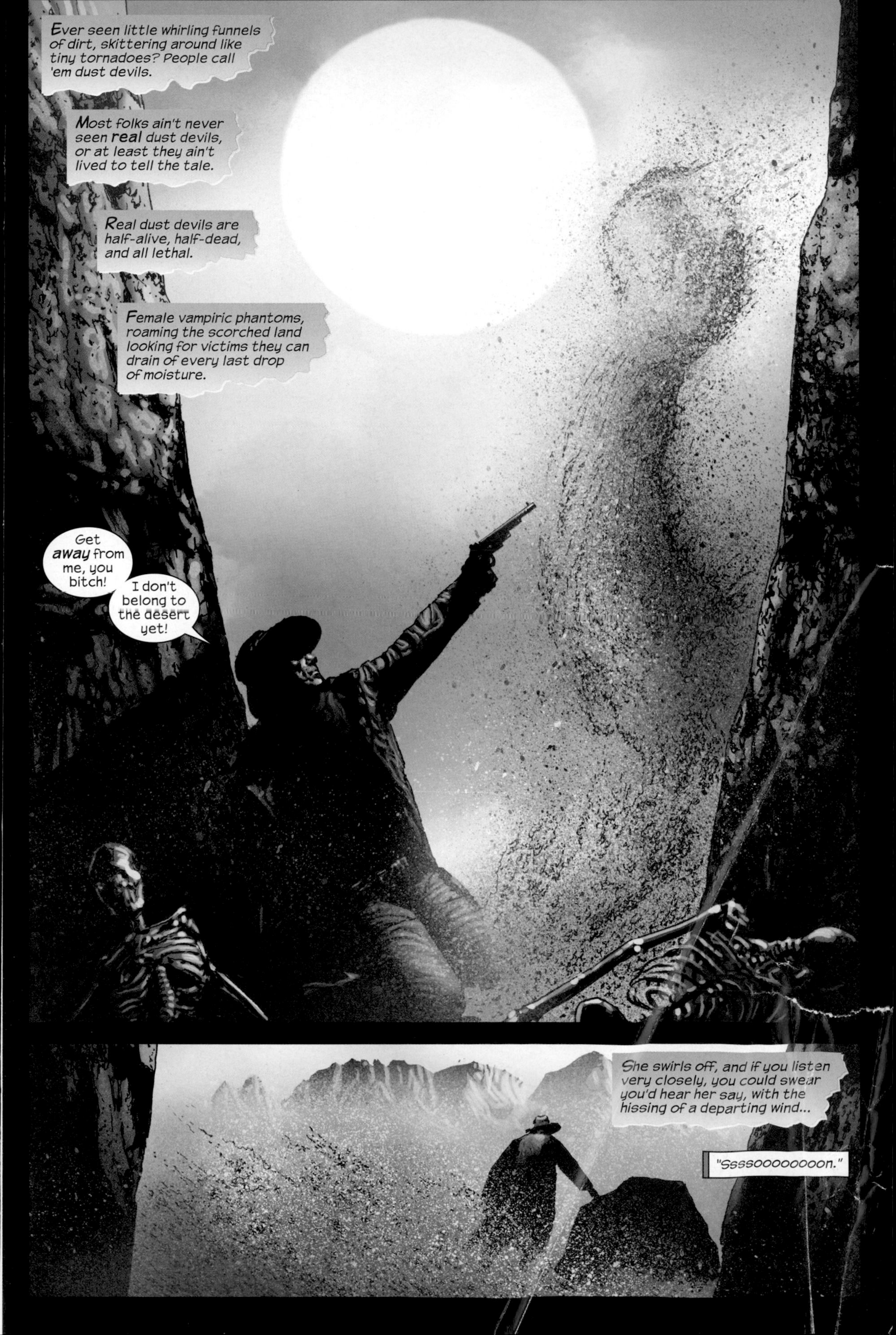
Ever seen little whirling funnels of dirt, skittering around like tiny tornadoes? People call 'em dust devils.
Most folks ain't never seen **real** dust devils, or at least they ain't lived to tell the tale.
Real dust devils are half-alive, half-dead, and all lethal.
Female vampiric phantoms, roaming the scorched land looking for victims they can drain of every last drop of moisture.
Get **away** from me, you bitch!
I don't belong to the desert yet!
She swirls off, and if you listen very closely, you could swear you'd hear her say, with the hissing of a departing wind...
"Sssso000000oon."

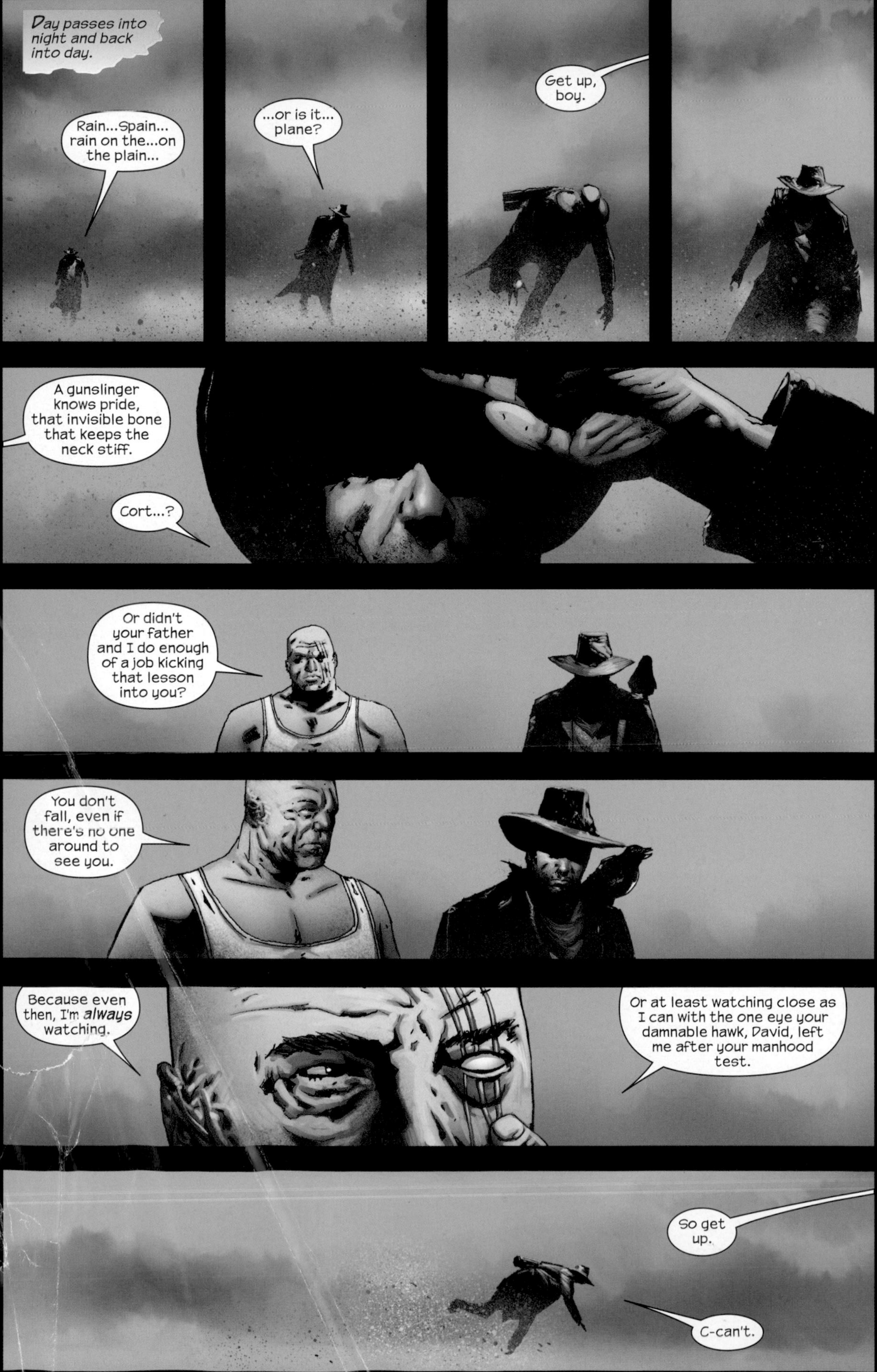
Day passes into night and back into day.
Rain...Spain... rain on the...on the plain...
...or is it... plane?
Get up, boy.
A gunslinger knows pride, that invisible bone that keeps the neck stiff.
Cort...?
Or didn't your father and I do enough of a job kicking that lesson into you?
You don't fall, even if there's no one around to see you.
Because even then, I'm *always* watching.
Or at least watching close as I can with the one eye your damnable hawk, David, left me after your manhood test.
So get up.
C-can't.

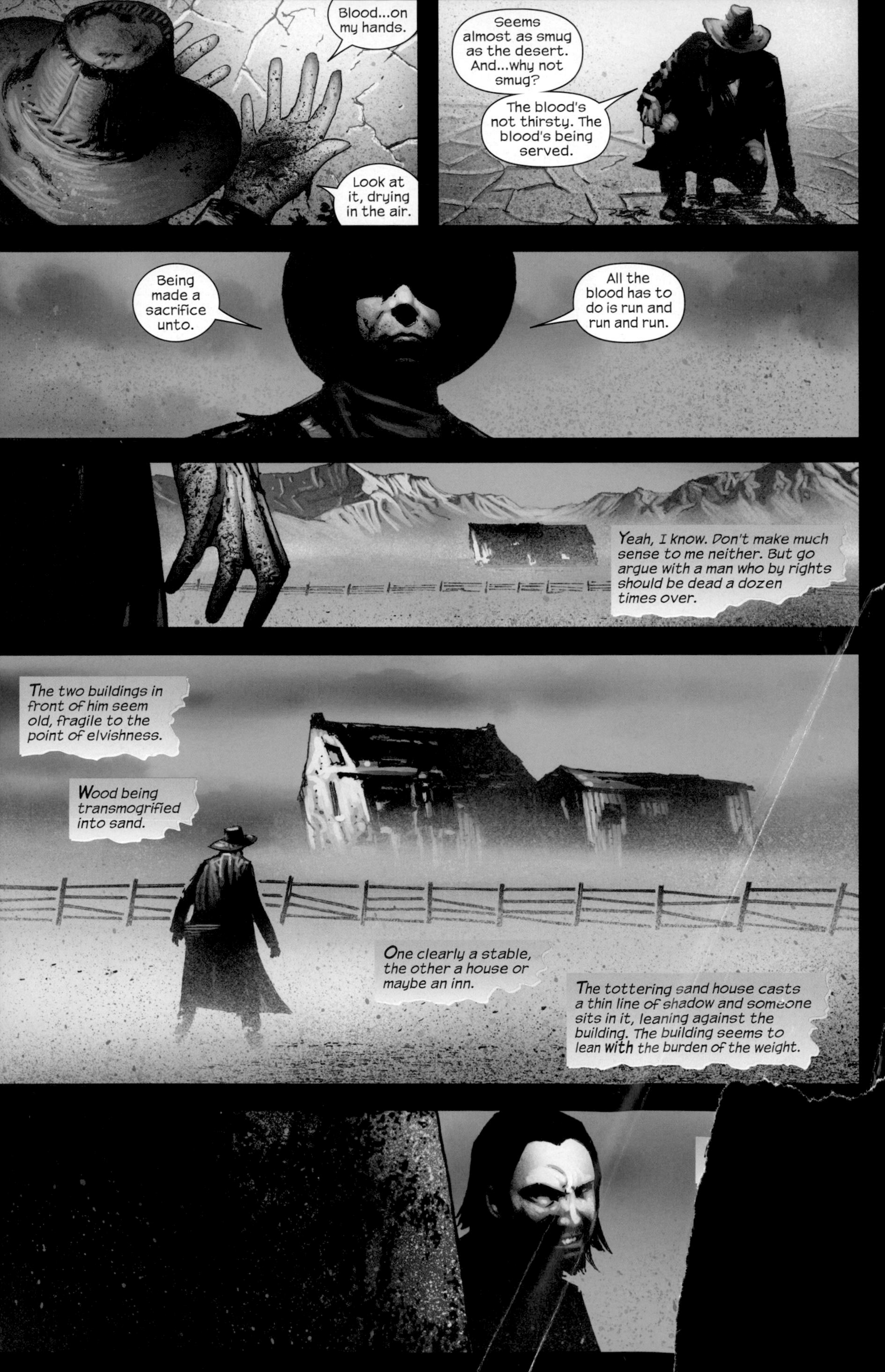
Blood...on my hands.
Look at it, drying in the air.
Seems almost as smug as the desert. And...why not smug?
The blood's not thirsty. The blood's being served.
Being made a sacrifice unto.
All the blood has to do is run and run and run.
Yeah, I know. Don't make much sense to me neither. But go argue with a man who by rights should be dead a dozen times over.
The two buildings in front of him seem old, fragile to the point of elvishness.
Wood being transmogrified into sand.
One clearly a stable, the other a house or maybe an inn.
The tottering sand house casts a thin line of shadow and someone sits in it, leaning against the building. The building seems to lean with the burden of the weight.

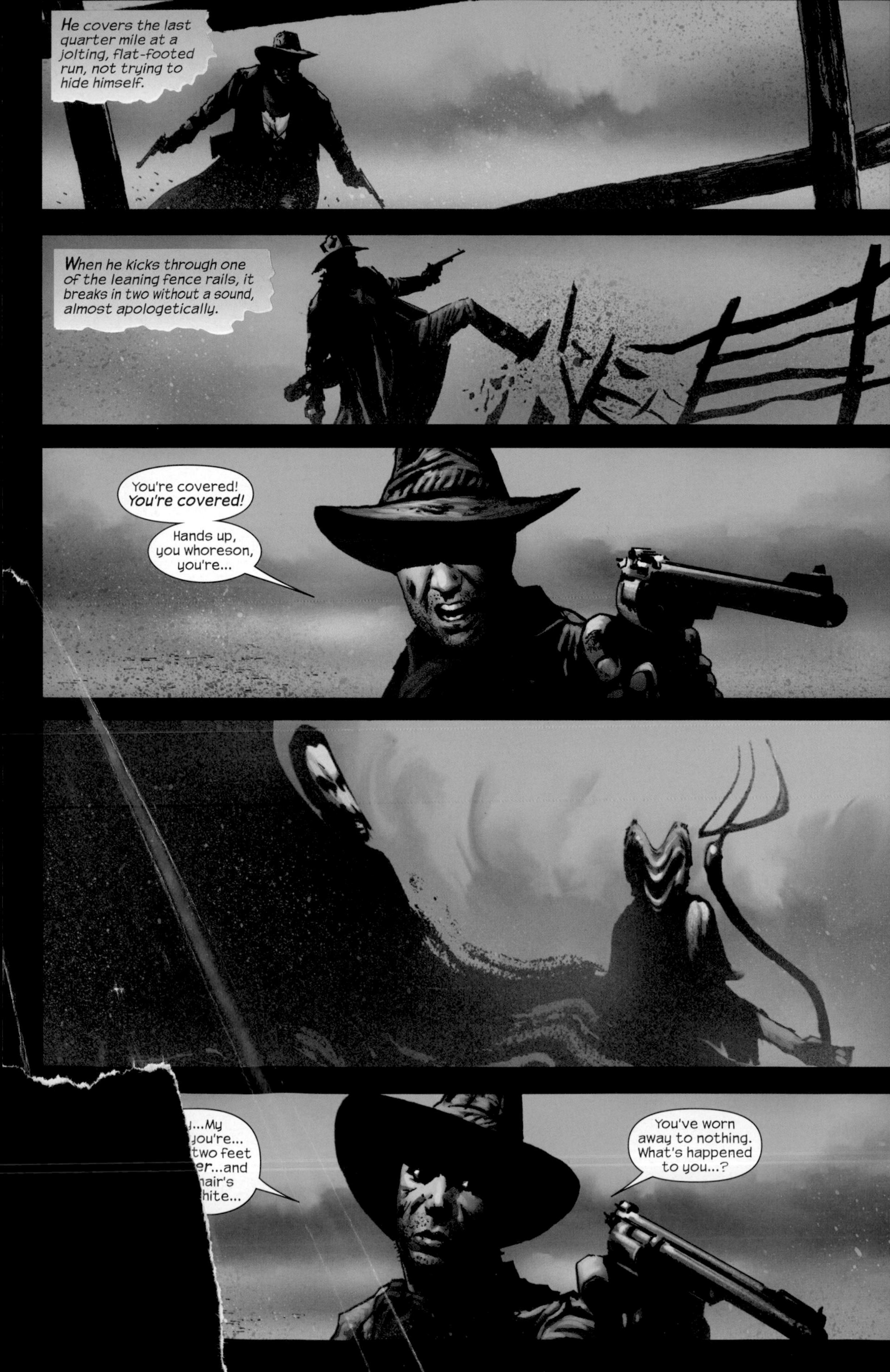
He covers the last quarter mile at a jolting, flat-footed run, not trying to hide himself.
When he kicks through one of the leaning fence rails, it breaks in two without a sound, almost apologetically.
You're covered! You're covered!
Hands up, you whoreson, you're...
...My you're... two feet er...and hair's hite...
You've worn away to nothing. What's happened to you...?

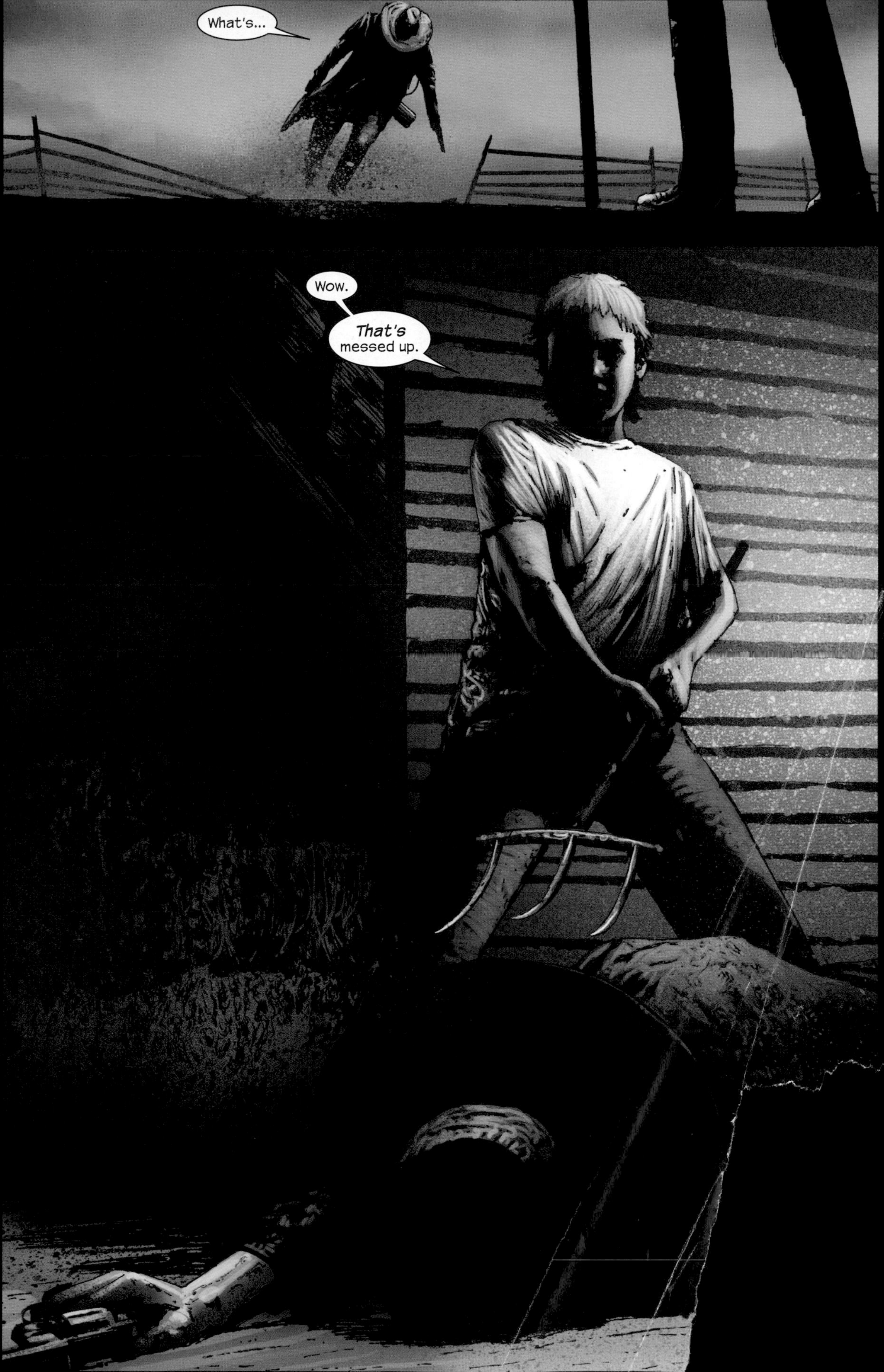
What's...
Wow.
That's messed up.

STEPHEN KING
THE DARK TOWER
~THE GUNSLINGER~

THE WAY STATION

CHAPTER TWO

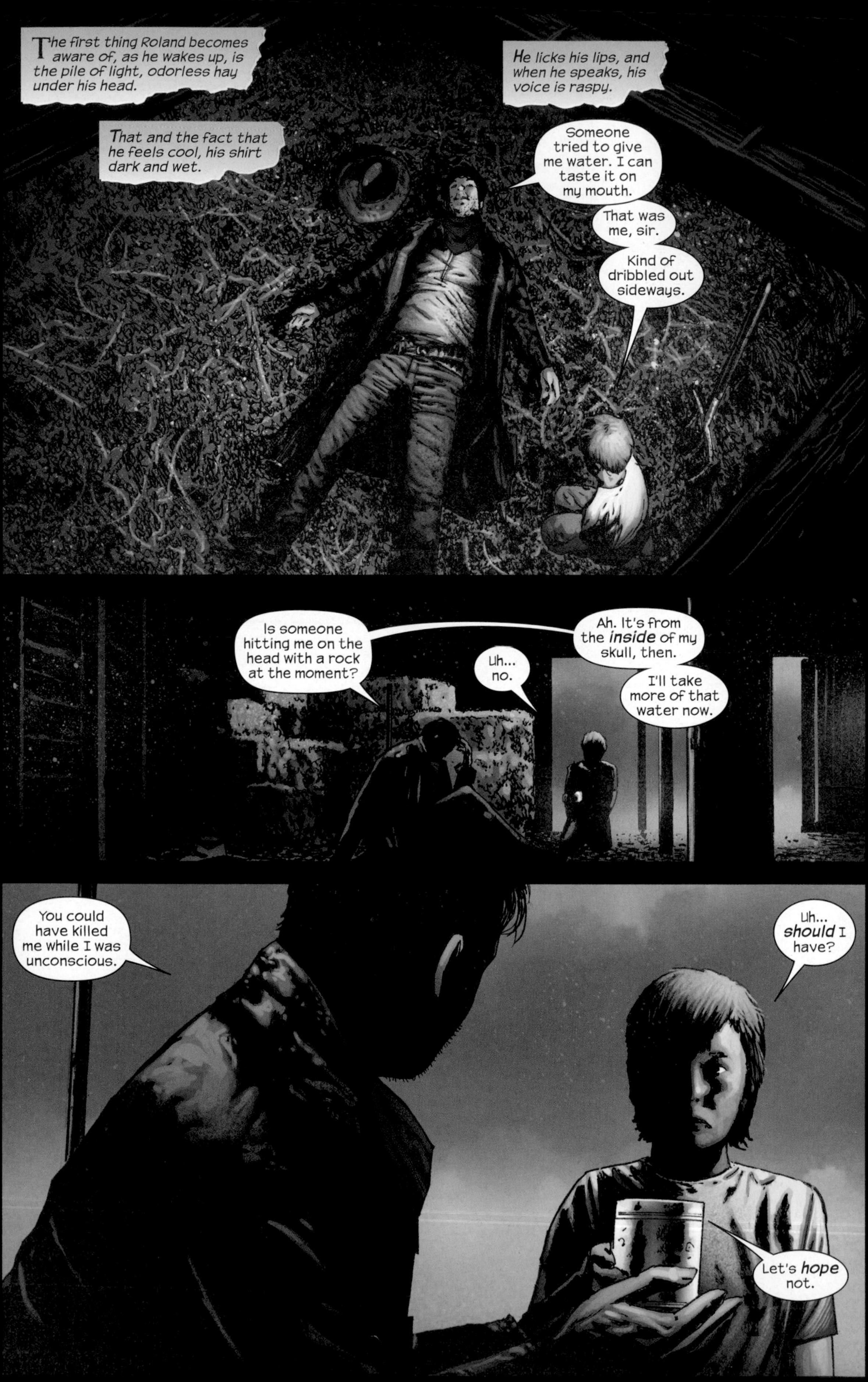
The first thing Roland becomes aware of, as he wakes up, is the pile of light, odorless hay under his head.
That and the fact that he feels cool, his shirt dark and wet.
He licks his lips, and when he speaks, his voice is raspy.
Someone tried to give me water. I can taste it on my mouth.
That was me, sir.
Kind of dribbled out sideways.
Is someone hitting me on the head with a rock at the moment?
Uh... no.
Ah. It's from the inside of my skull, then.
I'll take more of that water now.
You could have killed me while I was unconscious.
Uh... should I have?
Let's hope not.

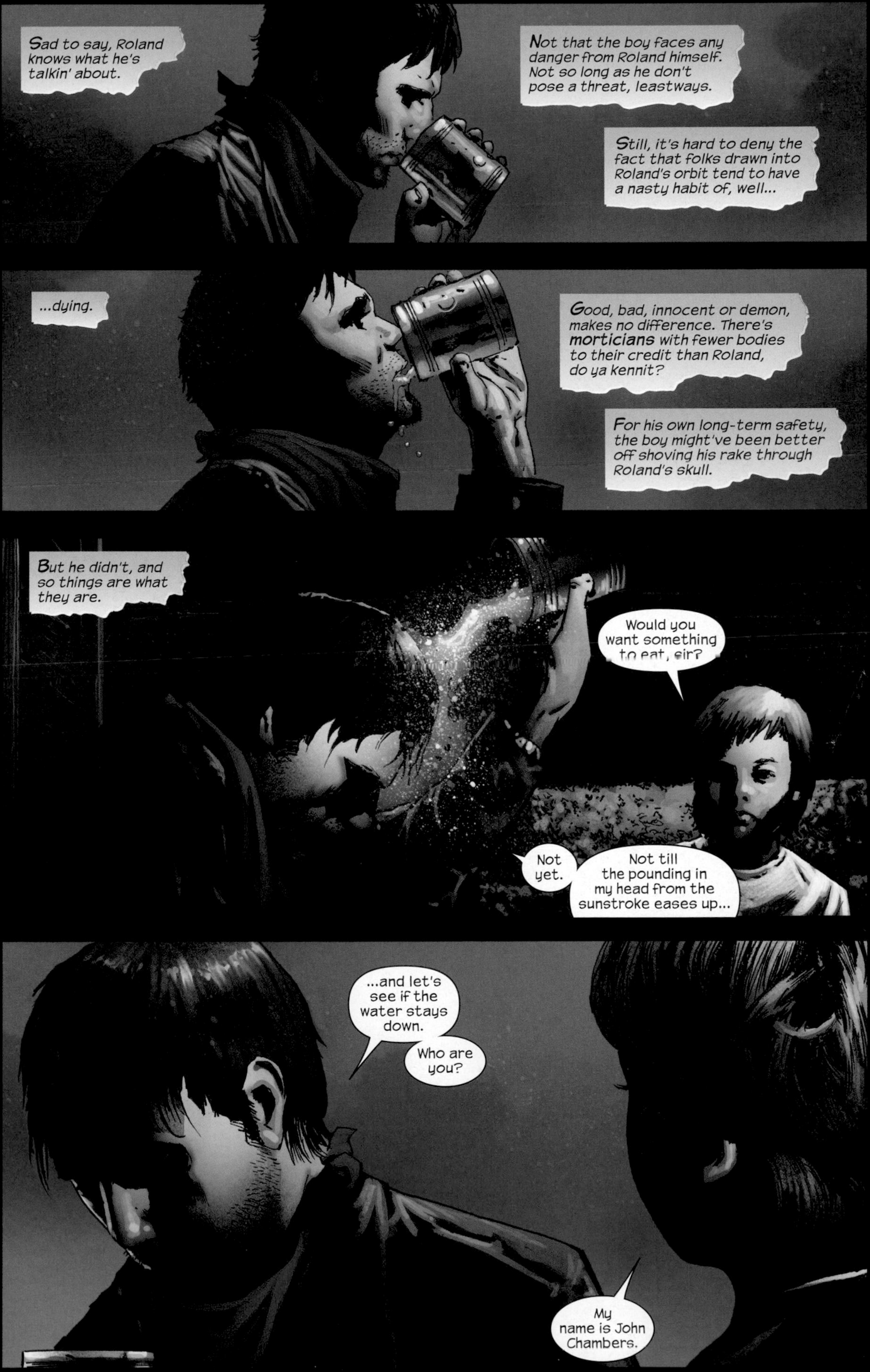

Sad to say, Roland knows what he's talkin' about.
Not that the boy faces any danger from Roland himself. Not so long as he don't pose a threat, leastways.
Still, it's hard to deny the fact that folks drawn into Roland's orbit tend to have a nasty habit of, well...
...dying.
Good, bad, innocent or demon, makes no difference. There's **morticians** with fewer bodies to their credit than Roland, do ya kennit?
For his own long-term safety, the boy might've been better off shoving his rake through Roland's skull.
But he didn't, and so things are what they are.
Would you want something to eat, sir?
Not yet.
Not till the pounding in my head from the sunstroke eases up...
...and let's see if the water stays down.
Who are you?
My name is John Chambers.

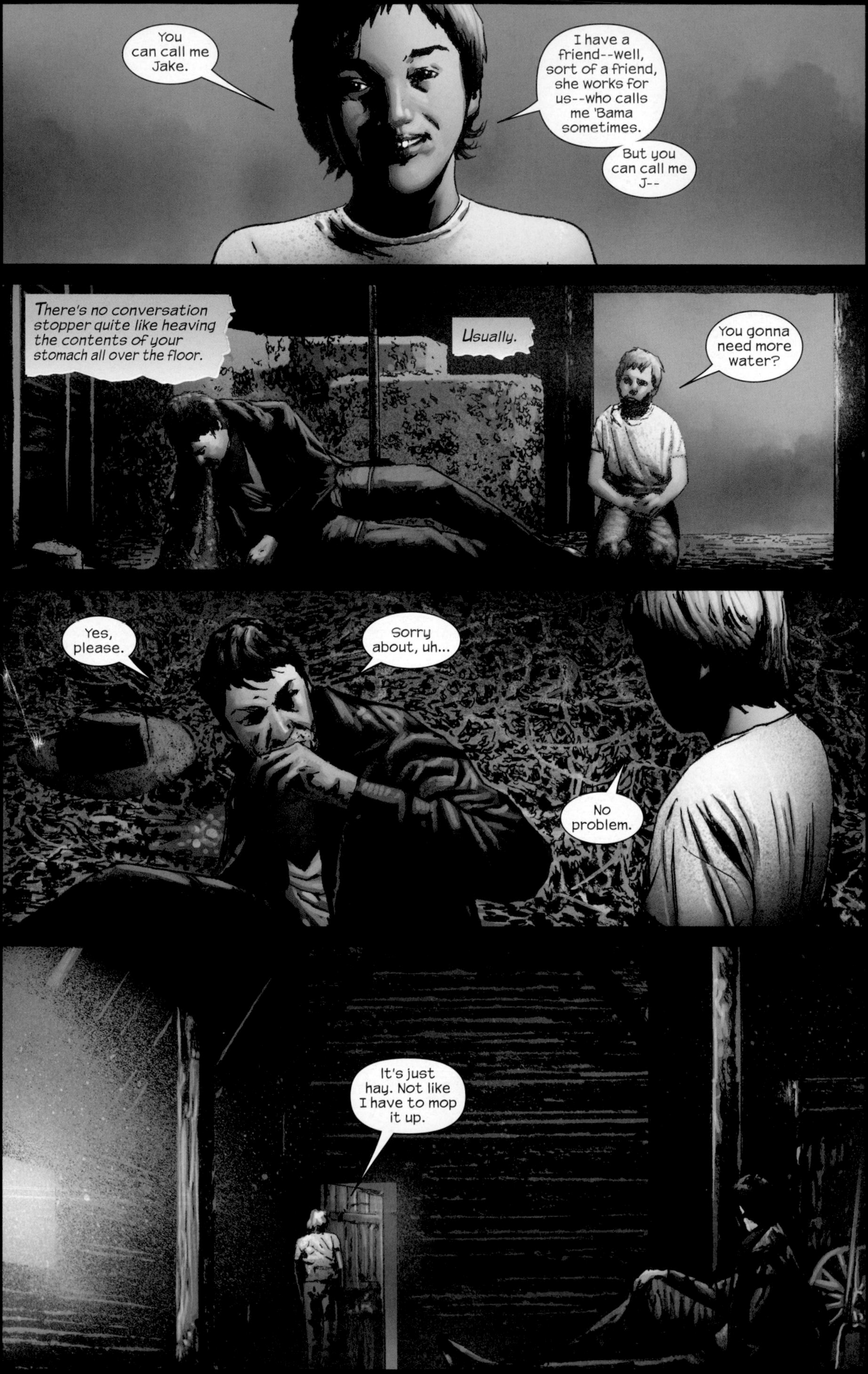
You can call me Jake.
I have a friend--well, sort of a friend, she works for us--who calls me 'Bama sometimes.
But you can call me J--
There's no conversation stopper quite like heaving the contents of your stomach all over the floor.
Usually.
You gonna need more water?
Yes, please.
Sorry about, uh...
No problem.
It's just hay. Not like I have to mop it up.

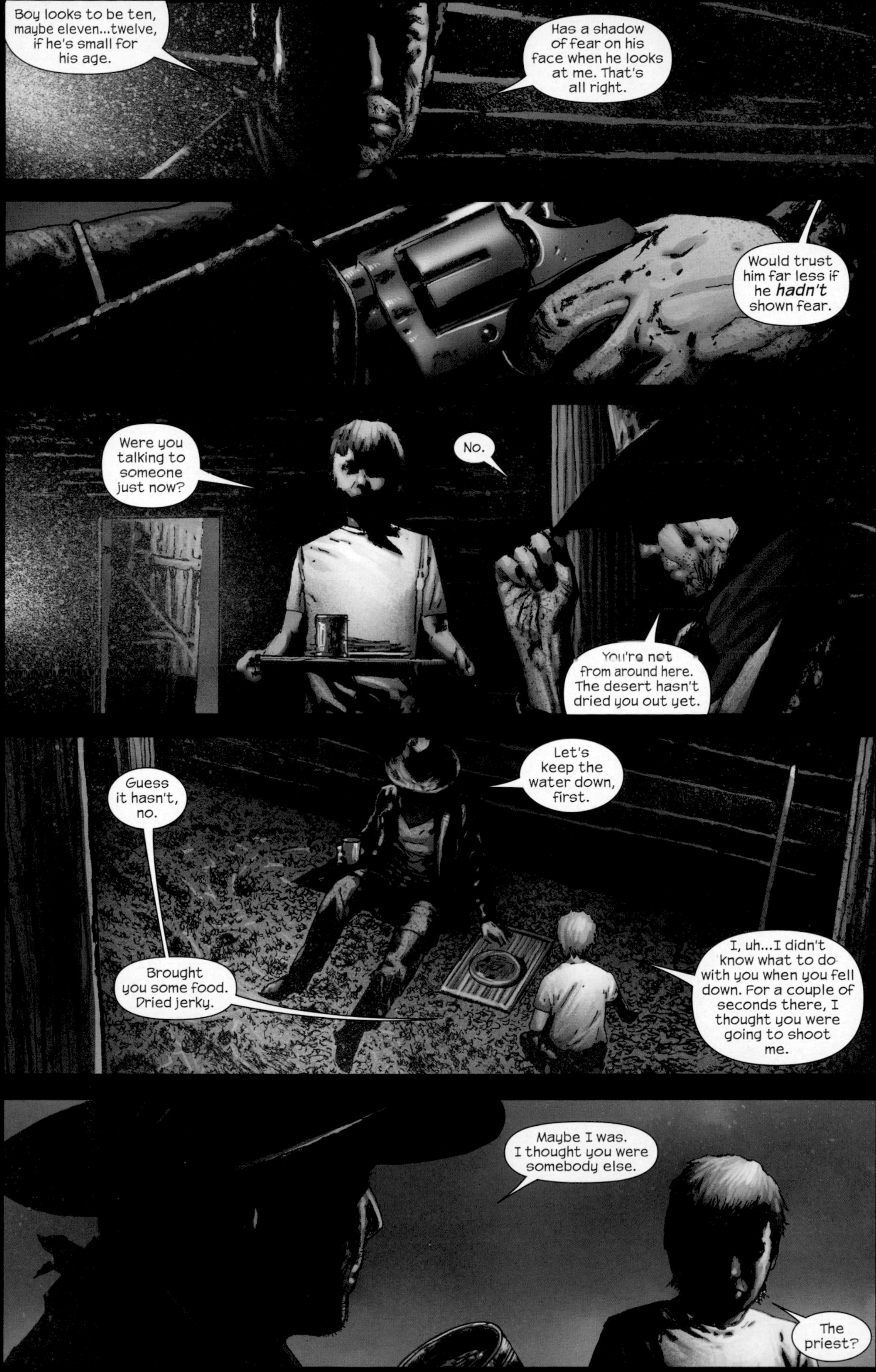
Boy looks to be ten, maybe eleven...twelve, if he's small for his age.
Has a shadow of fear on his face when he looks at me. That's all right.
Would trust him far less if he ***hadn't*** shown fear.
Were you talking to someone just now?
No.
You're not from around here. The desert hasn't dried you out yet.
Guess it hasn't, no.
Let's keep the water down, first.
Brought you some food. Dried jerky.
I, uh...I didn't know what to do with you when you fell down. For a couple of seconds there, I thought you were going to shoot me.
Maybe I was. I thought you were somebody else.
The priest?

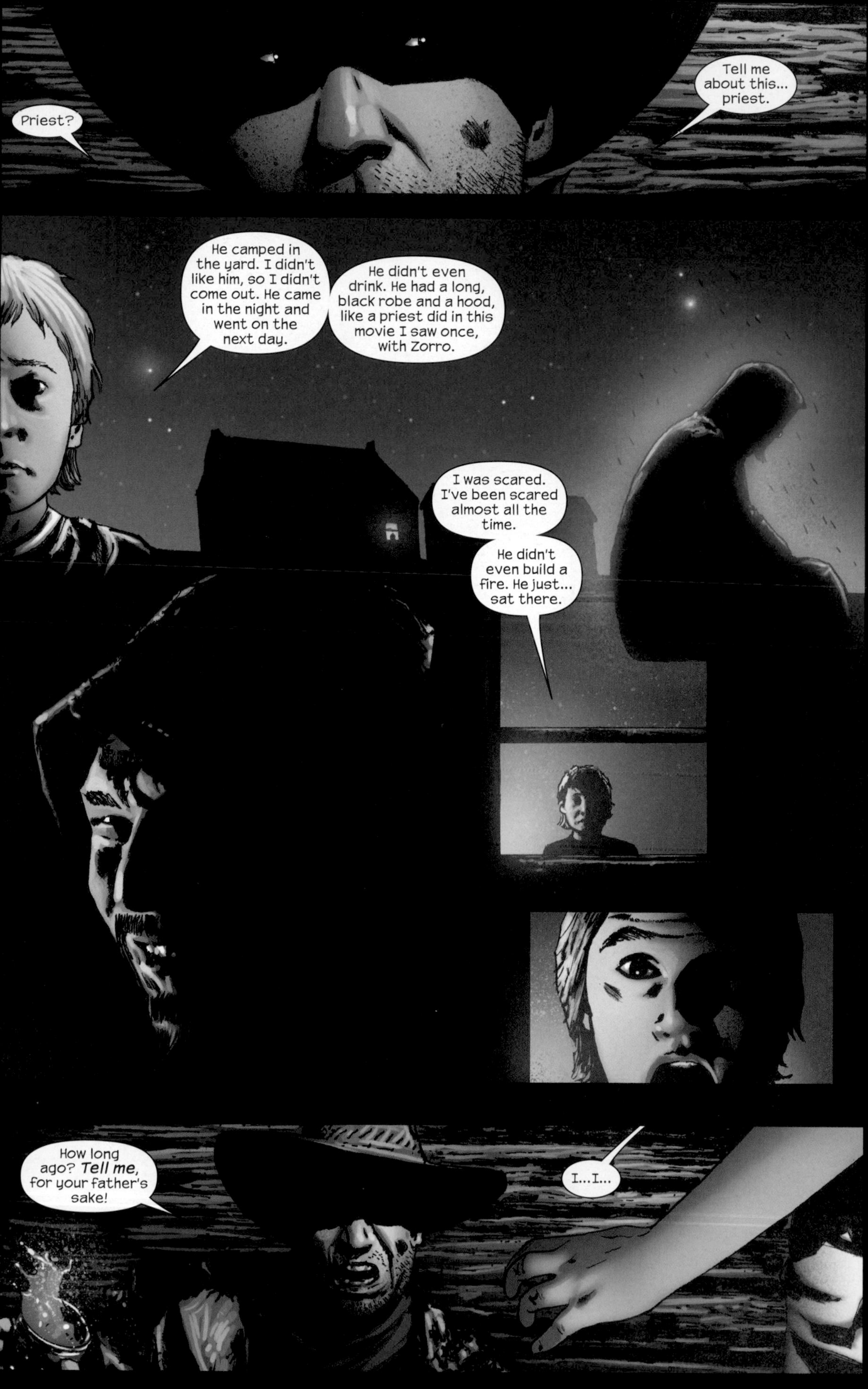
Priest?
Tell me about this... priest.
He camped in the yard. I didn't like him, so I didn't come out. He came in the night and went on the next day.
He didn't even drink. He had a long, black robe and a hood, like a priest did in this movie I saw once, with Zorro.
I was scared. I've been scared almost all the time.
He didn't even build a fire. He just... sat there.
How long ago? *Tell me*, for your father's sake!
I...I...

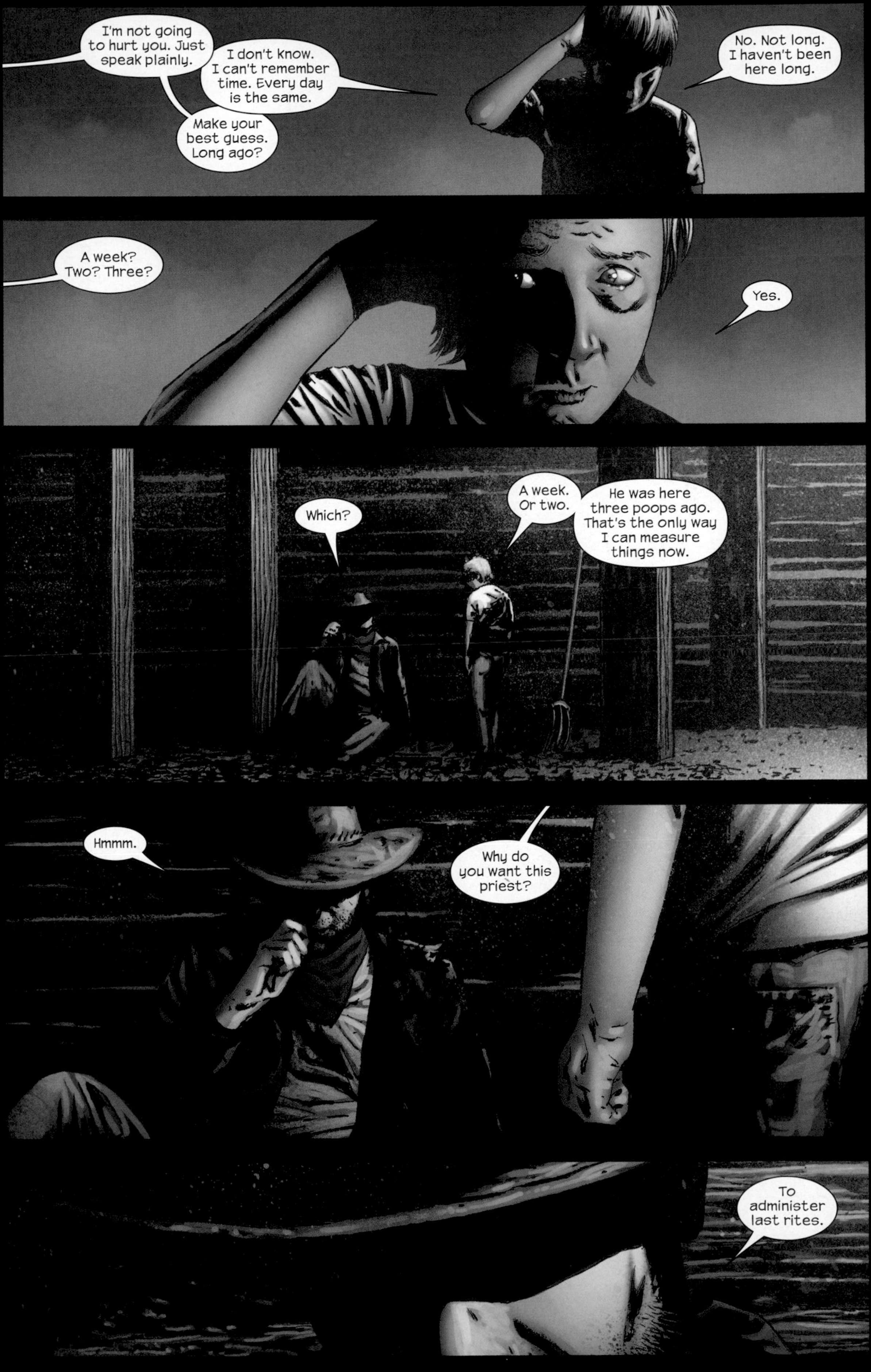
I'm not going to hurt you. Just speak plainly.
I don't know. I can't remember time. Every day is the same.
Make your best guess. Long ago?
No. Not long. I haven't been here long.
A week? Two? Three?
Yes.
Which?
A week. Or two.
He was here three poops ago. That's the only way I can measure things now.
Hmmm.
Why do you want this priest?
To administer last rites.

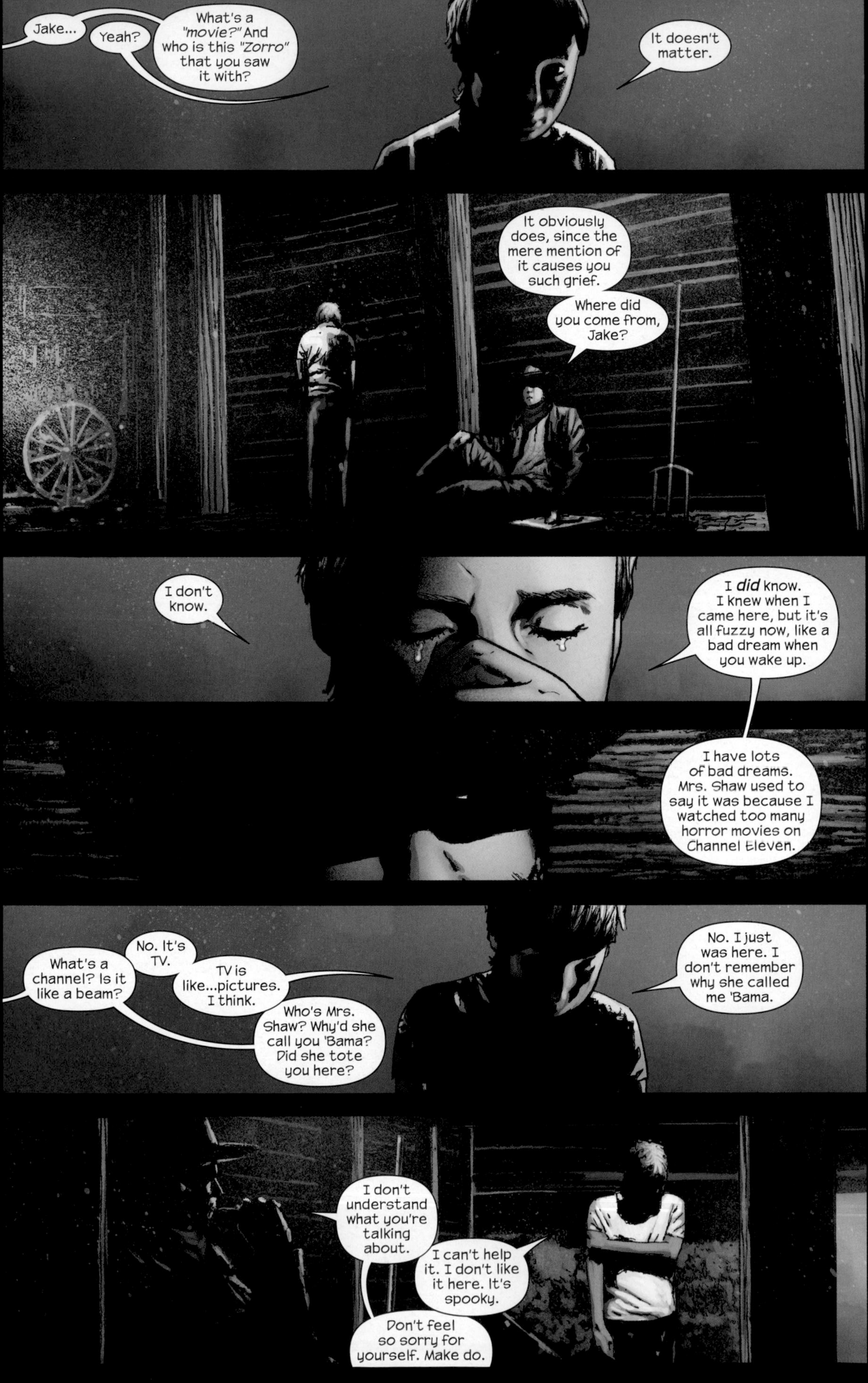
Jake...
Yeah?
What's a "movie?" And who is this "Zorro" that you saw it with?
It doesn't matter.
It obviously does, since the mere mention of it causes you such grief.
Where did you come from, Jake?
I don't know.
I did know. I knew when I came here, but it's all fuzzy now, like a bad dream when you wake up.
I have lots of bad dreams. Mrs. Shaw used to say it was because I watched too many horror movies on Channel Eleven.
What's a channel? Is it like a beam?
No. It's TV.
TV is like...pictures. I think.
Who's Mrs. Shaw? Why'd she call you 'Bama? Did she tote you here?
No. I just was here. I don't remember why she called me 'Bama.
I don't understand what you're talking about.
I can't help it. I don't like it here. It's spooky.
Don't feel so sorry for yourself. Make do.

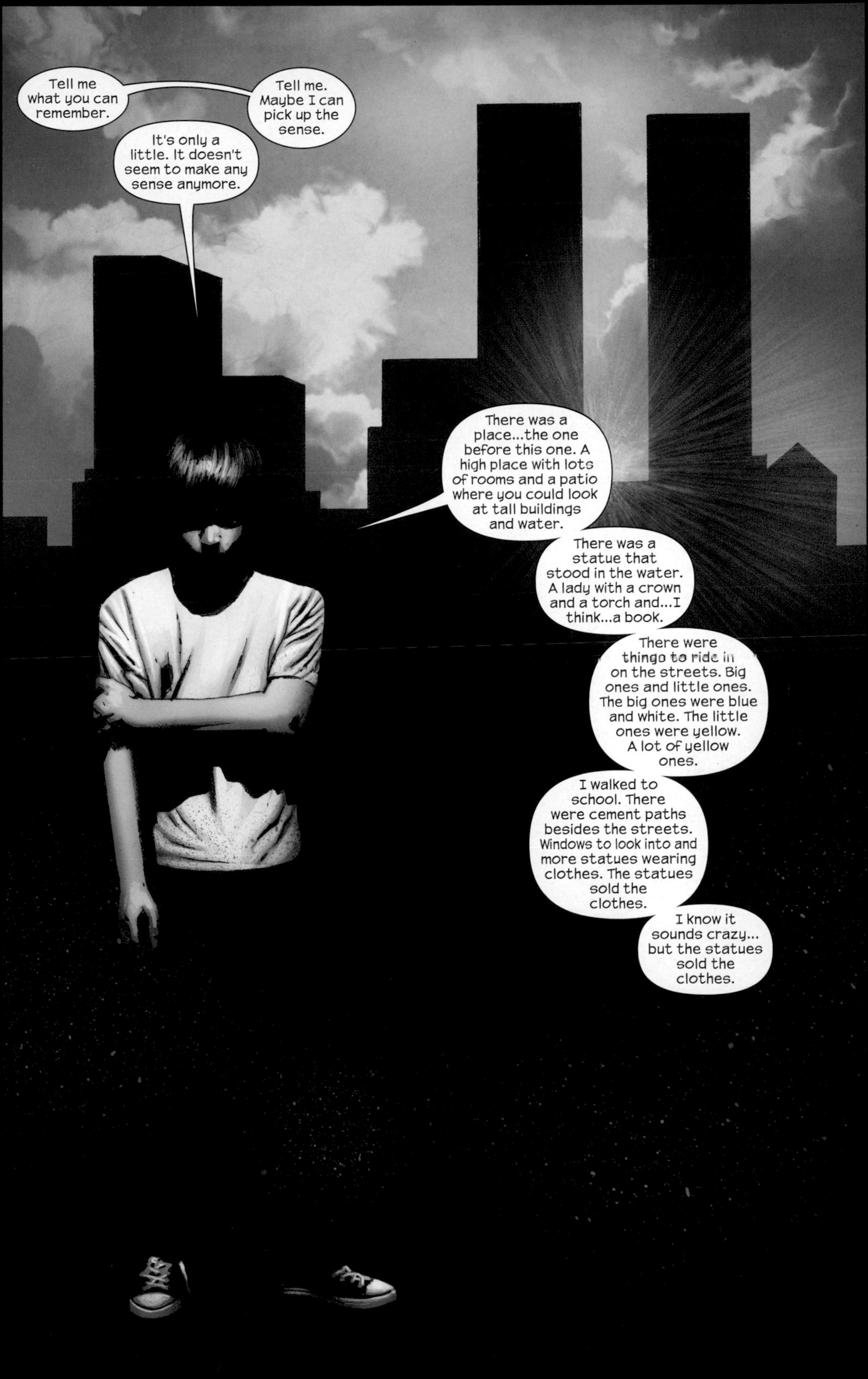
Tell me what you can remember.
Tell me. Maybe I can pick up the sense.
It's only a little. It doesn't seem to make any sense anymore.
There was a place...the one before this one. A high place with lots of rooms and a patio where you could look at tall buildings and water.
There was a statue that stood in the water. A lady with a crown and a torch and...I think...a book.
There were things to ride in on the streets. Big ones and little ones. The big ones were blue and white. The little ones were yellow. A lot of yellow ones.
I walked to school. There were cement paths besides the streets. Windows to look into and more statues wearing clothes. The statues sold the clothes.
I know it sounds crazy... but the statues sold the clothes.

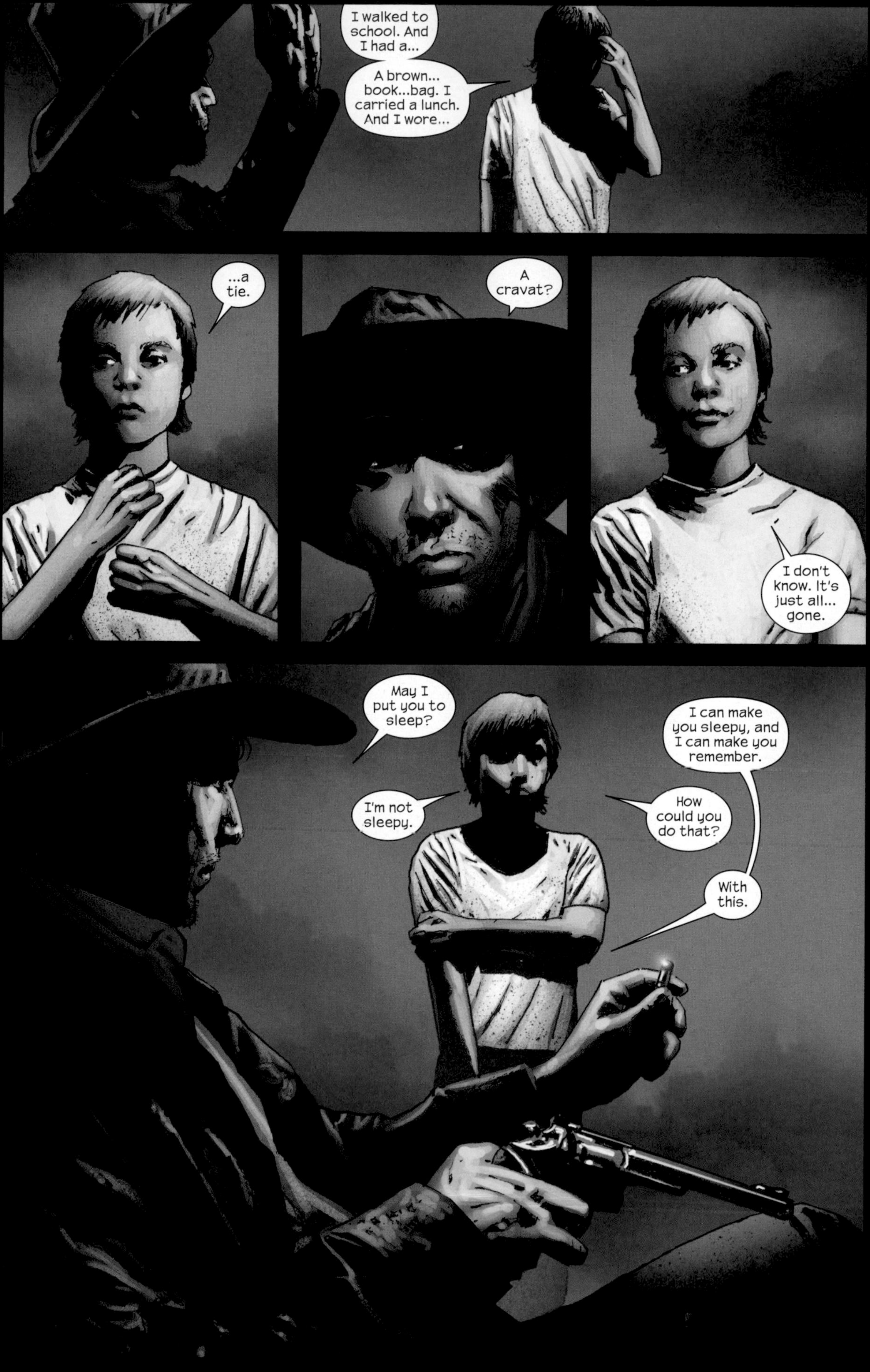

I walked to school. And I had a...
A brown... book...bag. I carried a lunch. And I wore...
...a tie.
A cravat?
I don't know. It's just all... gone.
May I put you to sleep?
I'm not sleepy.
I can make you sleepy, and I can make you remember.
How could you do that?
With this.

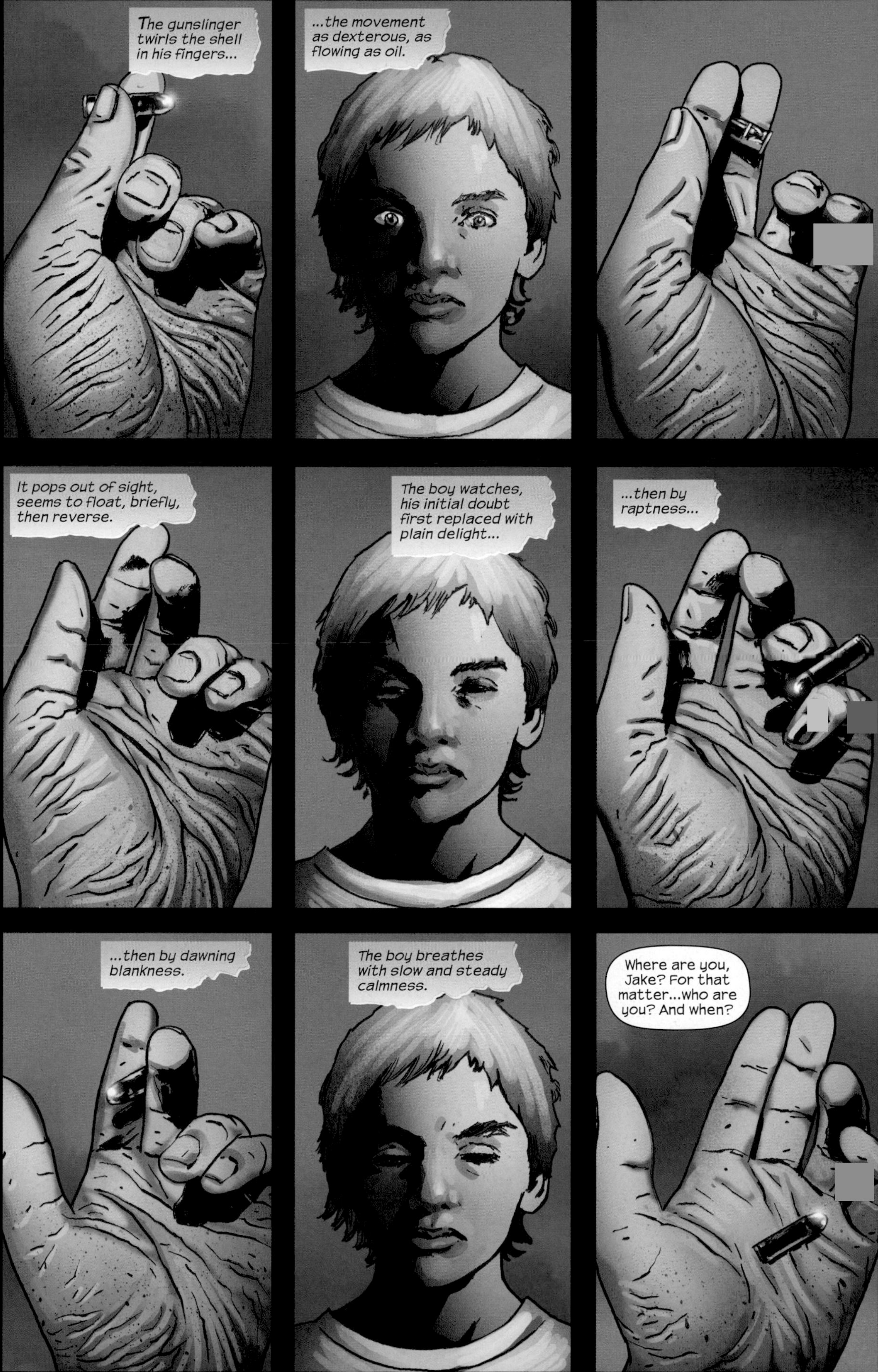
The gunslinger twirls the shell in his fingers...
...the movement as dexterous, as flowing as oil.
It pops out of sight, seems to float, briefly, then reverse.
The boy watches, his initial doubt first replaced with plain delight...
...then by raptness...
...then by dawning blankness.
The boy breathes with slow and steady calmness.
Where are you, Jake? For that matter...who are you? And when?

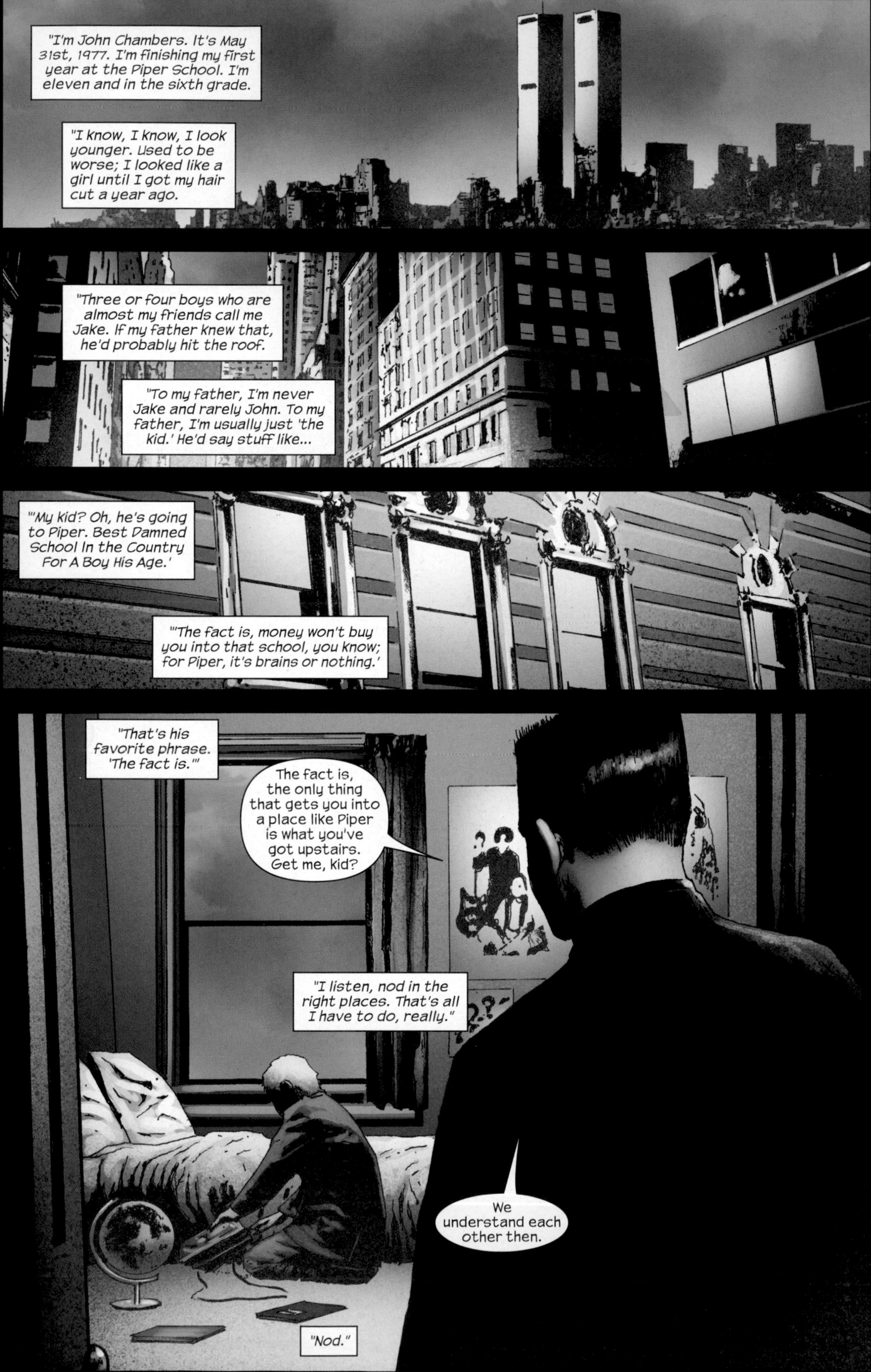
"I'm John Chambers. It's May 31st, 1977. I'm finishing my first year at the Piper School. I'm eleven and in the sixth grade.
"I know, I know, I look younger. Used to be worse; I looked like a girl until I got my hair cut a year ago.
"Three or four boys who are almost my friends call me Jake. If my father knew that, he'd probably hit the roof.
"To my father, I'm never Jake and rarely John. To my father, I'm usually just 'the kid.' He'd say stuff like...
"'My kid? Oh, he's going to Piper. Best Damned School In the Country For A Boy His Age.'
"'The fact is, money won't buy you into that school, you know; for Piper, it's brains or nothing.'
"That's his favorite phrase. 'The fact is.'"
The fact is, the only thing that gets you into a place like Piper is what you've got upstairs. Get me, kid?
"I listen, nod in the right places. That's all I have to do, really."
We understand each other then.
"Nod."

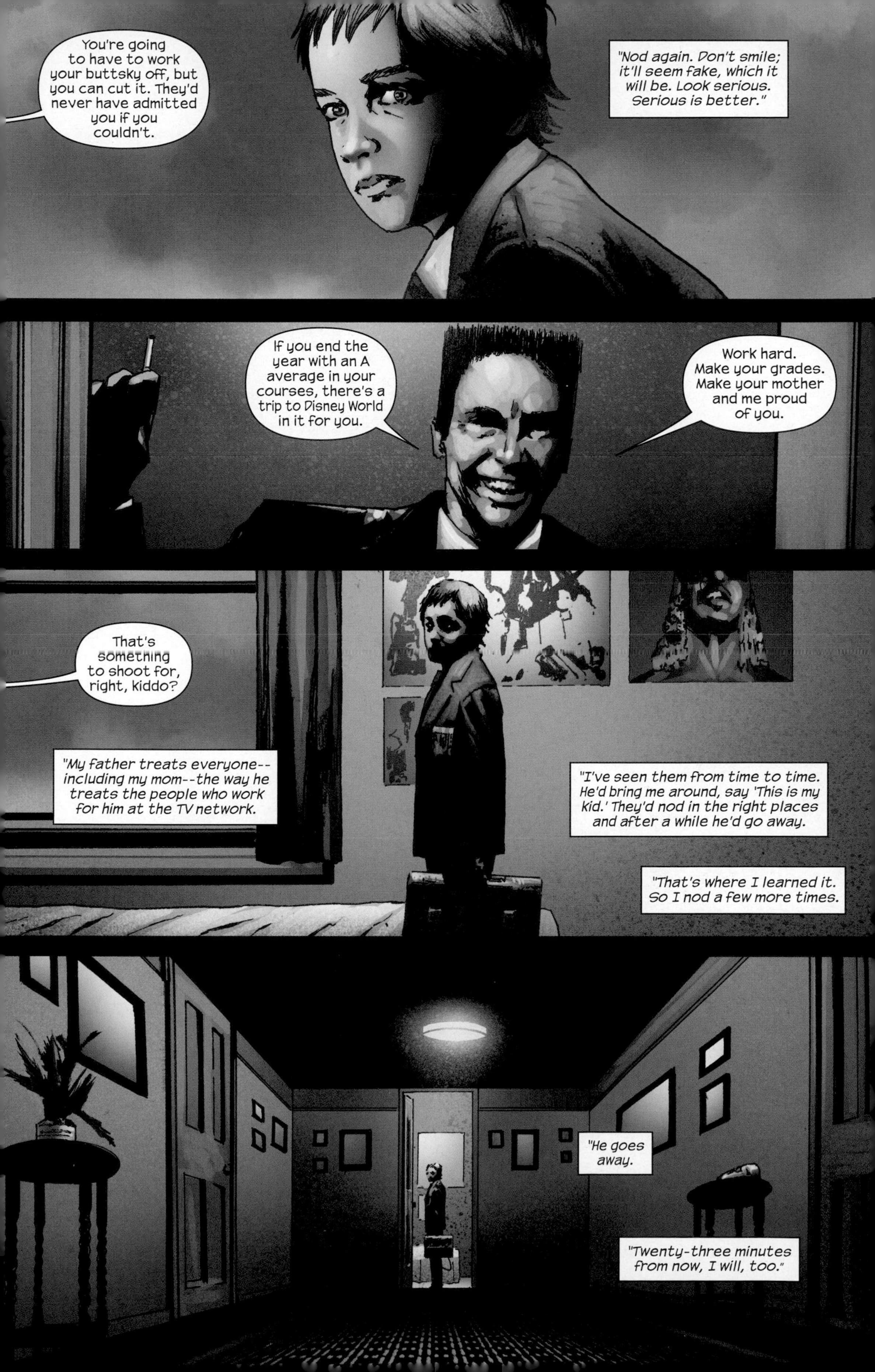
You're going to have to work your buttsky off, but you can cut it. They'd never have admitted you if you couldn't.
"Nod again. Don't smile; it'll seem fake, which it will be. Look serious. Serious is better."
If you end the year with an A average in your courses, there's a trip to Disney World in it for you.
Work hard. Make your grades. Make your mother and me proud of you.
That's something to shoot for, right, kiddo?
"My father treats everyone--including my mom--the way he treats the people who work for him at the TV network.
"I've seen them from time to time. He'd bring me around, say 'This is my kid.' They'd nod in the right places and after a while he'd go away.
"That's where I learned it. So I nod a few more times.
"He goes away.
"Twenty-three minutes from now, I will, too."

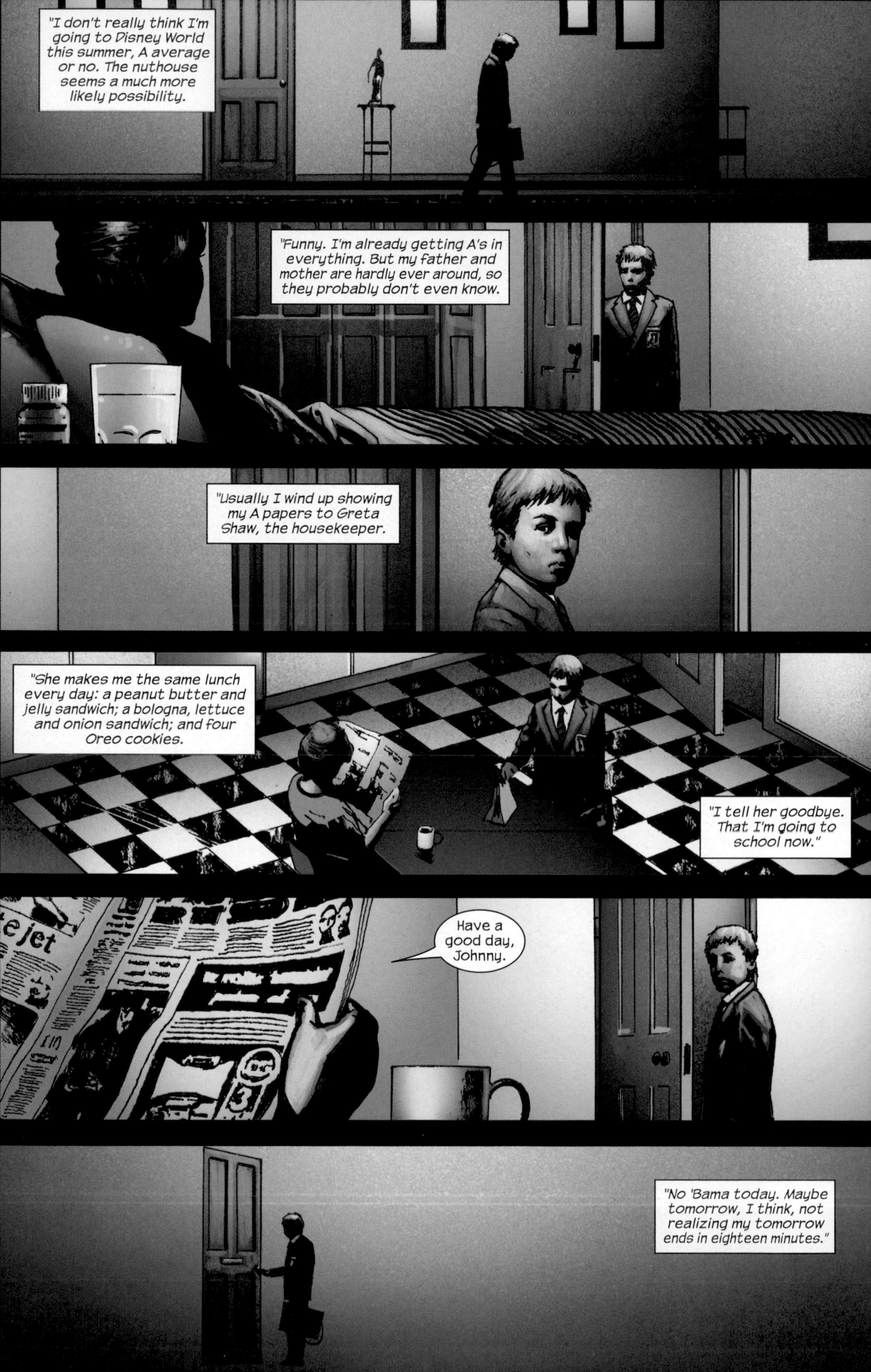
"I don't really think I'm going to Disney World this summer, A average or no. The nuthouse seems a much more likely possibility.
"Funny. I'm already getting A's in everything. But my father and mother are hardly ever around, so they probably don't even know.
"Usually I wind up showing my A papers to Greta Shaw, the housekeeper.
"She makes me the same lunch every day: a peanut butter and jelly sandwich; a bologna, lettuce and onion sandwich; and four Oreo cookies.
"I tell her goodbye. That I'm going to school now."
Have a good day, Johnny.
"No 'Bama today. Maybe tomorrow, I think, not realizing my tomorrow ends in eighteen minutes."

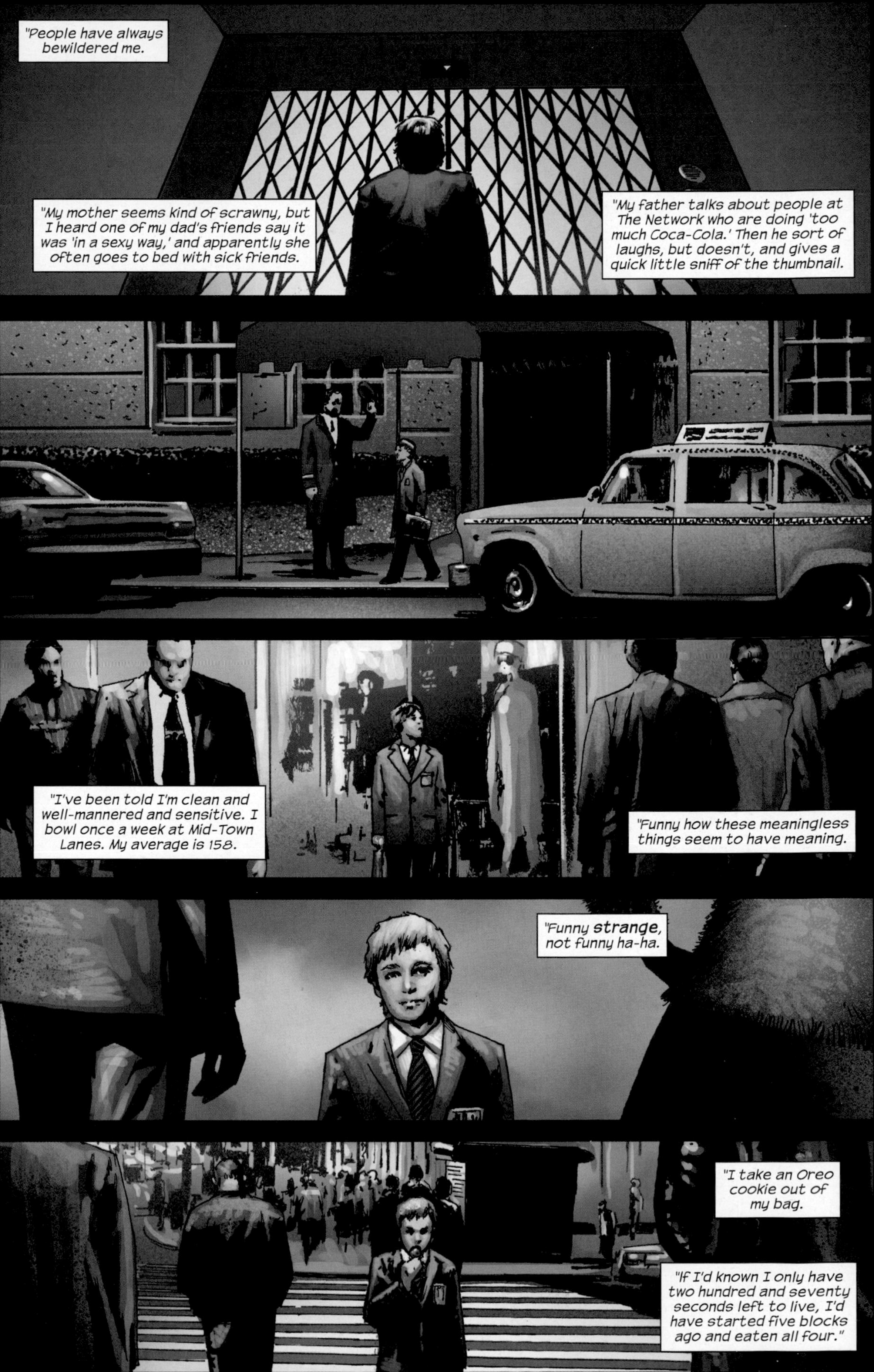
"People have always bewildered me.
"My mother seems kind of scrawny, but I heard one of my dad's friends say it was 'in a sexy way,' and apparently she often goes to bed with sick friends.
"My father talks about people at The Network who are doing 'too much Coca-Cola.' Then he sort of laughs, but doesn't, and gives a quick little sniff of the thumbnail.
"I've been told I'm clean and well-mannered and sensitive. I bowl once a week at Mid-Town Lanes. My average is 158.
"Funny how these meaningless things seem to have meaning.
"Funny **strange**, not funny ha-ha.
"I take an Oreo cookie out of my bag.
"If I'd known I only have two hundred and seventy seconds left to live, I'd have started five blocks ago and eaten all four."

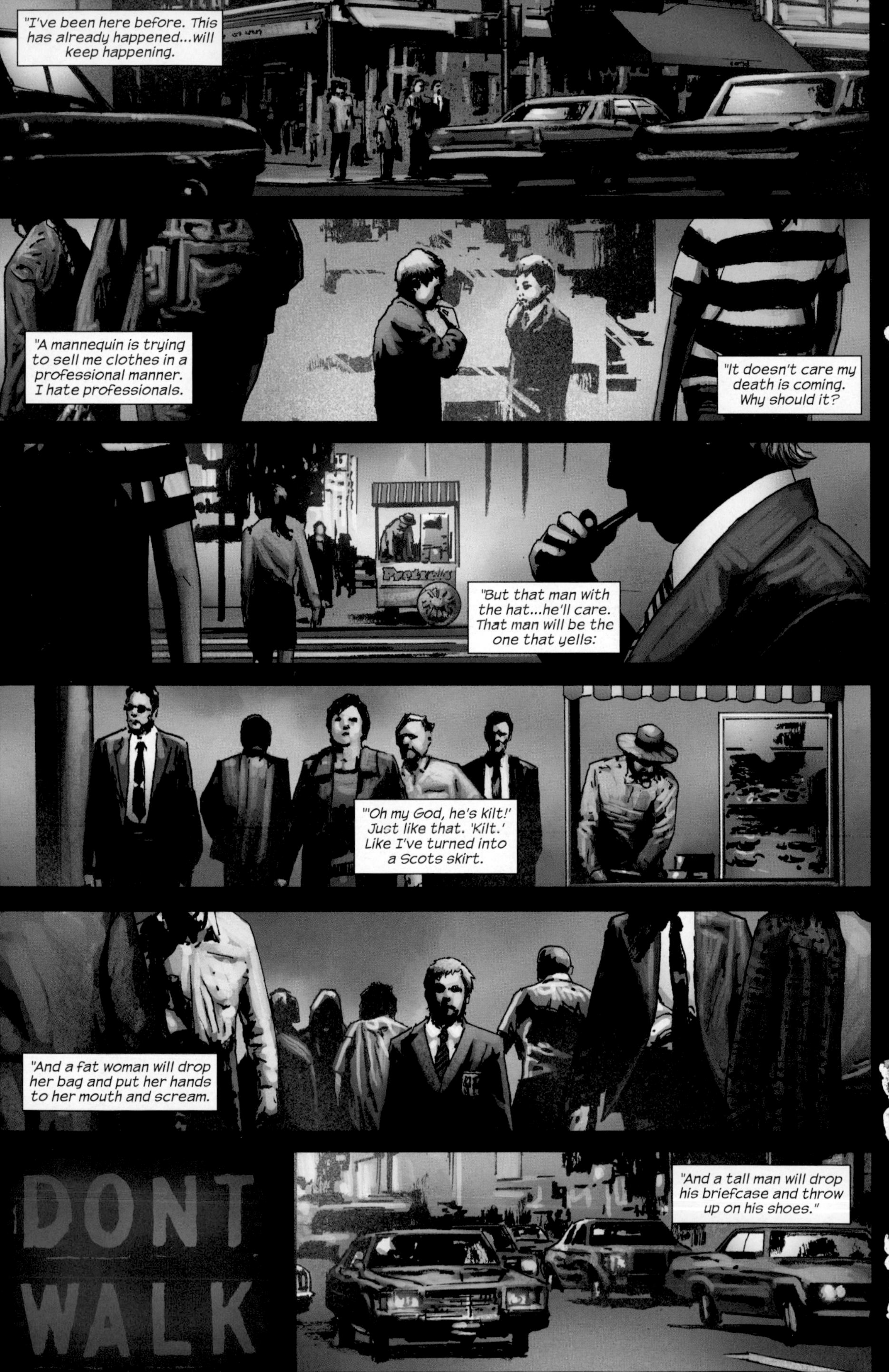
"I've been here before. This has already happened...will keep happening.
"A mannequin is trying to sell me clothes in a professional manner. I hate professionals.
"It doesn't care my death is coming. Why should it?
"But that man with the hat...he'll care. That man will be the one that yells:
"'Oh my God, he's kilt!' Just like that. 'Kilt.' Like I've turned into a Scots skirt.
"And a fat woman will drop her bag and put her hands to her mouth and scream.
DONT WALK
"And a tall man will drop his briefcase and throw up on his shoes."

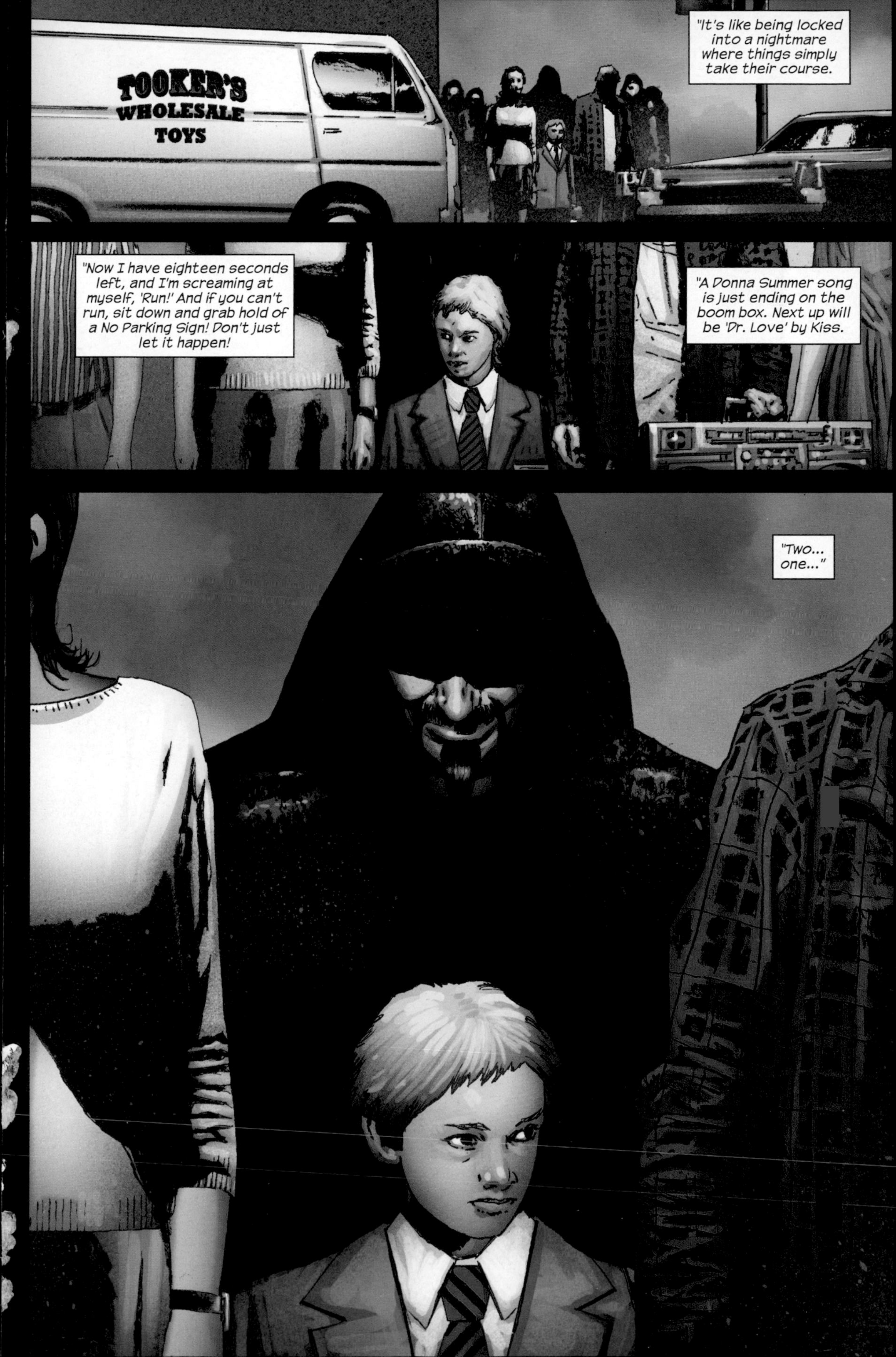
TOOKER'S WHOLESALE TOYS
"It's like being locked into a nightmare where things simply take their course.
"Now I have eighteen seconds left, and I'm screaming at myself, 'Run!' And if you can't run, sit down and grab hold of a No Parking Sign! Don't just let it happen!
"A Donna Summer song is just ending on the boom box. Next up will be 'Dr. Love' by Kiss.
"Two... one..."

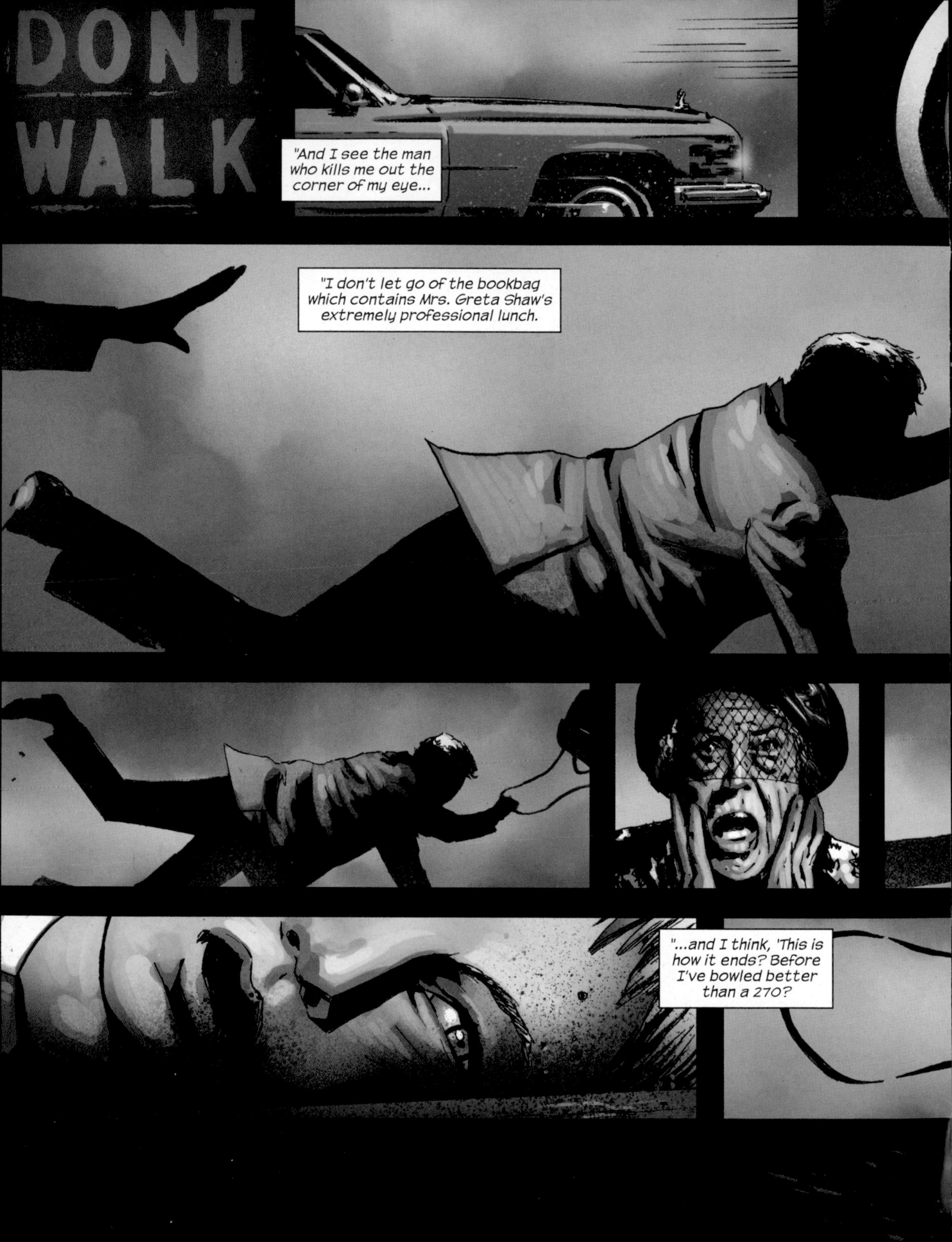
DONT
WALK
"And I see the man who kills me out the corner of my eye...
"I don't let go of the bookbag which contains Mrs. Greta Shaw's extremely professional lunch.
"...and I think, 'This is how it ends? Before I've bowled better than a 270?

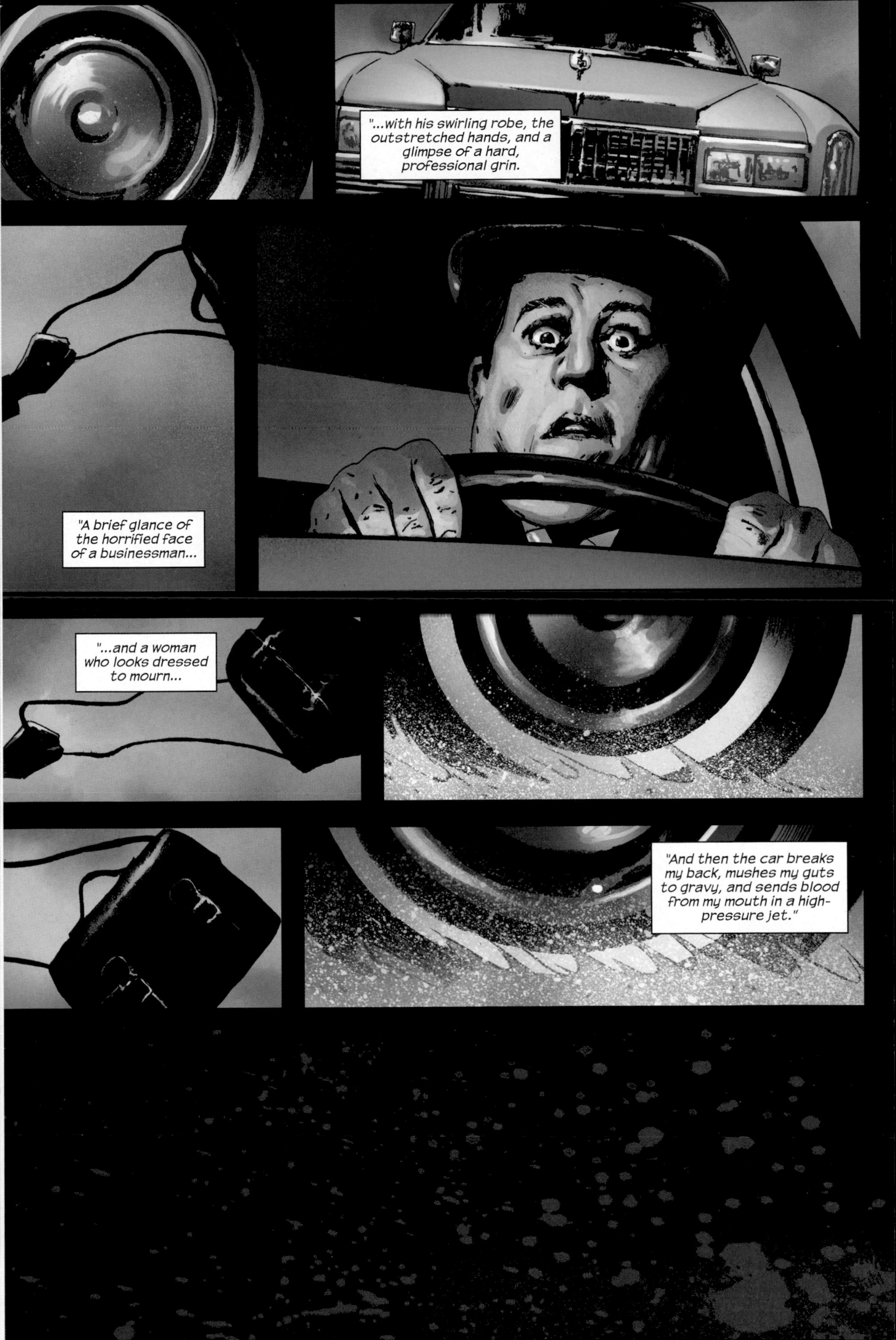
"...with his swirling robe, the outstretched hands, and a glimpse of a hard, professional grin.
"A brief glance of the horrified face of a businessman...
"...and a woman who looks dressed to mourn...
"And then the car breaks my back, mushes my guts to gravy, and sends blood from my mouth in a high-pressure jet."

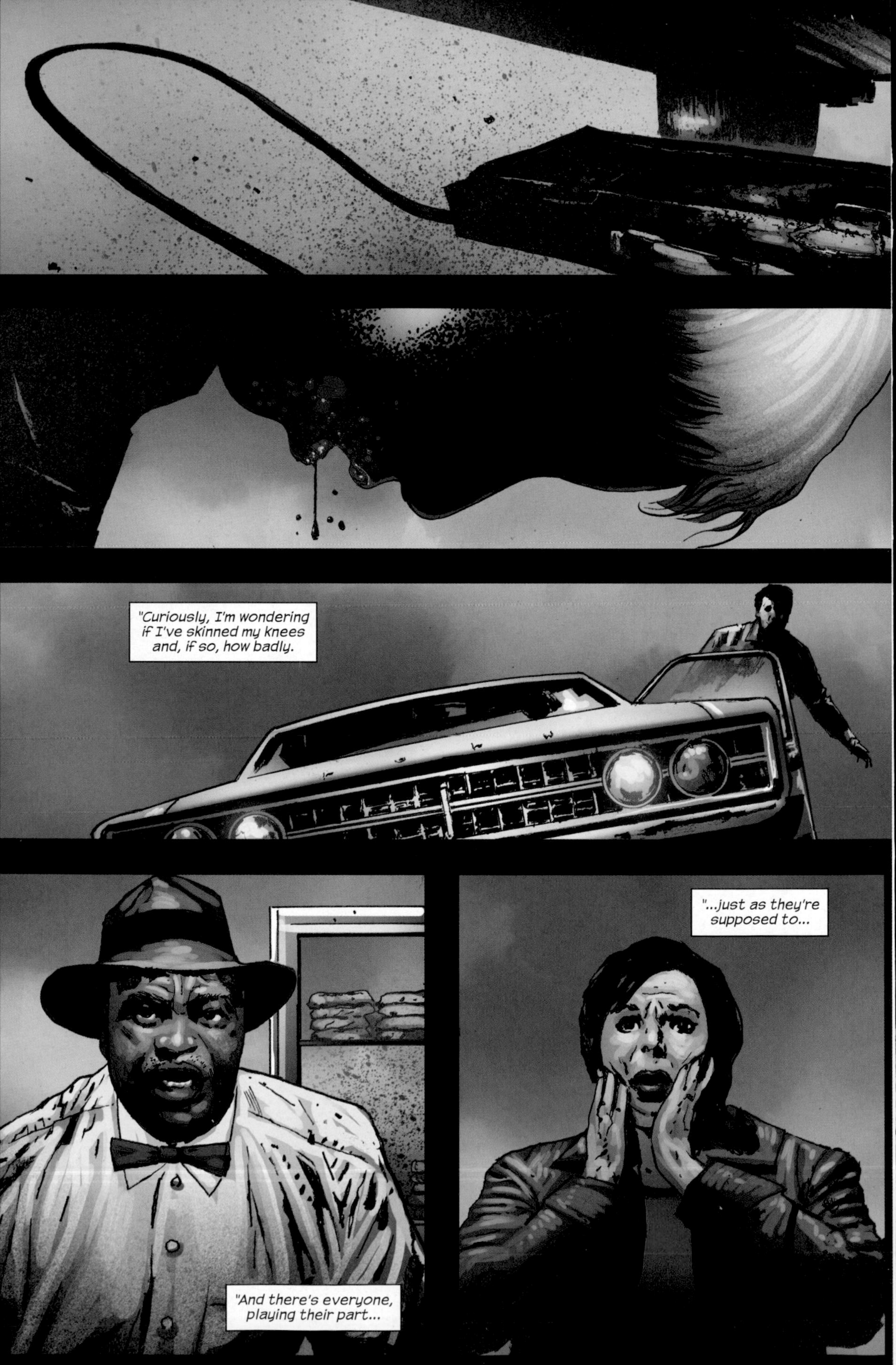
"Curiously, I'm wondering if I've skinned my knees and, if so, how badly.
"And there's everyone, playing their part...
"...just as they're supposed to...

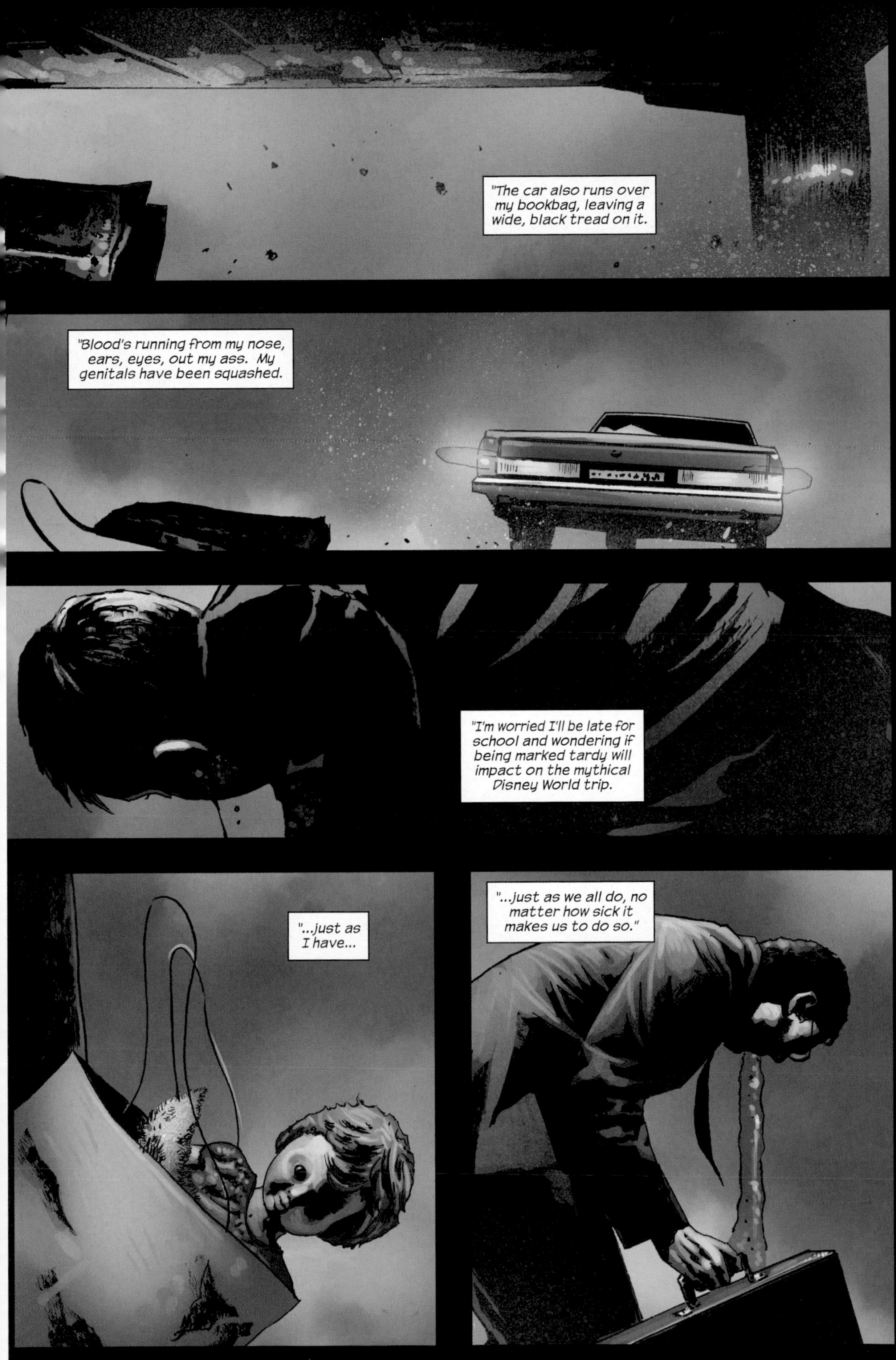
"The car also runs over my bookbag, leaving a wide, black tread on it.
"Blood's running from my nose, ears, eyes, out my ass. My genitals have been squashed.
"I'm worried I'll be late for school and wondering if being marked tardy will impact on the mythical Disney World trip.
"...just as I have...
"...just as we all do, no matter how sick it makes us to do so."

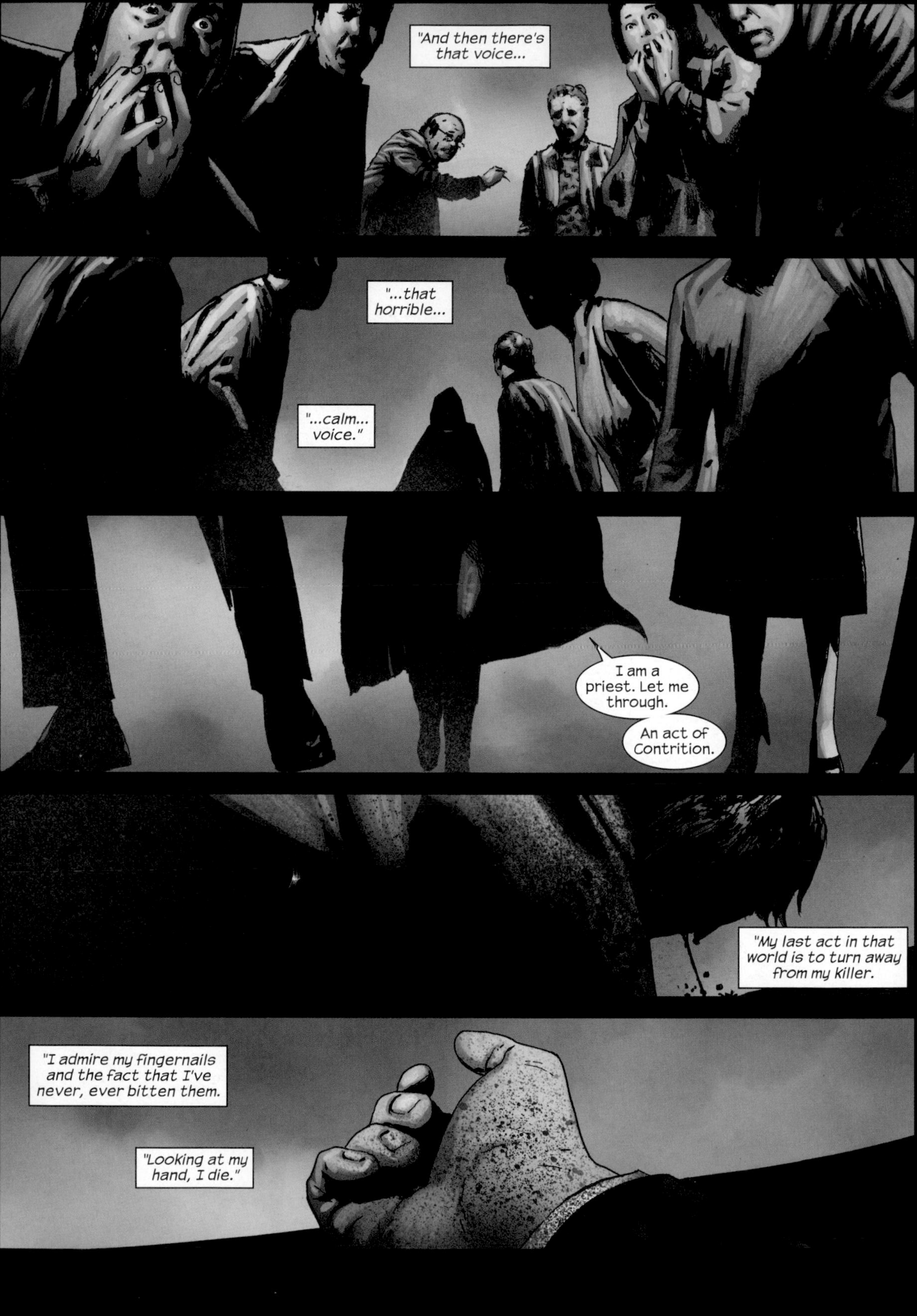
"And then there's that voice...
"...that horrible...
"...calm... voice."
I am a priest. Let me through.
An act of Contrition.
"My last act in that world is to turn away from my killer.
"I admire my fingernails and the fact that I've never, ever bitten them.
"Looking at my hand, I die."

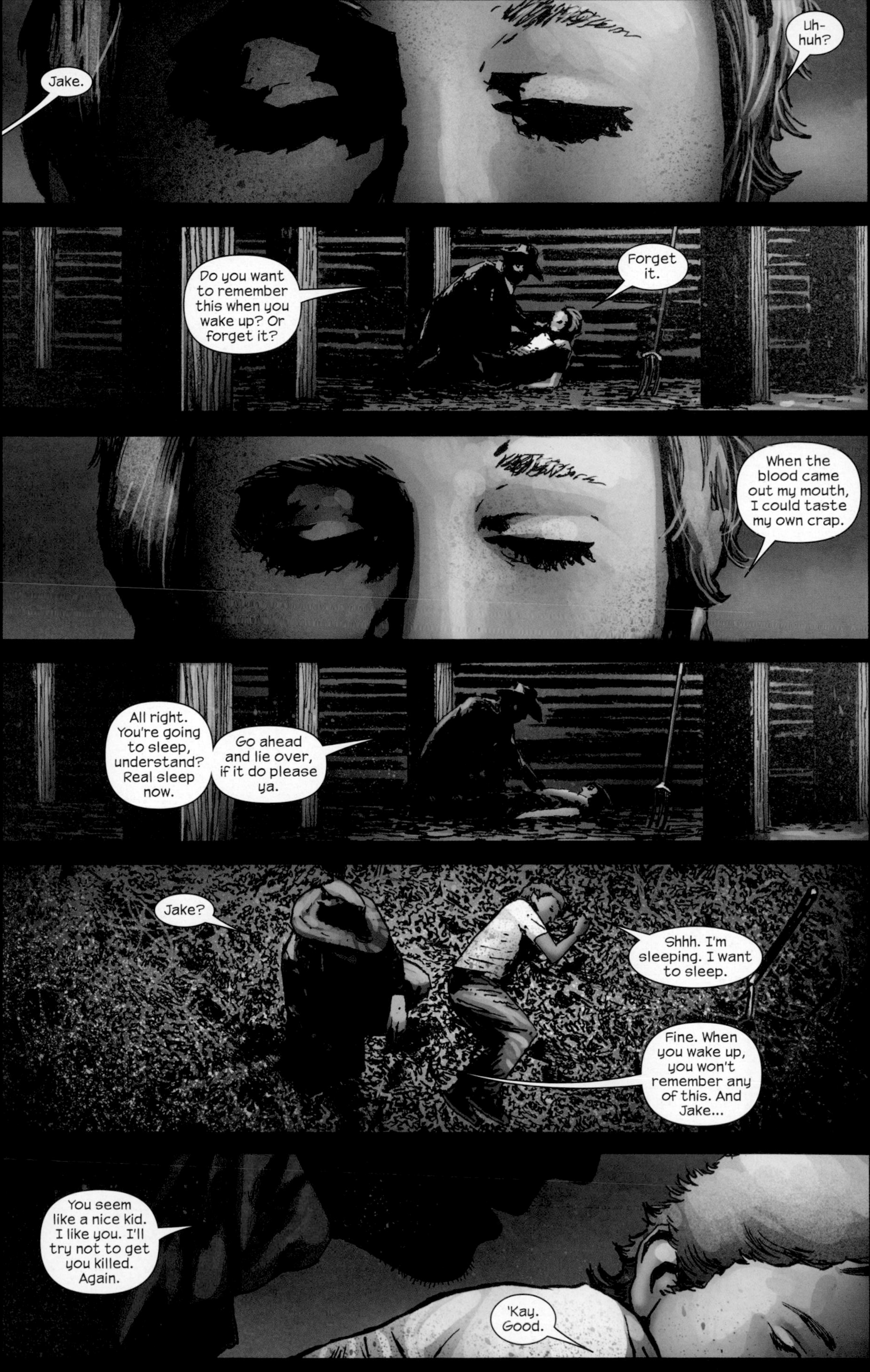
Jake.
Uh-huh?
Do you want to remember this when you wake up? Or forget it?
Forget it.
When the blood came out my mouth, I could taste my own crap.
All right. You're going to sleep, understand? Real sleep now.
Go ahead and lie over, if it do please ya.
Jake?
Shhh. I'm sleeping. I want to sleep.
Fine. When you wake up, you won't remember any of this. And Jake...
You seem like a nice kid. I like you. I'll try not to get you killed. Again.
'Kay. Good.

THE DARK TOWER
~ THE GUNSLINGER ~
STEPHEN KING

THE WAY STATION

CHAPTER THREE

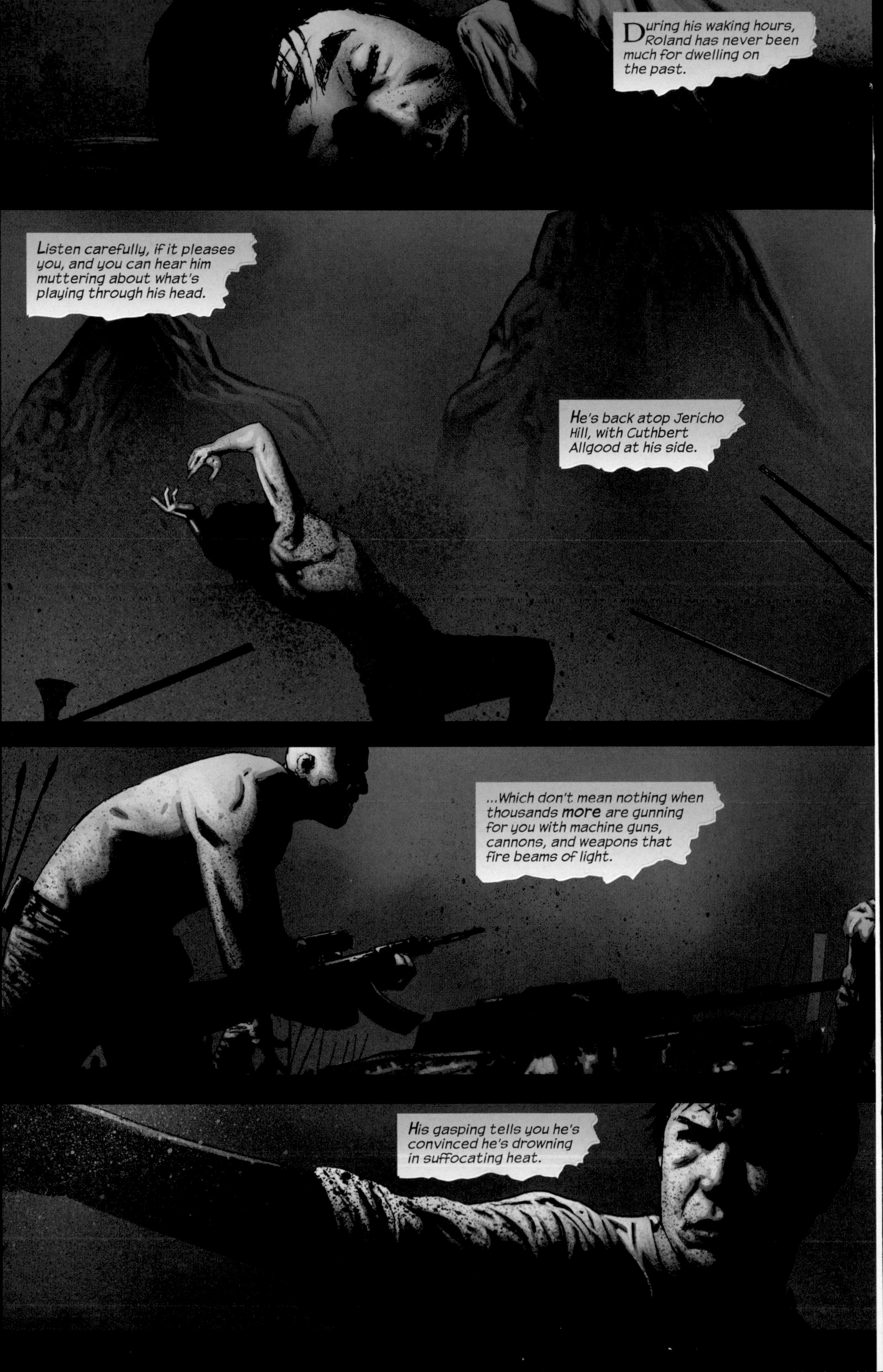
During his waking hours, Roland has never been much for dwelling on the past.
Listen carefully, if it pleases you, and you can hear him muttering about what's playing through his head.
He's back atop Jericho Hill, with Cuthbert Allgood at his side.
...Which don't mean nothing when thousands more are gunning for you with machine guns, cannons, and weapons that fire beams of light.
His gasping tells you he's convinced he's drowning in suffocating heat.

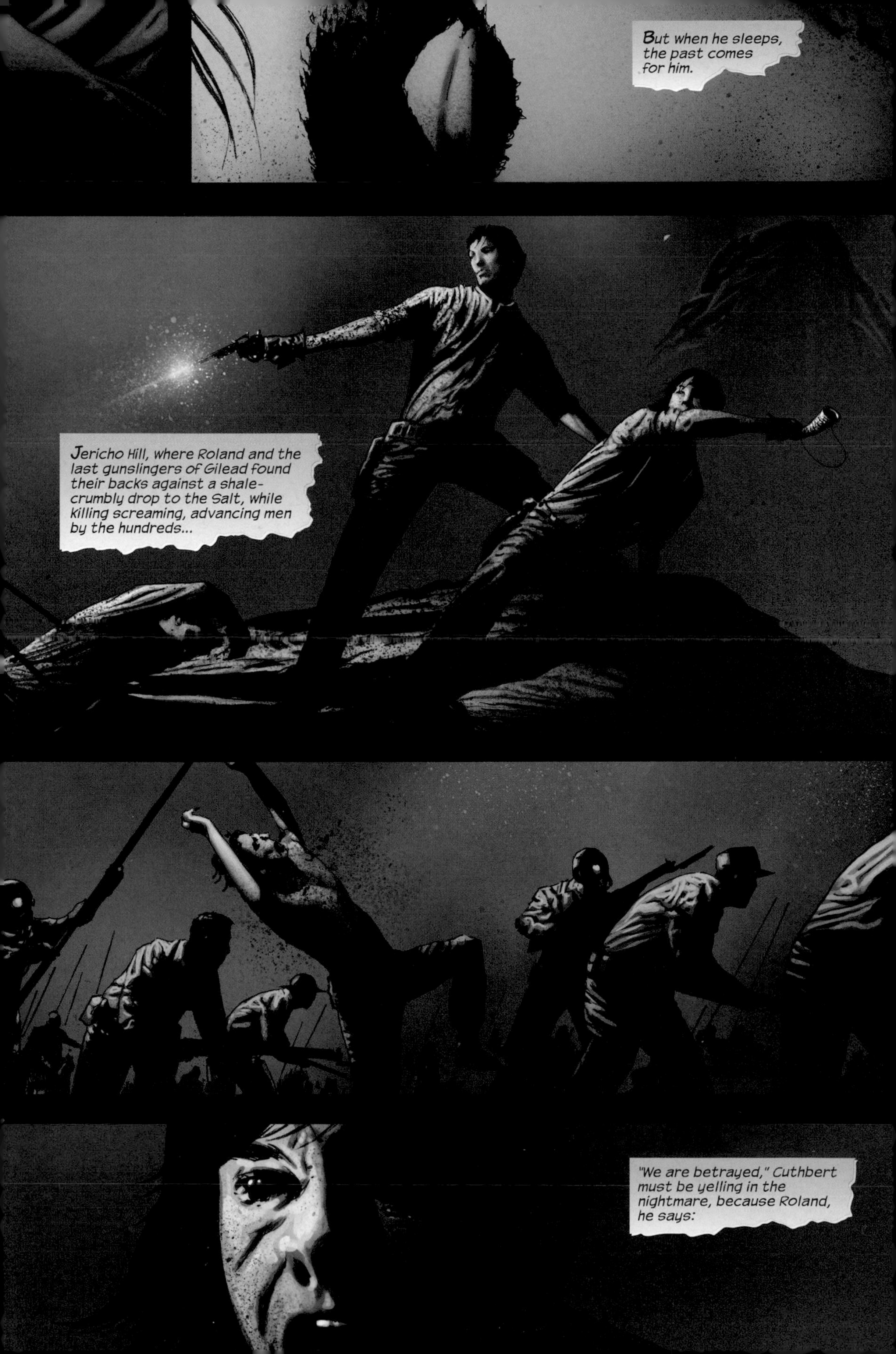

But when he sleeps, the past comes for him.
Jericho Hill, where Roland and the last gunslingers of Gilead found their backs against a shale-crumbly drop to the Salt, while killing screaming, advancing men by the hundreds...
"We are betrayed," Cuthbert must be yelling in the nightmare, because Roland, he says:

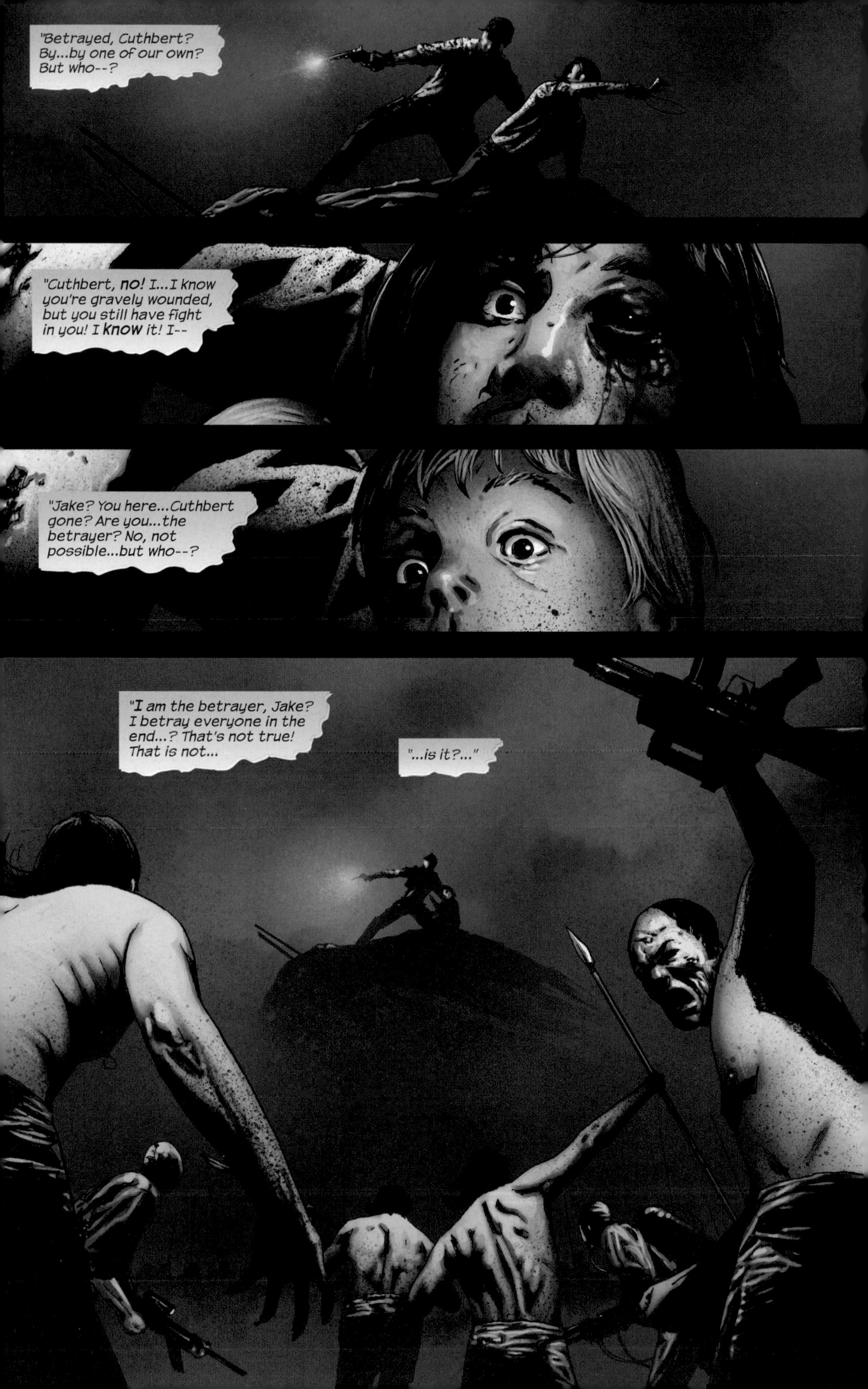
"Betrayed, Cuthbert? By...by one of our own? But who--?
"Cuthbert, no! I...I know you're gravely wounded, but you still have fight in you! I KNOW it! I--
"Jake? You here...Cuthbert gone? Are you...the betrayer? No, not possible...but who--?
"I am the betrayer, Jake? I betray everyone in the end...? That's not true! That is not...
"...is it?..."

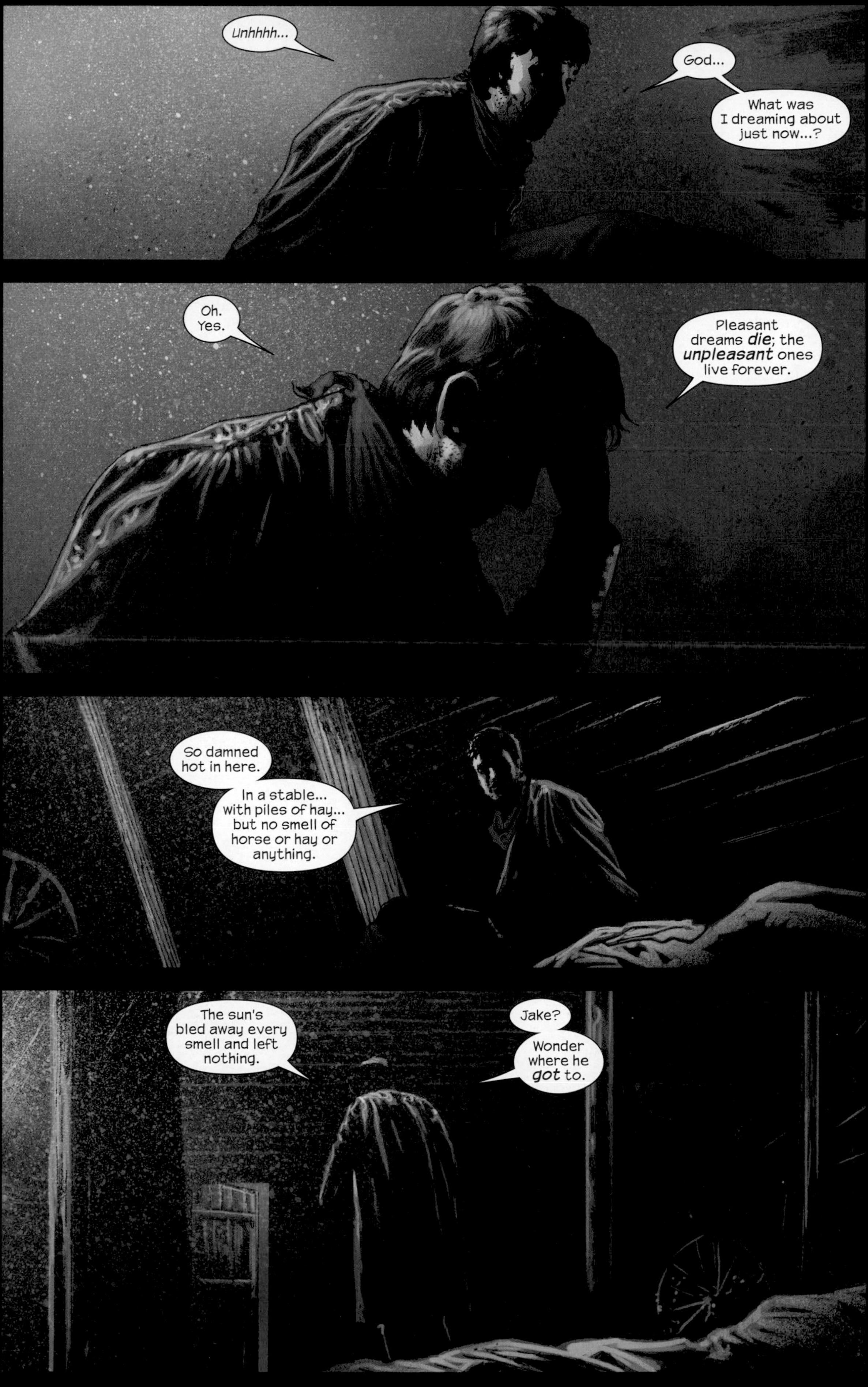
Unhhhh...
God...
What was I dreaming about just now...?
Oh. Yes.
Pleasant dreams *die*; the *unpleasant* ones live forever.
So damned hot in here.
In a stable... with piles of hay... but no smell of horse or hay or anything.
The sun's bled away every smell and left nothing.
Jake?
Wonder where he *got* to.

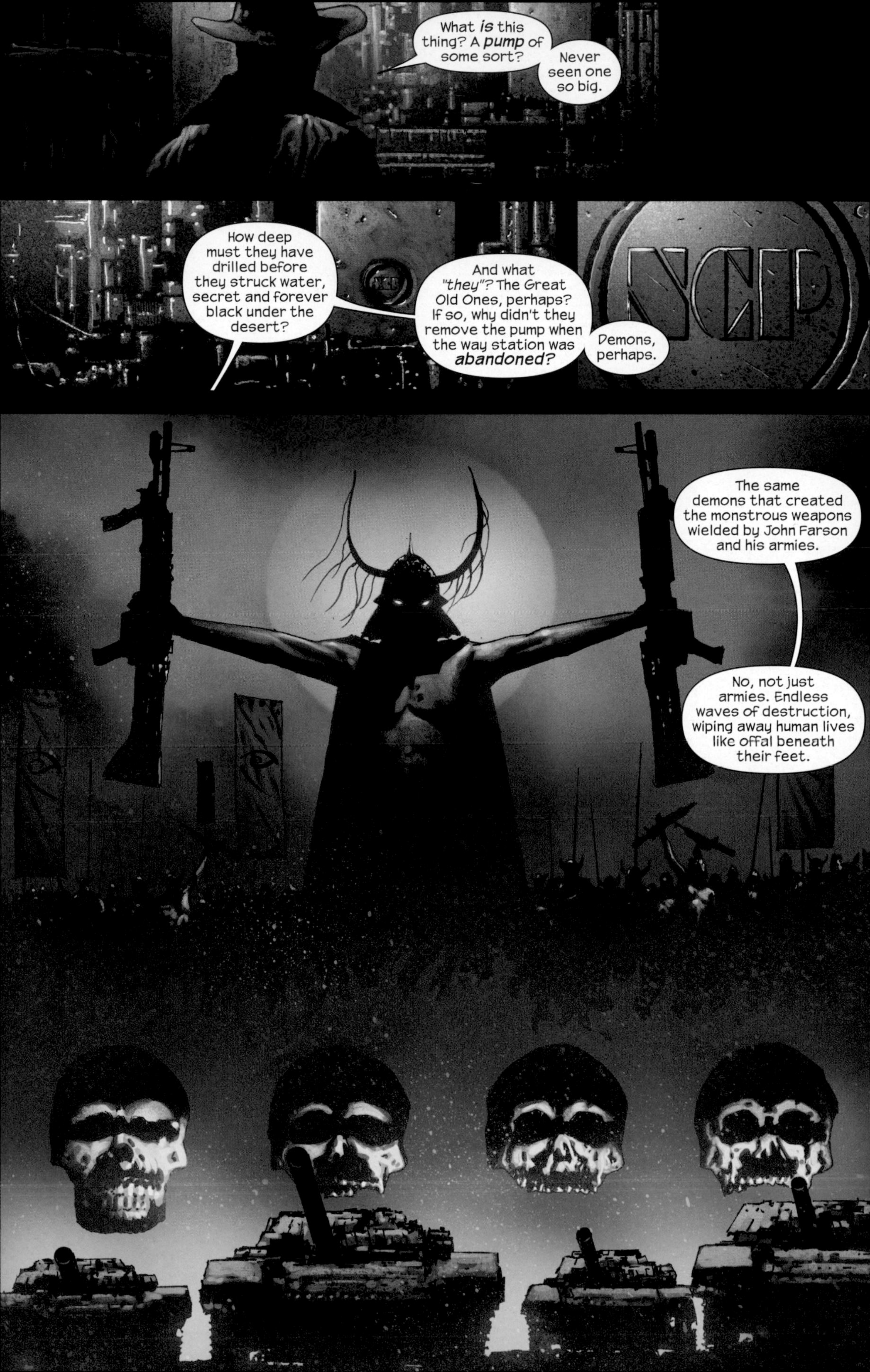
What *is* this thing? A *pump* of some sort?
Never seen one so big.
How deep must they have drilled before they struck water, secret and forever black under the desert?
And what "*they*"? The Great Old Ones, perhaps? If so, why didn't they remove the pump when the way station was ***abandoned?***
NCP
Demons, perhaps.
The same demons that created the monstrous weapons wielded by John Farson and his armies.
No, not just armies. Endless waves of destruction, wiping away human lives like offal beneath their feet.

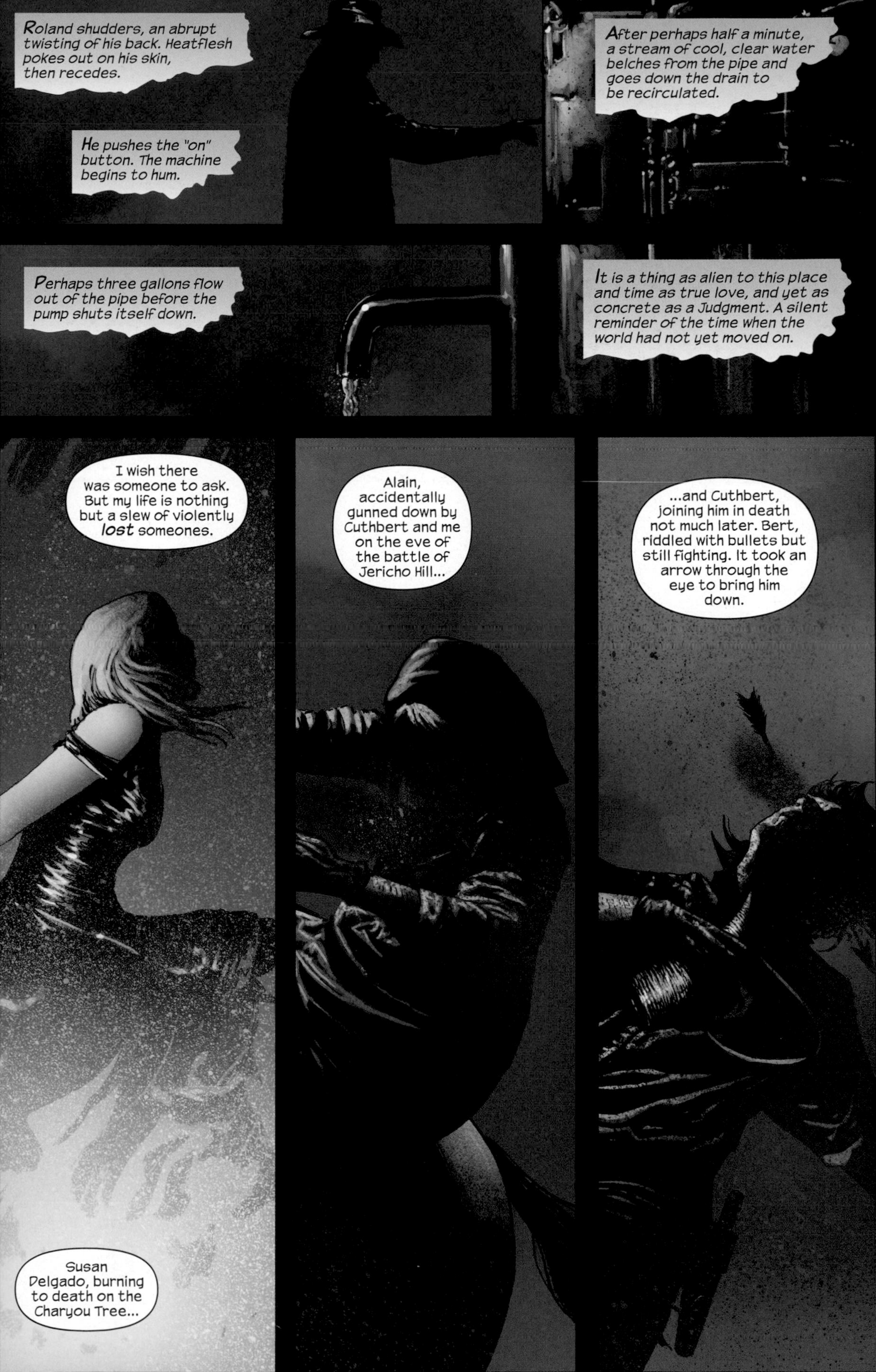
Roland shudders, an abrupt twisting of his back. Heatflesh pokes out on his skin, then recedes.
He pushes the "on" button. The machine begins to hum.
After perhaps half a minute, a stream of cool, clear water belches from the pipe and goes down the drain to be recirculated.
Perhaps three gallons flow out of the pipe before the pump shuts itself down.
It is a thing as alien to this place and time as true love, and yet as concrete as a Judgment. A silent reminder of the time when the world had not yet moved on.
I wish there was someone to ask. But my life is nothing but a slew of violently *lost* someones.
Susan Delgado, burning to death on the Charyou Tree...
Alain, accidentally gunned down by Cuthbert and me on the eve of the battle of Jericho Hill...
...and Cuthbert, joining him in death not much later. Bert, riddled with bullets but still fighting. It took an arrow through the eye to bring him down.

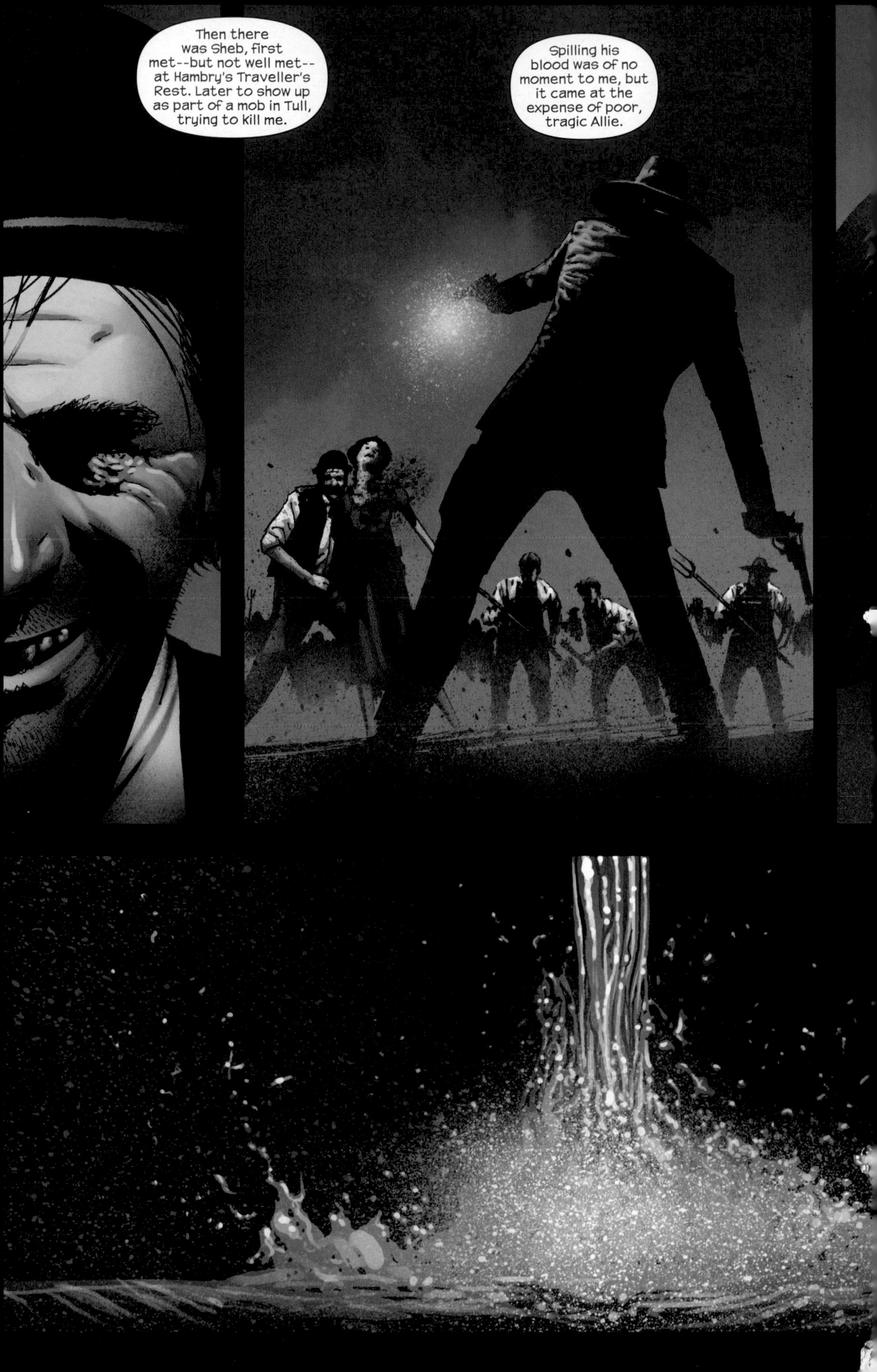
Then there was Sheb, first met--but not well met--at Hambry's Traveller's Rest. Later to show up as part of a mob in Tull, trying to kill me.
Spilling his blood was of no moment to me, but it came at the expense of poor, tragic Allie.

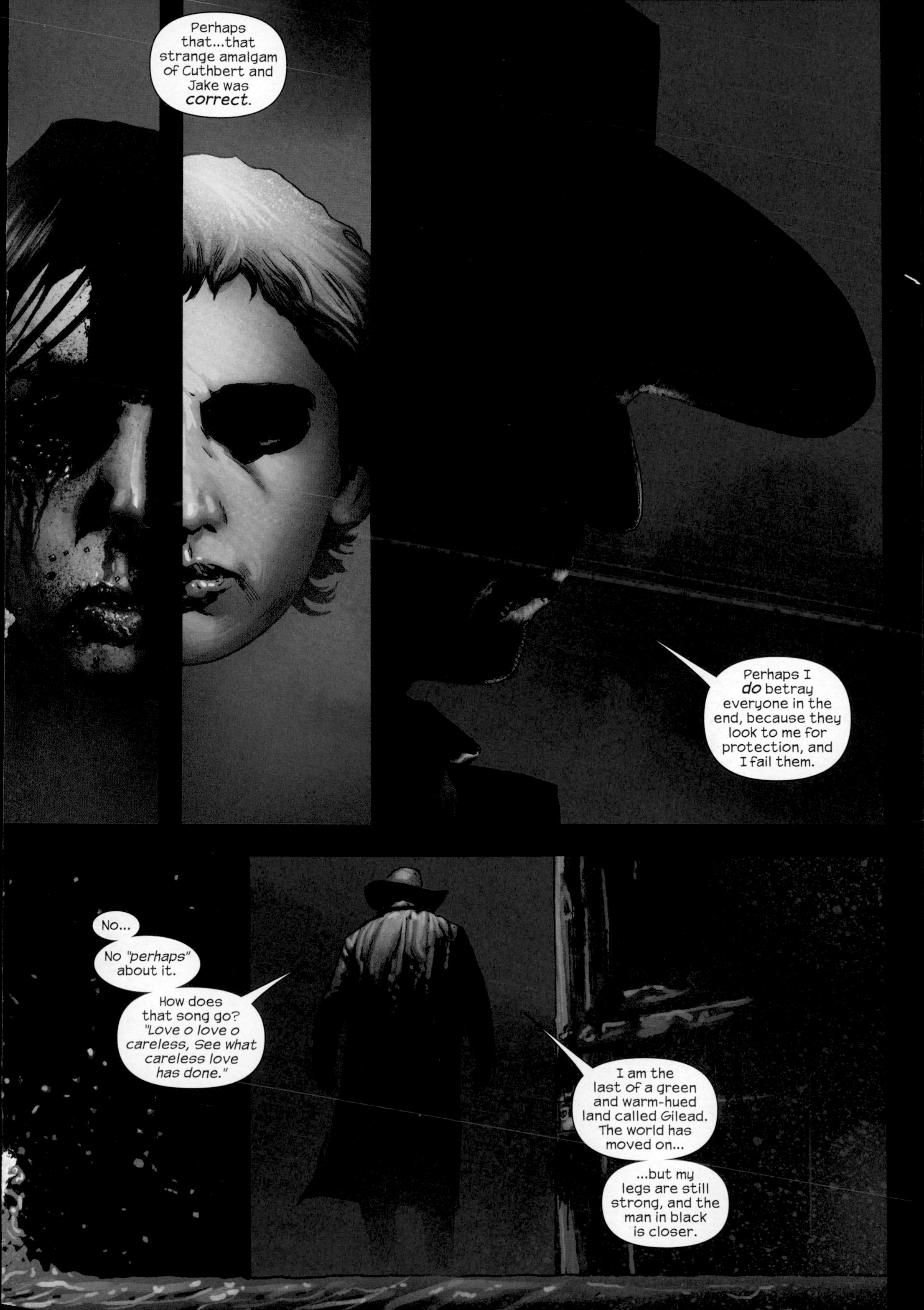
Perhaps that...that strange amalgam of Cuthbert and Jake was *correct*.
Perhaps I *do* betray everyone in the end, because they look to me for protection, and I fail them.
No...
No *"perhaps"* about it.
How does that song go? *"Love o love o careless, See what careless love has done."*
I am the last of a green and warm-hued land called Gilead. The world has moved on...
...but my legs are still strong, and the man in black is closer.

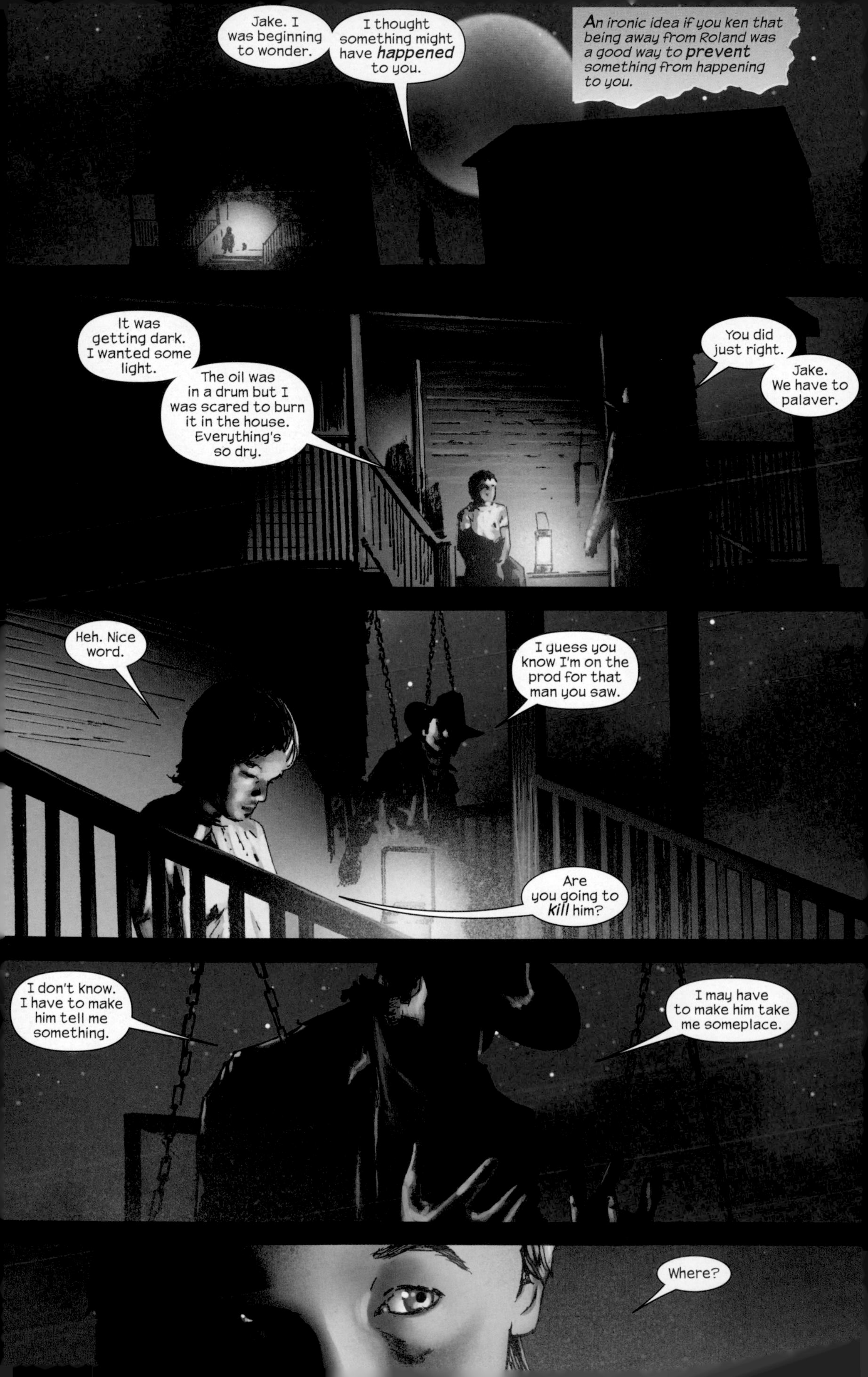
Jake. I was beginning to wonder.
I thought something might have *happened* to you.
An ironic idea if you ken that being away from Roland was a good way to **prevent** something from happening to you.
It was getting dark. I wanted some light.
The oil was in a drum but I was scared to burn it in the house. Everything's so dry.
You did just right.
Jake. We have to palaver.
Heh. Nice word.
I guess you know I'm on the prod for that man you saw.
Are you going to ***kill*** him?
I don't know. I have to make him tell me something.
I may have to make him take me someplace.
Where?

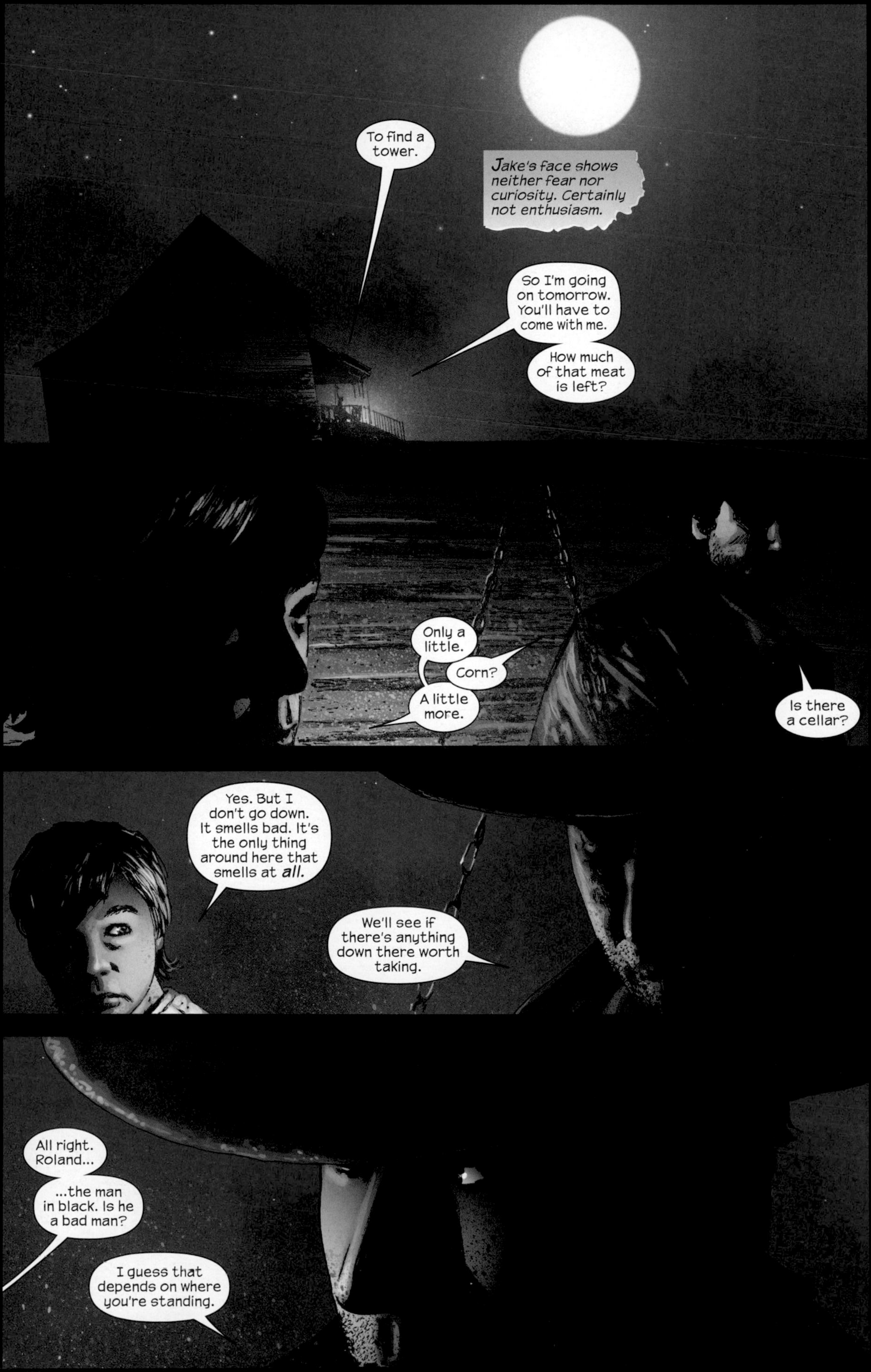
To find a tower.
Jake's face shows neither fear nor curiosity. Certainly not enthusiasm.
So I'm going on tomorrow. You'll have to come with me.
How much of that meat is left?
Only a little.
Corn?
A little more.
Is there a cellar?
Yes. But I don't go down. It smells bad. It's the only thing around here that smells at *all.*
We'll see if there's anything down there worth taking.
All right. Roland...
...the man in black. Is he a bad man?
I guess that depends on where you're standing.

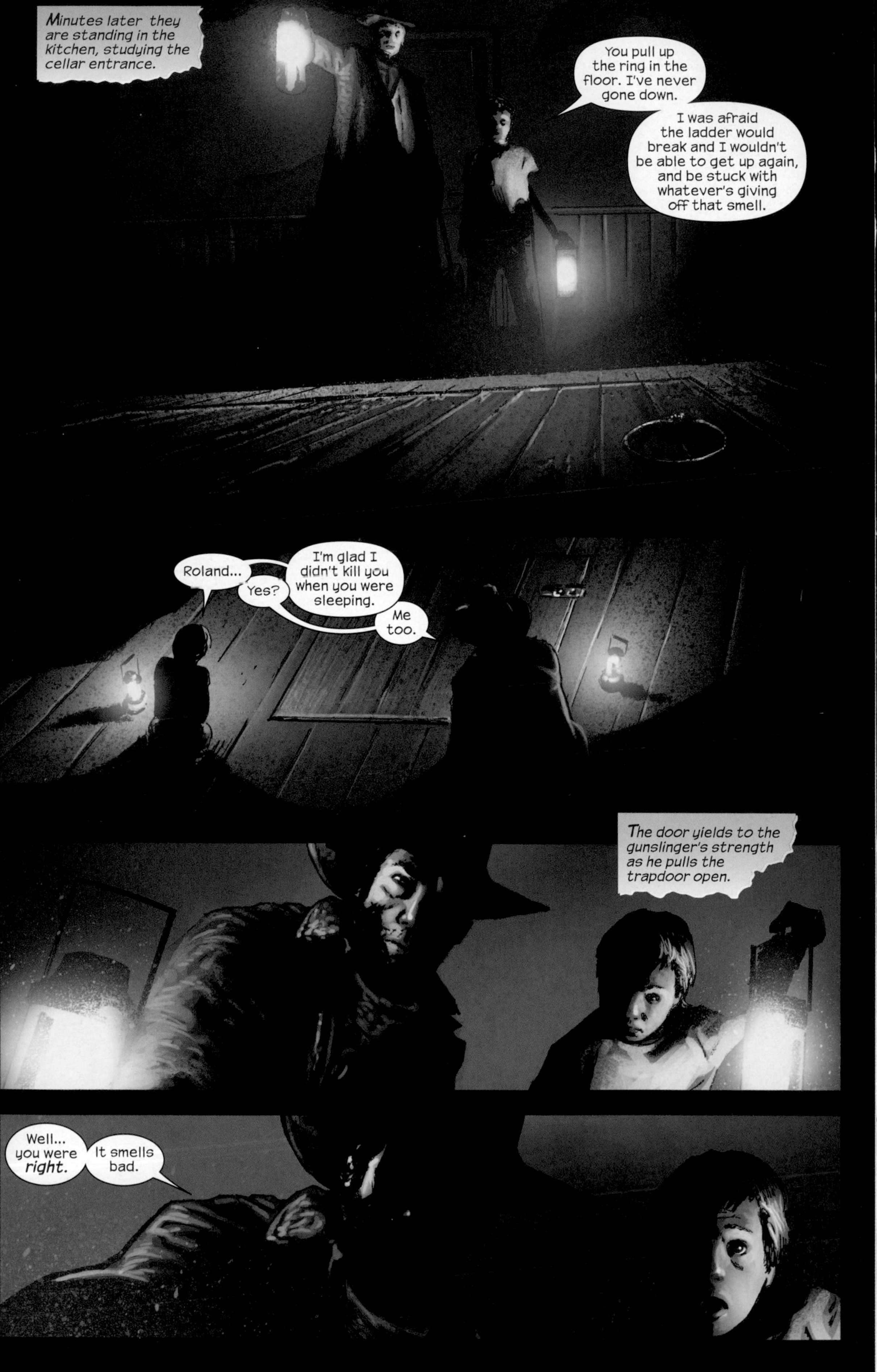

Minutes later they are standing in the kitchen, studying the cellar entrance.
You pull up the ring in the floor. I've never gone down.
I was afraid the ladder would break and I wouldn't be able to get up again, and be stuck with whatever's giving off that smell.
Roland...
Yes?
I'm glad I didn't kill you when you were sleeping.
Me too.
The door yields to the gunslinger's strength as he pulls the trapdoor open.
Well... you were *right*.
It smells bad.

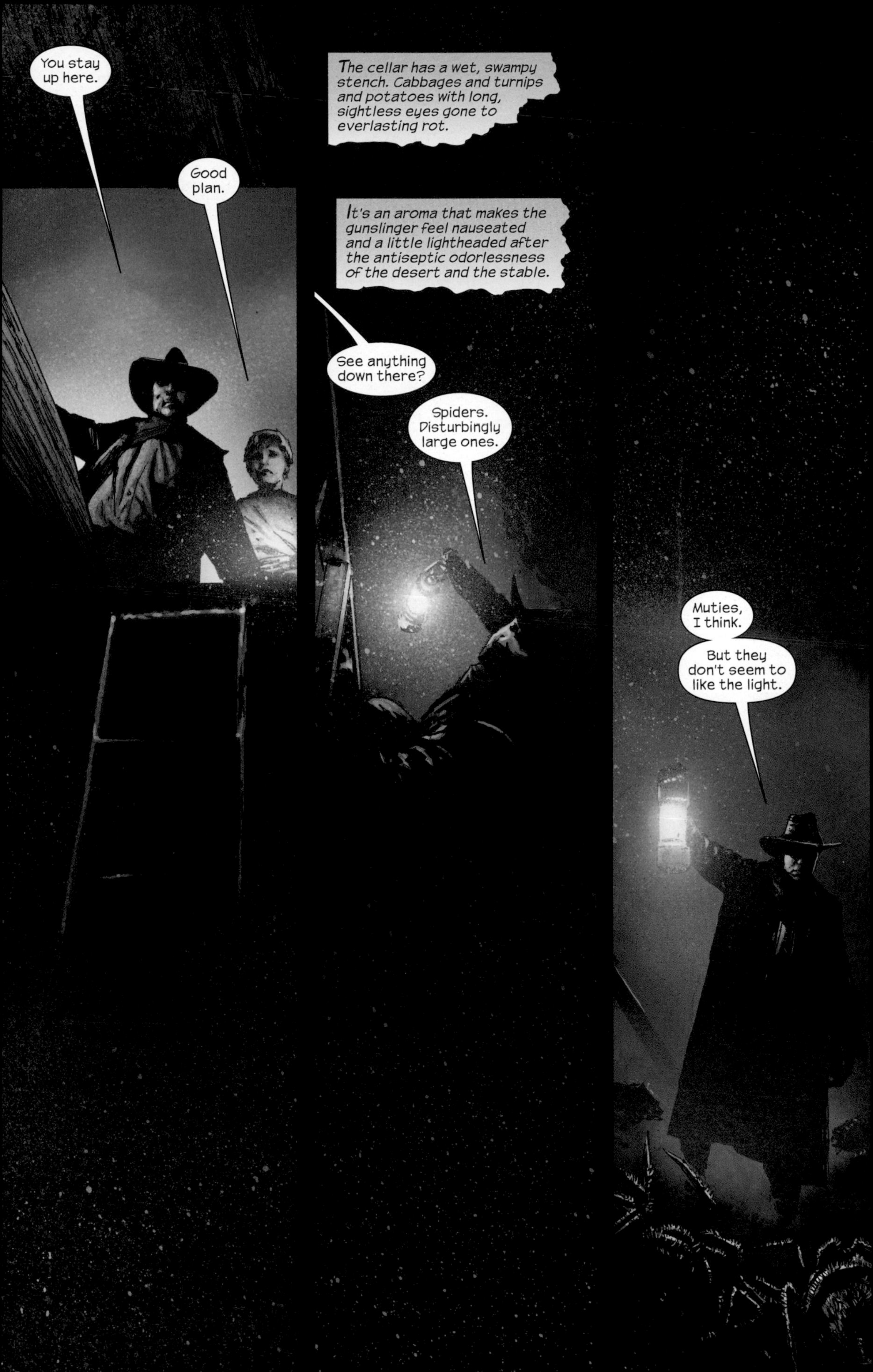
You stay up here.
Good plan.
The cellar has a wet, swampy stench. Cabbages and turnips and potatoes with long, sightless eyes gone to everlasting rot.
It's an aroma that makes the gunslinger feel nauseated and a little lightheaded after the antiseptic odorlessness of the desert and the stable.
See anything down there?
Spiders. Disturbingly large ones.
Muties, I think.
But they don't seem to like the light.

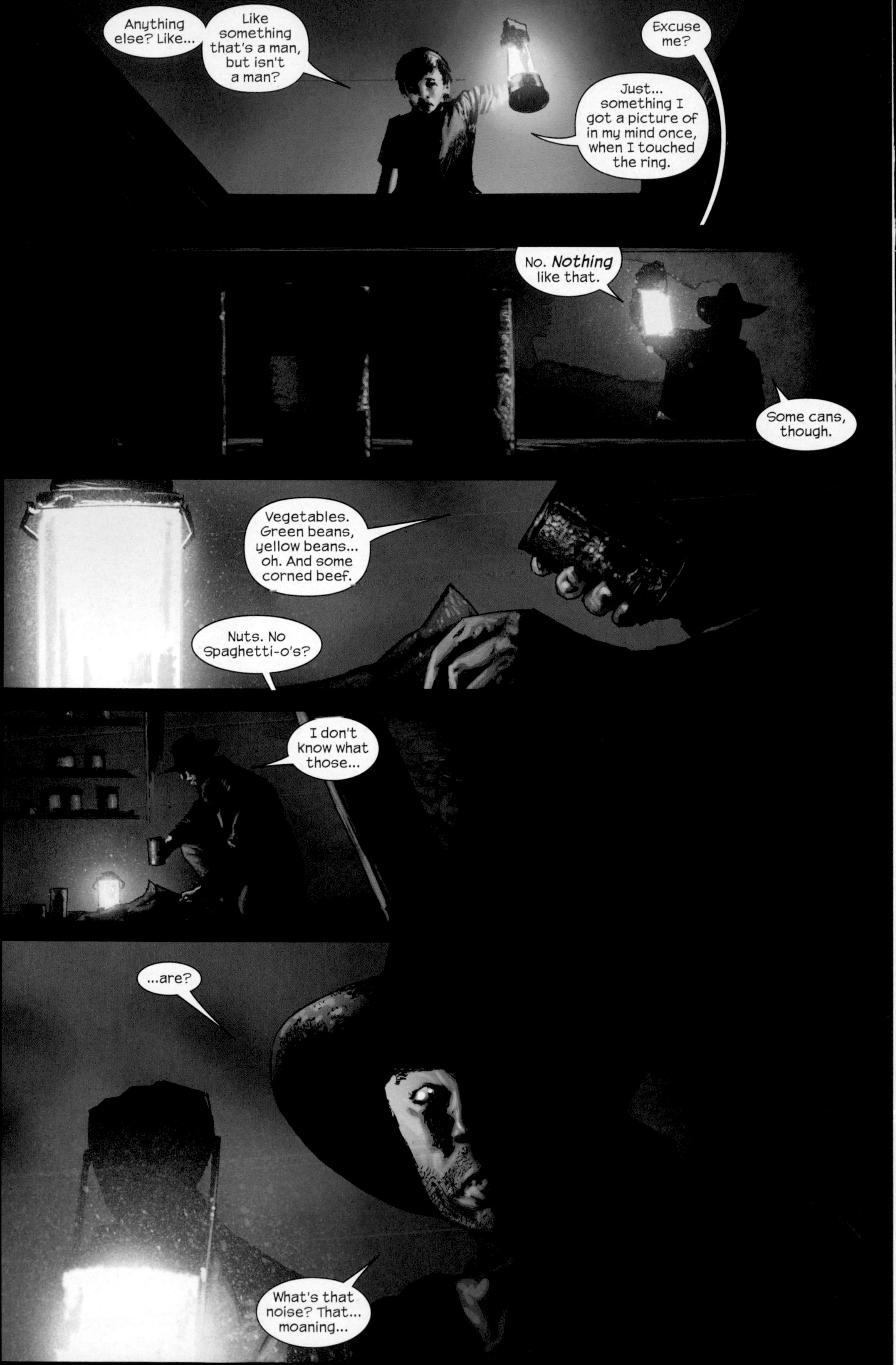
Anything else? Like...
Like something that's a man, but isn't a man?
Excuse me?
Just... something I got a picture of in my mind once, when I touched the ring.
No. *Nothing* like that.
Some cans, though.
Vegetables. Green beans, yellow beans... oh. And some corned beef.
Nuts. No Spaghetti-o's?
I don't know what those...
...are?
What's that noise? That... moaning...

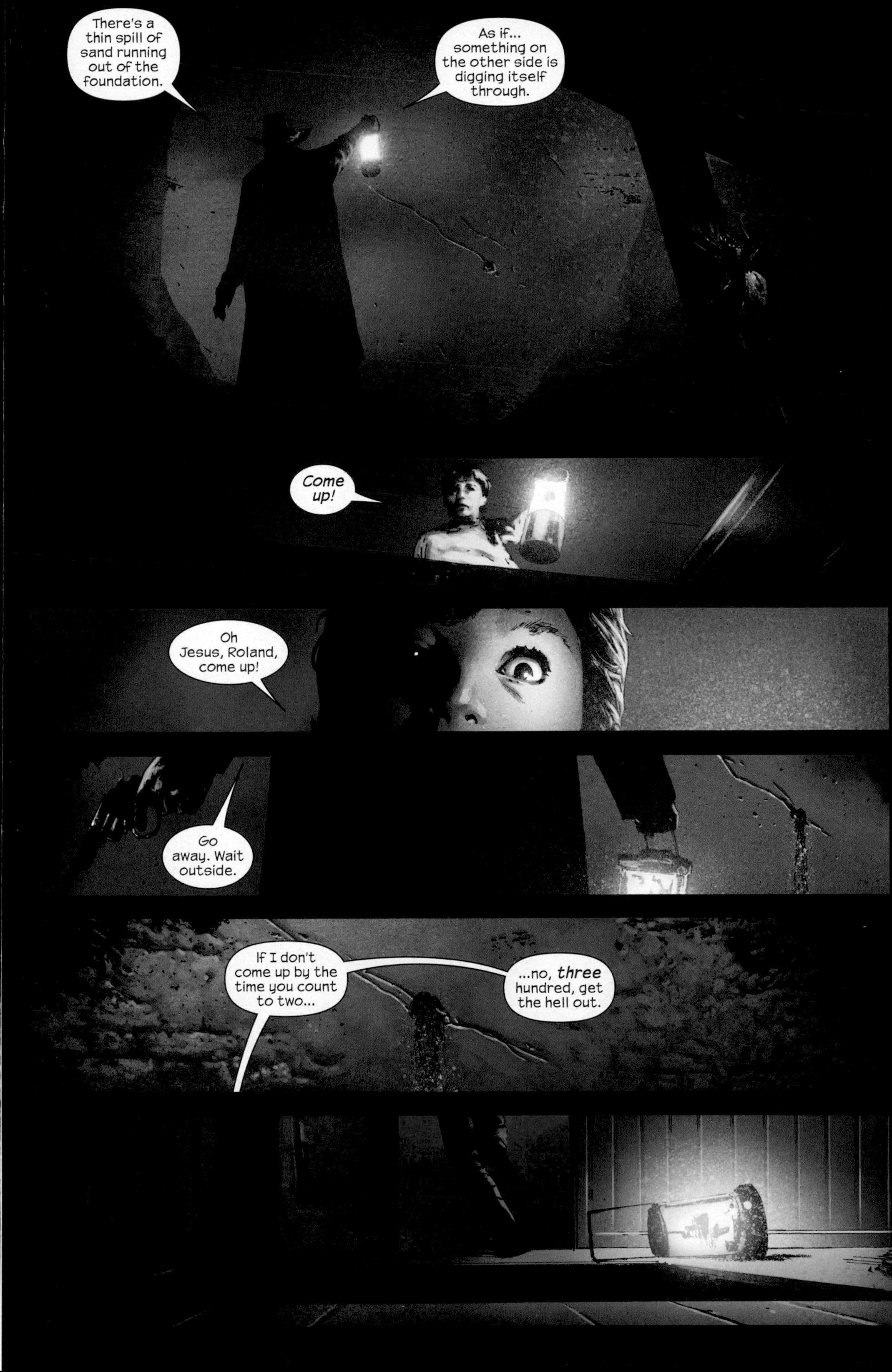
There's a thin spill of sand running out of the foundation.
As if... something on the other side is digging itself through.
Come up!
Oh Jesus, Roland, come up!
Go away. Wait outside.
If I don't come up by the time you count to two...
...no, *three* hundred, get the hell out.

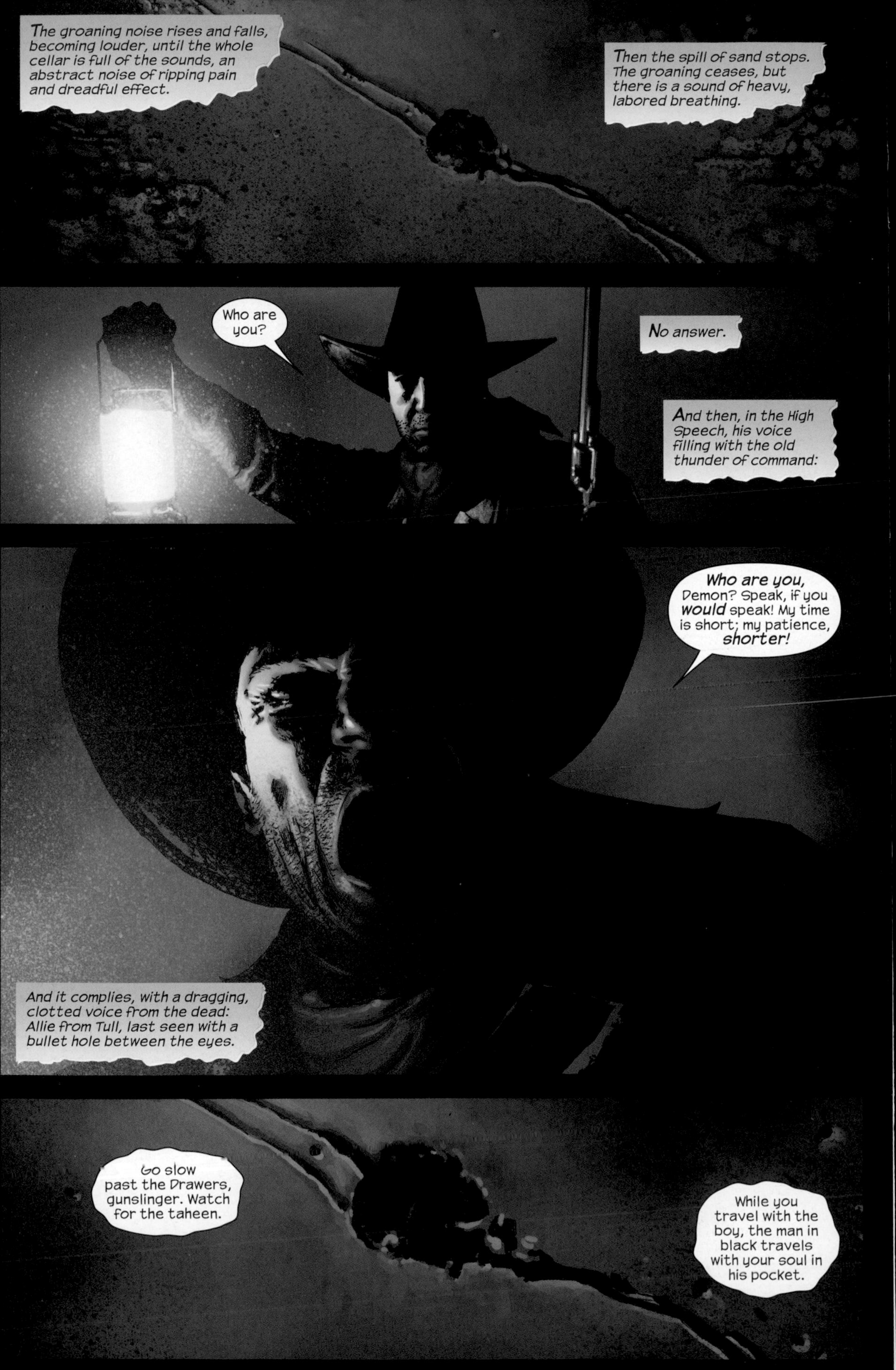
The groaning noise rises and falls, becoming louder, until the whole cellar is full of the sounds, an abstract noise of ripping pain and dreadful effect.
Then the spill of sand stops. The groaning ceases, but there is a sound of heavy, labored breathing.
Who are you?
No answer.
And then, in the High Speech, his voice filling with the old thunder of command:
Who are you, Demon? Speak, if you would speak! My time is short; my patience, shorter!
And it complies, with a dragging, clotted voice from the dead: Allie from Tull, last seen with a bullet hole between the eyes.
Go slow past the Drawers, gunslinger. Watch for the taheen.
While you travel with the boy, the man in black travels with your soul in his pocket.

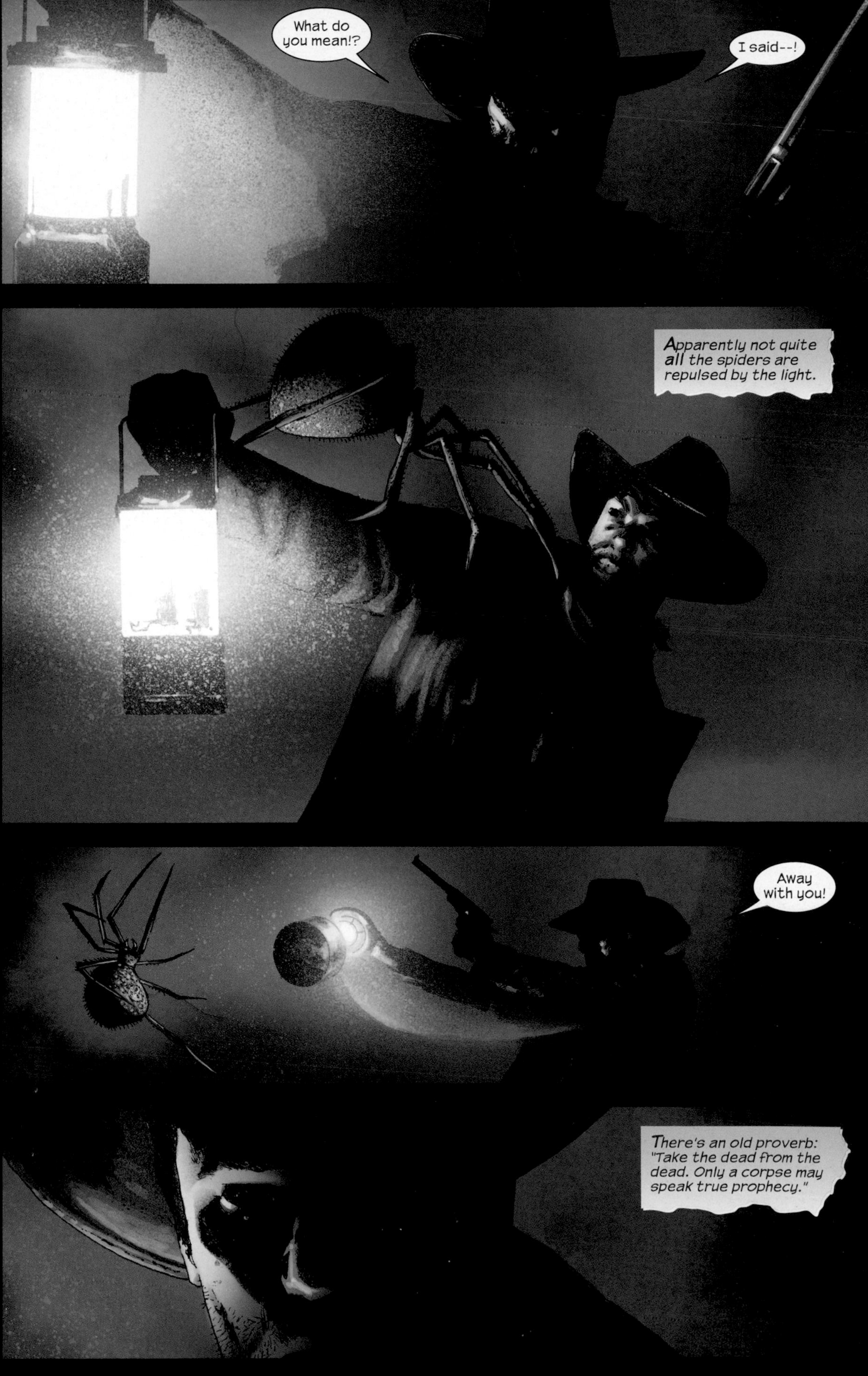
What do you mean!?
I said--!
Apparently not quite all the spiders are repulsed by the light.
Away with you!
There's an old proverb: "Take the dead from the dead. Only a corpse may speak true prophecy."

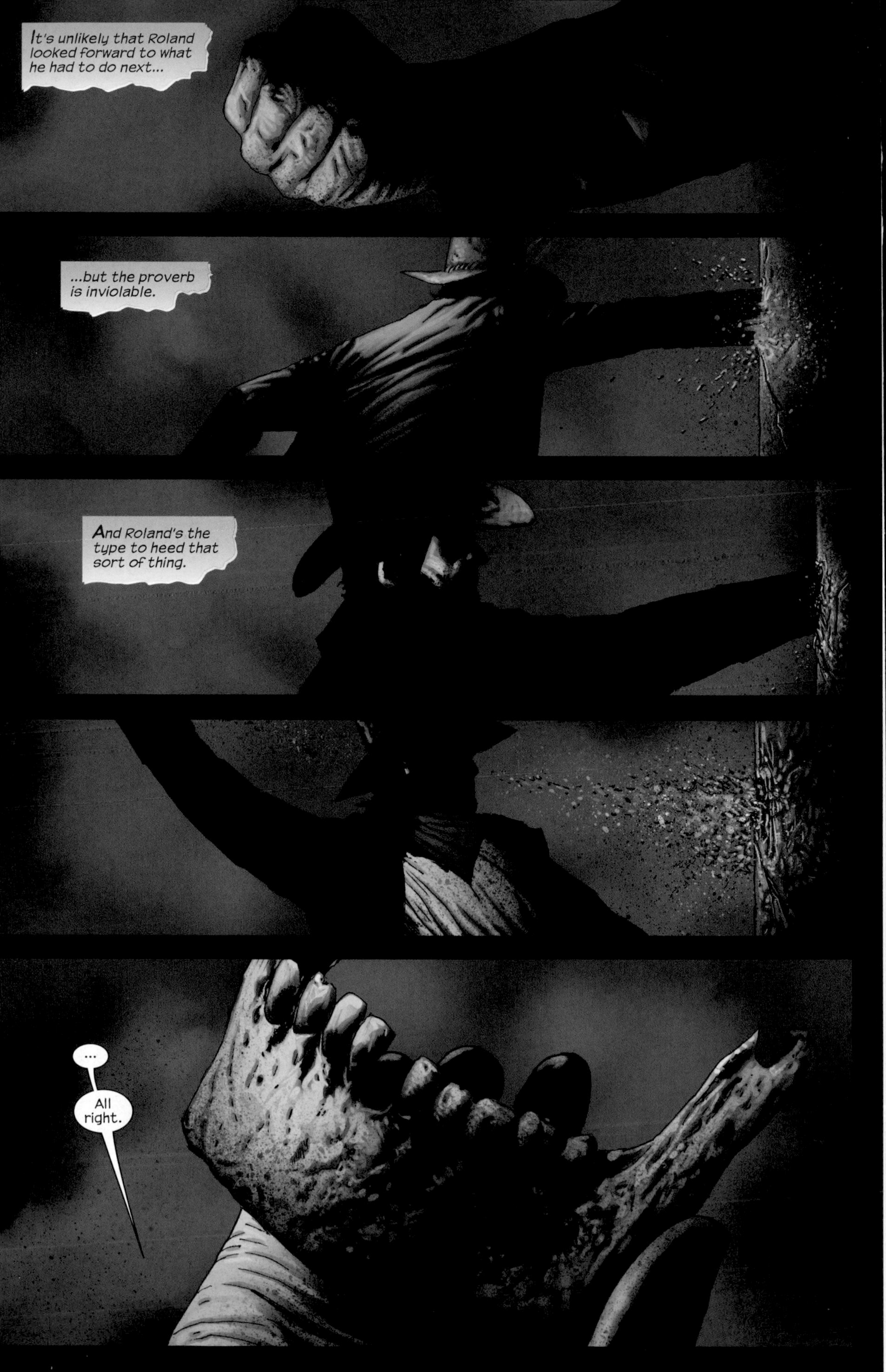
It's unlikely that Roland looked forward to what he had to do next...
...but the proverb is inviolable.
And Roland's the type to heed that sort of thing.
...
All right.

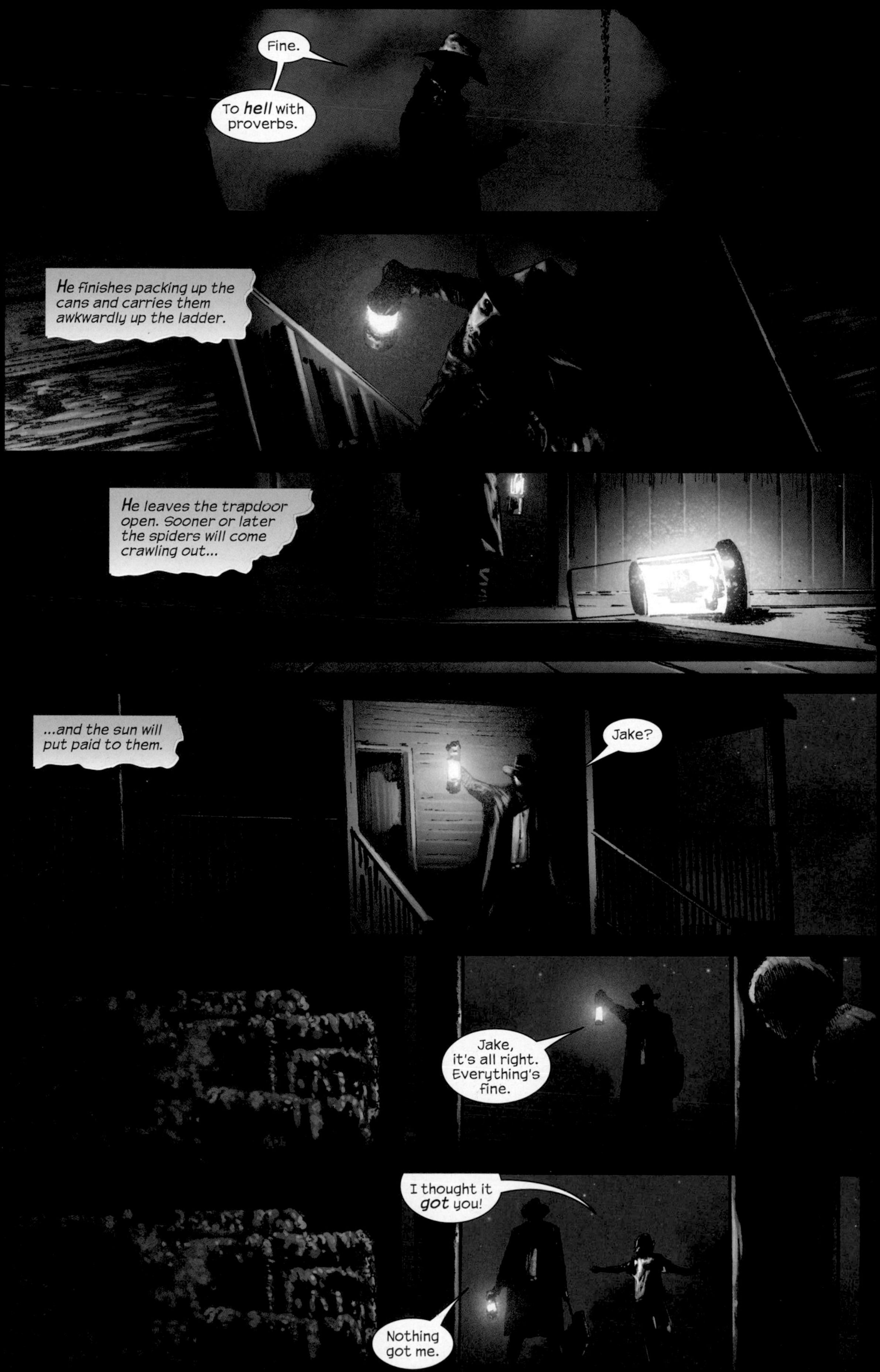
Fine.
To hell with proverbs.
He finishes packing up the cans and carries them awkwardly up the ladder.
He leaves the trapdoor open. Sooner or later the spiders will come crawling out...
...and the sun will put paid to them.
Jake?
Jake, it's all right. Everything's fine.
I thought it got you!
Nothing got me.

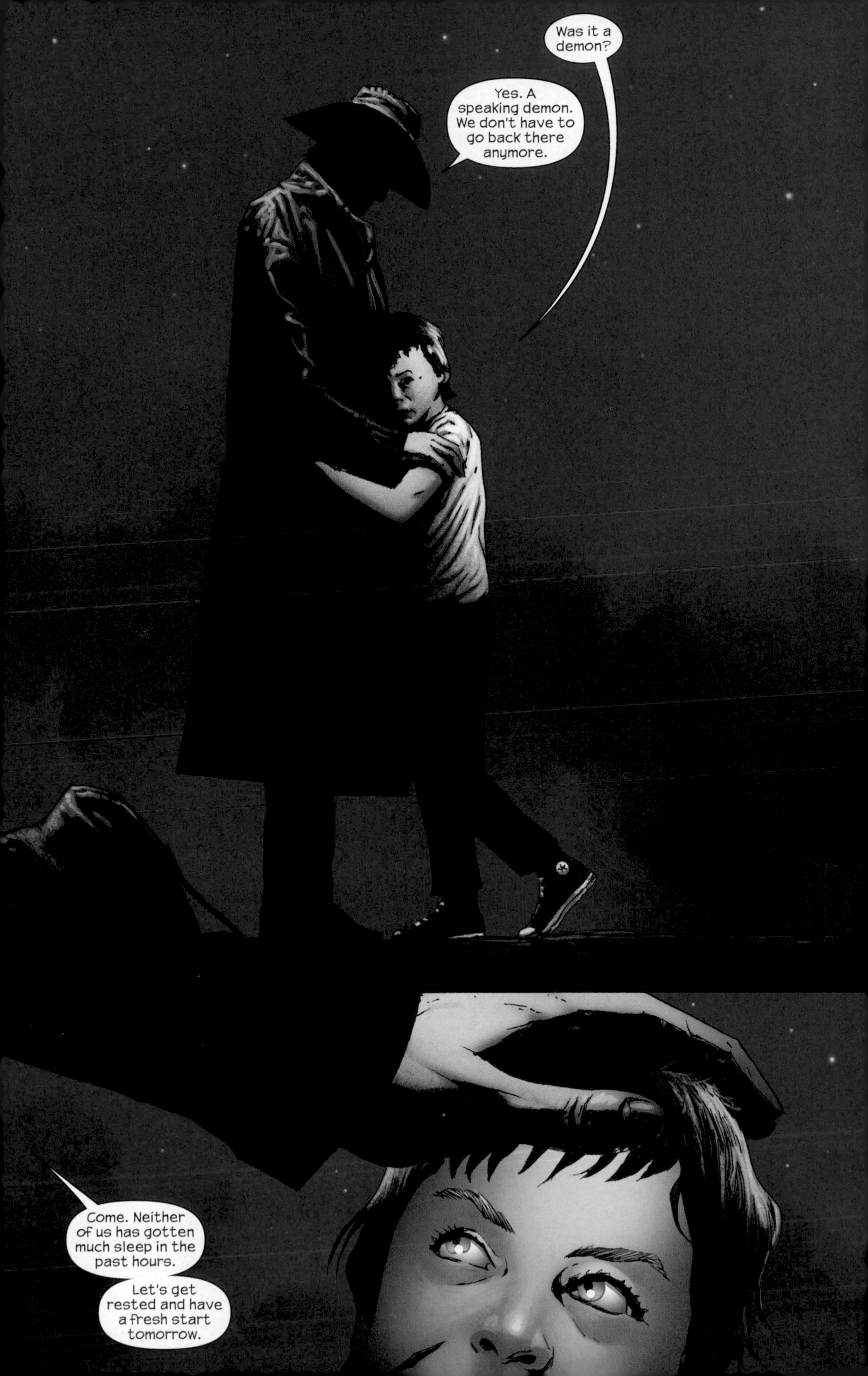
Was it a demon?
Yes. A speaking demon. We don't have to go back there anymore.
Come. Neither of us has gotten much sleep in the past hours.
Let's get rested and have a fresh start tomorrow.

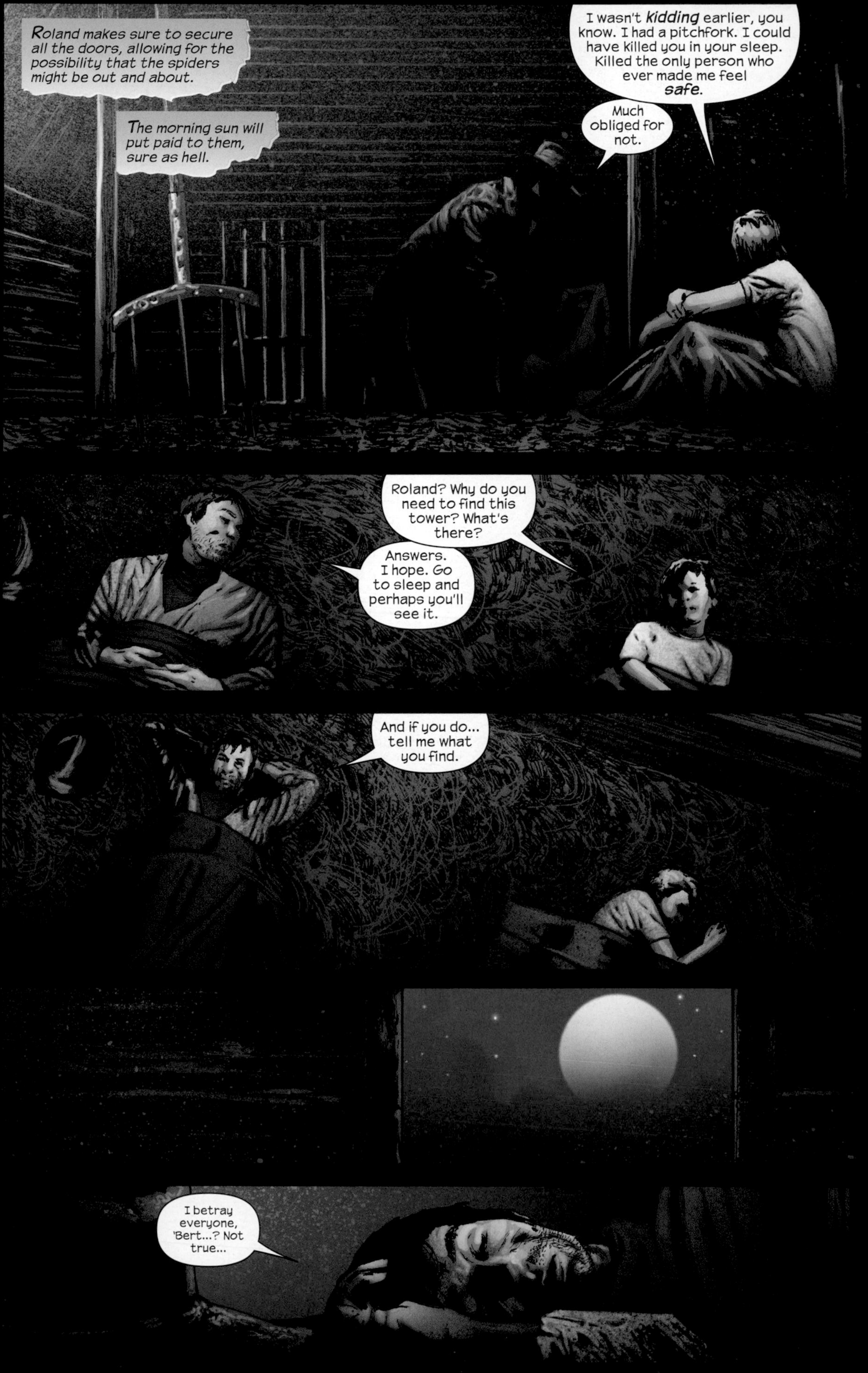
Roland makes sure to secure all the doors, allowing for the possibility that the spiders might be out and about.
The morning sun will put paid to them, sure as hell.
I wasn't kidding earlier, you know. I had a pitchfork. I could have killed you in your sleep. Killed the only person who ever made me feel safe.
Much obliged for not.
Roland? Why do you need to find this tower? What's there?
Answers. I hope. Go to sleep and perhaps you'll see it.
And if you do... tell me what you find.
I betray everyone, 'Bert...? Not true...

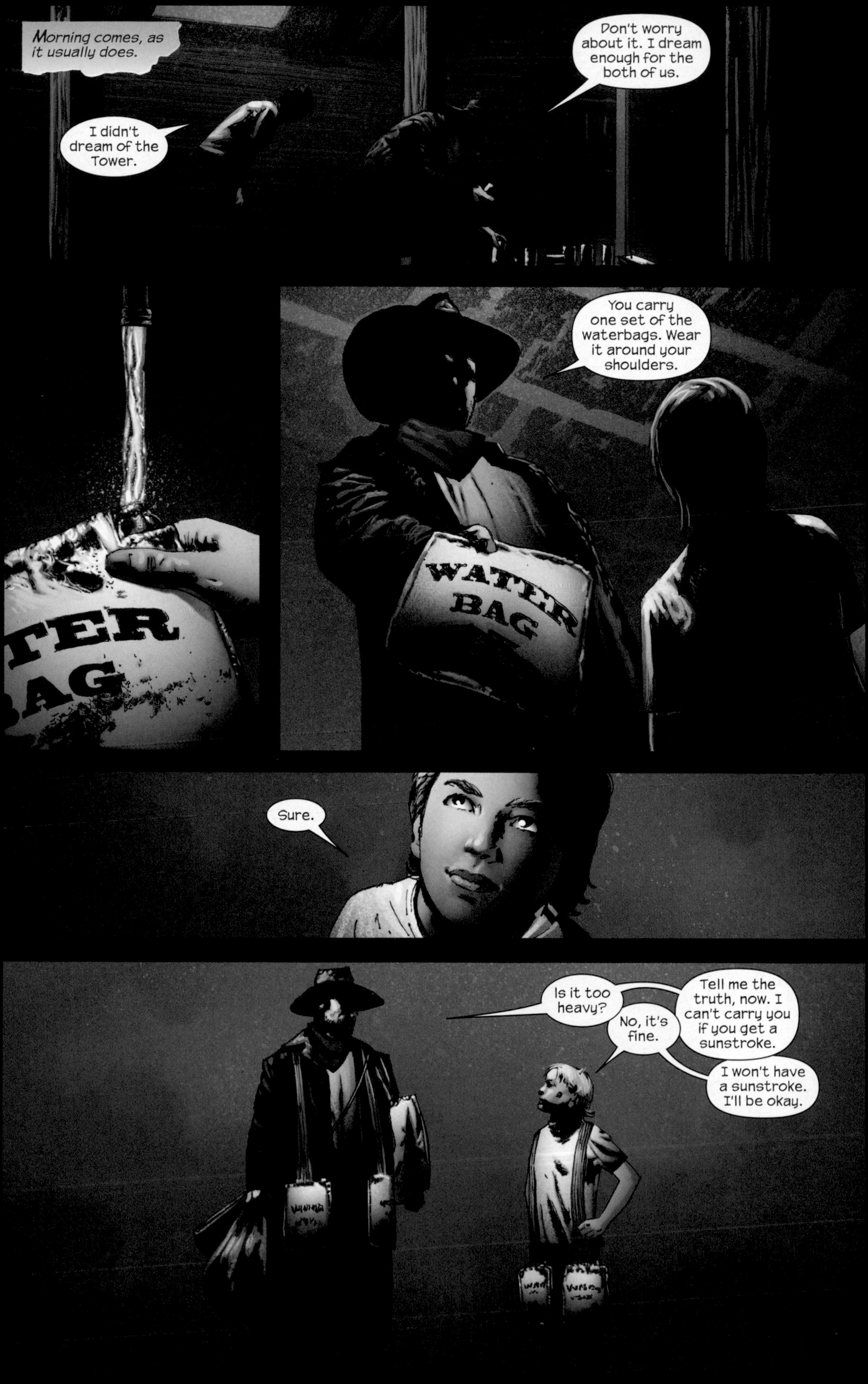
Morning comes, as it usually does.
I didn't dream of the Tower.
Don't worry about it. I dream enough for the both of us.
WATER BAG
You carry one set of the waterbags. Wear it around your shoulders.
WATER BAG
Sure.
Is it too heavy?
No, it's fine.
Tell me the truth, now. I can't carry you if you get a sunstroke.
I won't have a sunstroke. I'll be okay.

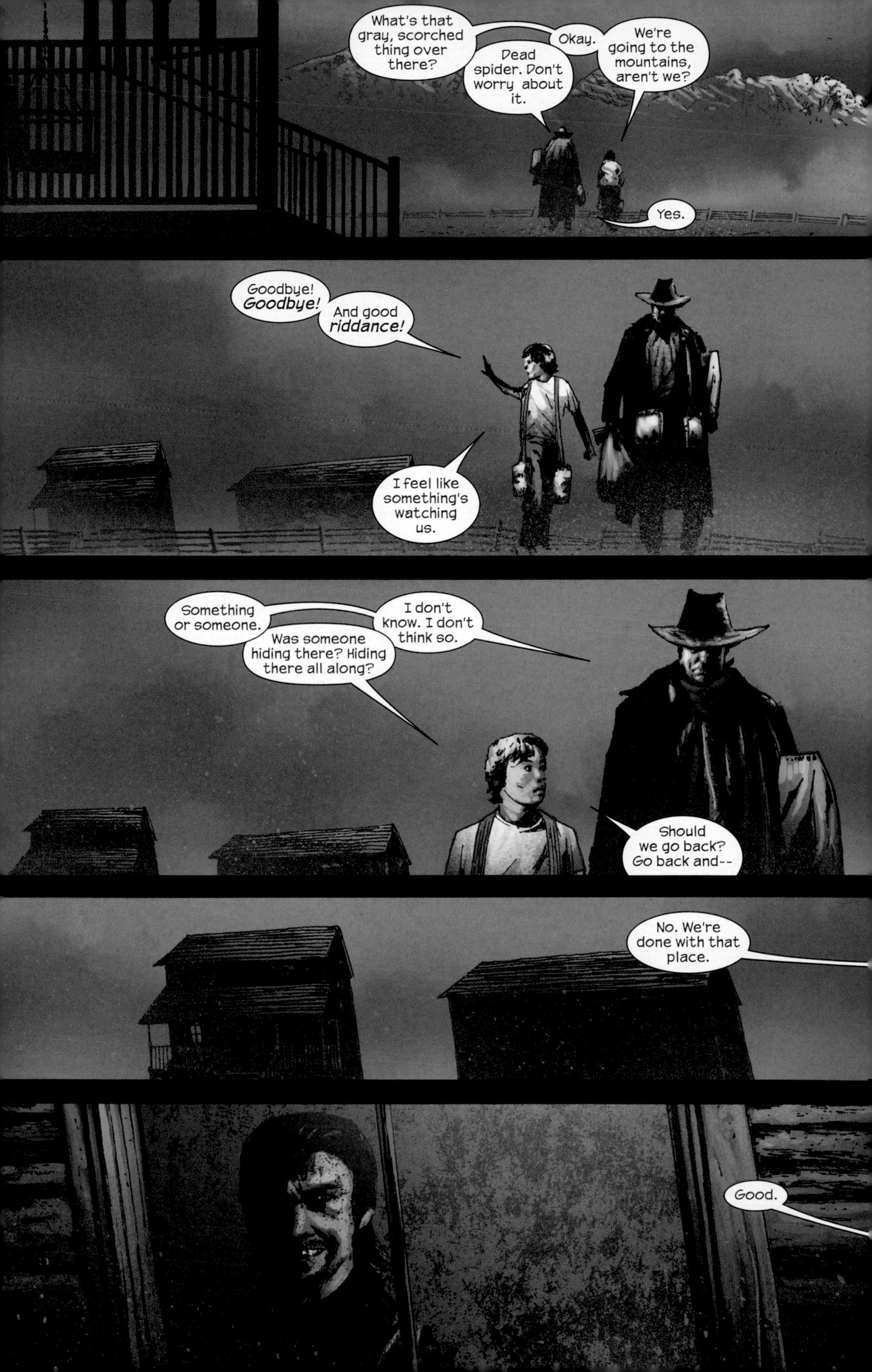
What's that gray, scorched thing over there?
Dead spider. Don't worry about it.
Okay.
We're going to the mountains, aren't we?
Yes.
Goodbye! *Goodbye!*
And good *riddance!*
I feel like something's watching us.
Something or someone.
Was someone hiding there? Hiding there all along?
I don't know. I don't think so.
Should we go back? Go back and--
No. We're done with that place.
Good.

STEPHEN KING

THE DARK TOWER
~THE GUNSLINGER~

THE WAY STATION

CHAPTER FOUR

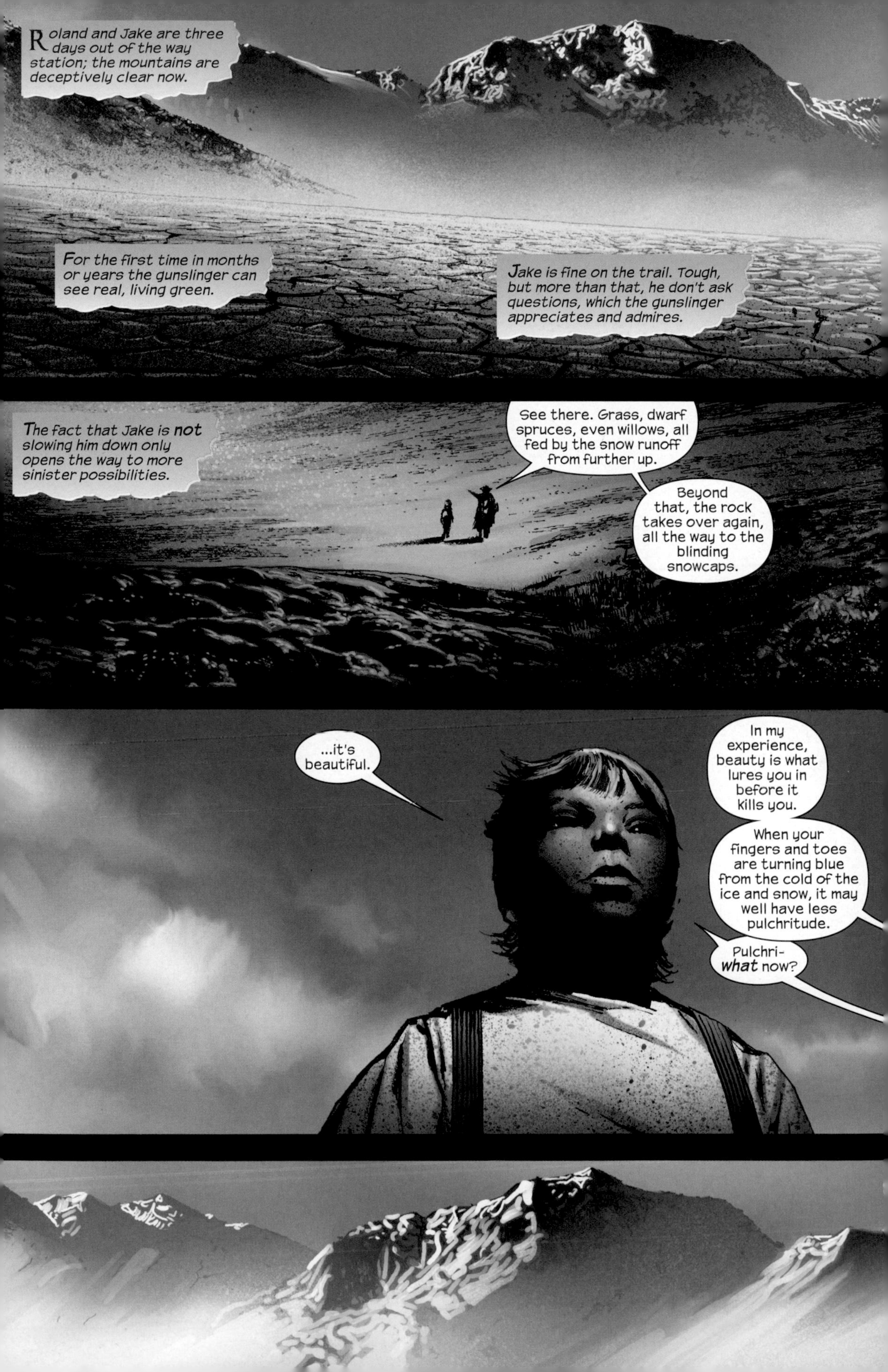

Roland and Jake are three days out of the way station; the mountains are deceptively clear now.
For the first time in months or years the gunslinger can see real, living green.
Jake is fine on the trail. Tough, but more than that, he don't ask questions, which the gunslinger appreciates and admires.
The fact that Jake is not slowing him down only opens the way to more sinister possibilities.
See there. Grass, dwarf spruces, even willows, all fed by the snow runoff from further up.
Beyond that, the rock takes over again, all the way to the blinding snowcaps.
...it's beautiful.
In my experience, beauty is what lures you in before it kills you.
When your fingers and toes are turning blue from the cold of the ice and snow, it may well have less pulchritude.
Pulchri-what now?

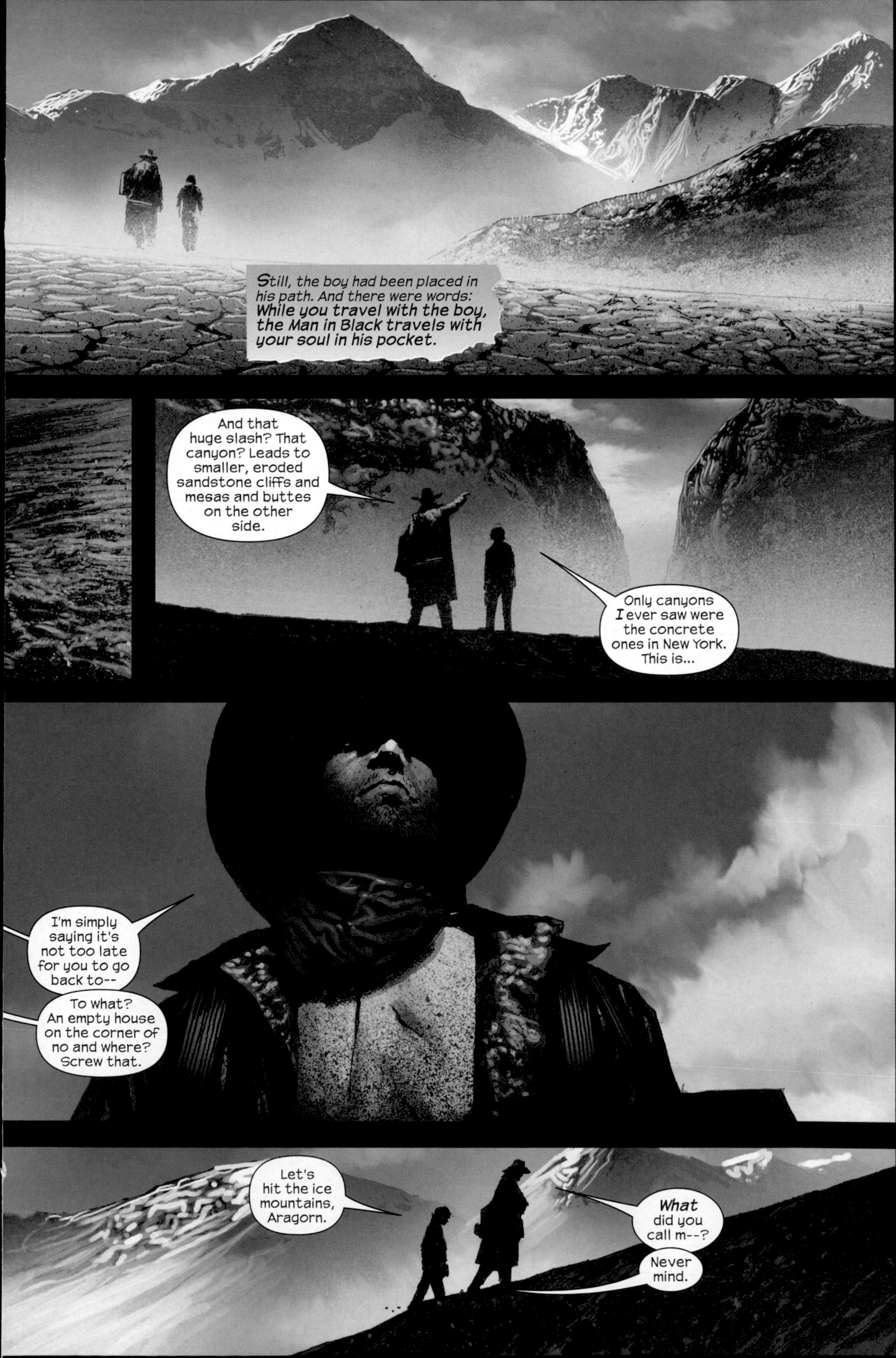
Still, the boy had been placed in his path. And there were words: While you travel with the boy, the Man in Black travels with your soul in his pocket.
And that huge slash? That canyon? Leads to smaller, eroded sandstone cliffs and mesas and buttes on the other side.
Only canyons I ever saw were the concrete ones in New York. This is...
I'm simply saying it's not too late for you to go back to--
To what? An empty house on the corner of no and where? Screw that.
Let's hit the ice mountains, Aragorn.
What did you call m--?
Never mind.

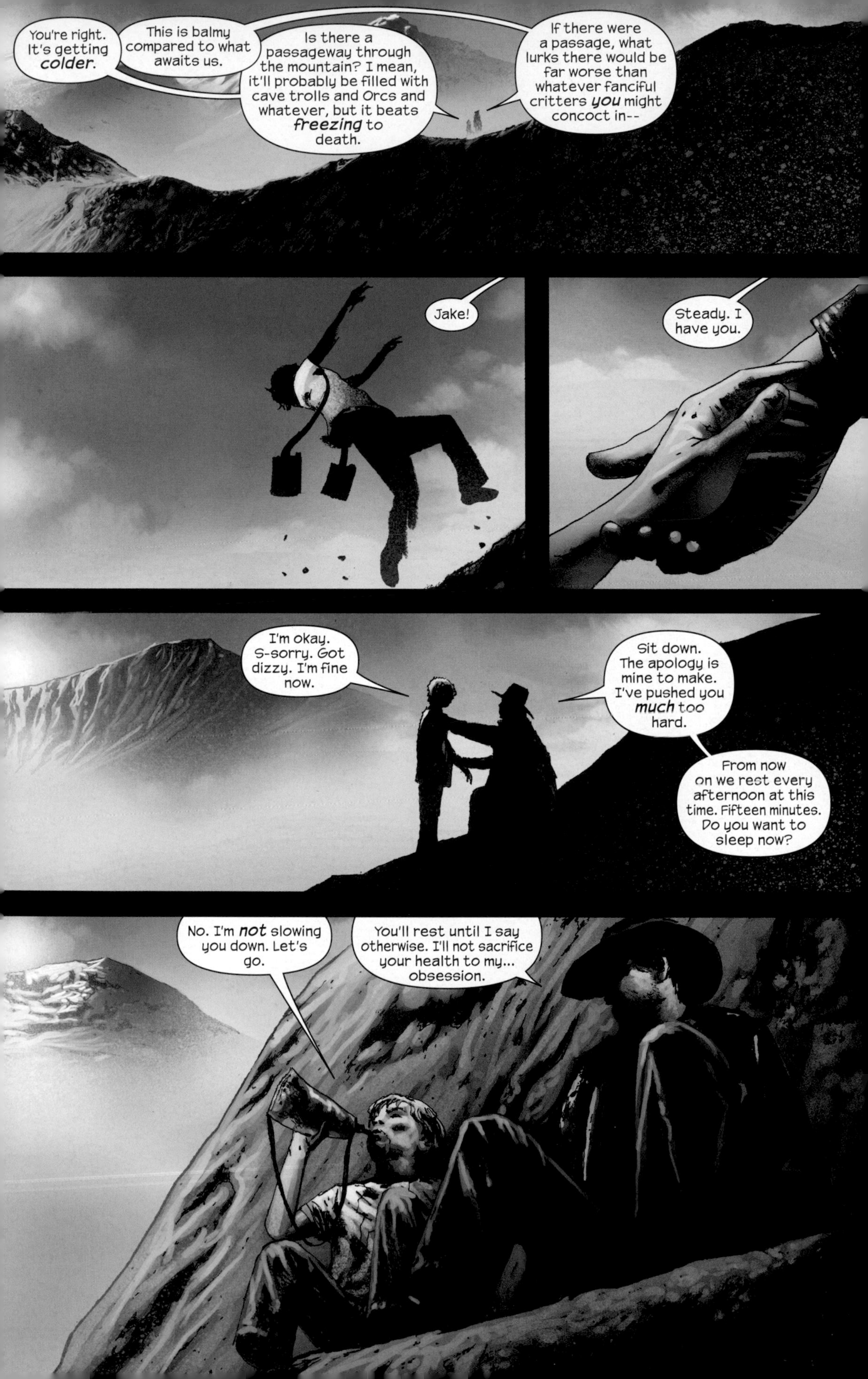
You're right. It's getting *colder*.
This is balmy compared to what awaits us.
Is there a passageway through the mountain? I mean, it'll probably be filled with cave trolls and Orcs and whatever, but it beats *freezing* to death.
If there were a passage, what lurks there would be far worse than whatever fanciful critters *you* might concoct in--
Jake!
Steady. I have you.
I'm okay. S-sorry. Got dizzy. I'm fine now.
Sit down. The apology is mine to make. I've pushed you *much* too hard.
From now on we rest every afternoon at this time. Fifteen minutes. Do you want to sleep now?
No. I'm *not* slowing you down. Let's go.
You'll rest until I say otherwise. I'll not sacrifice your health to my... obsession.

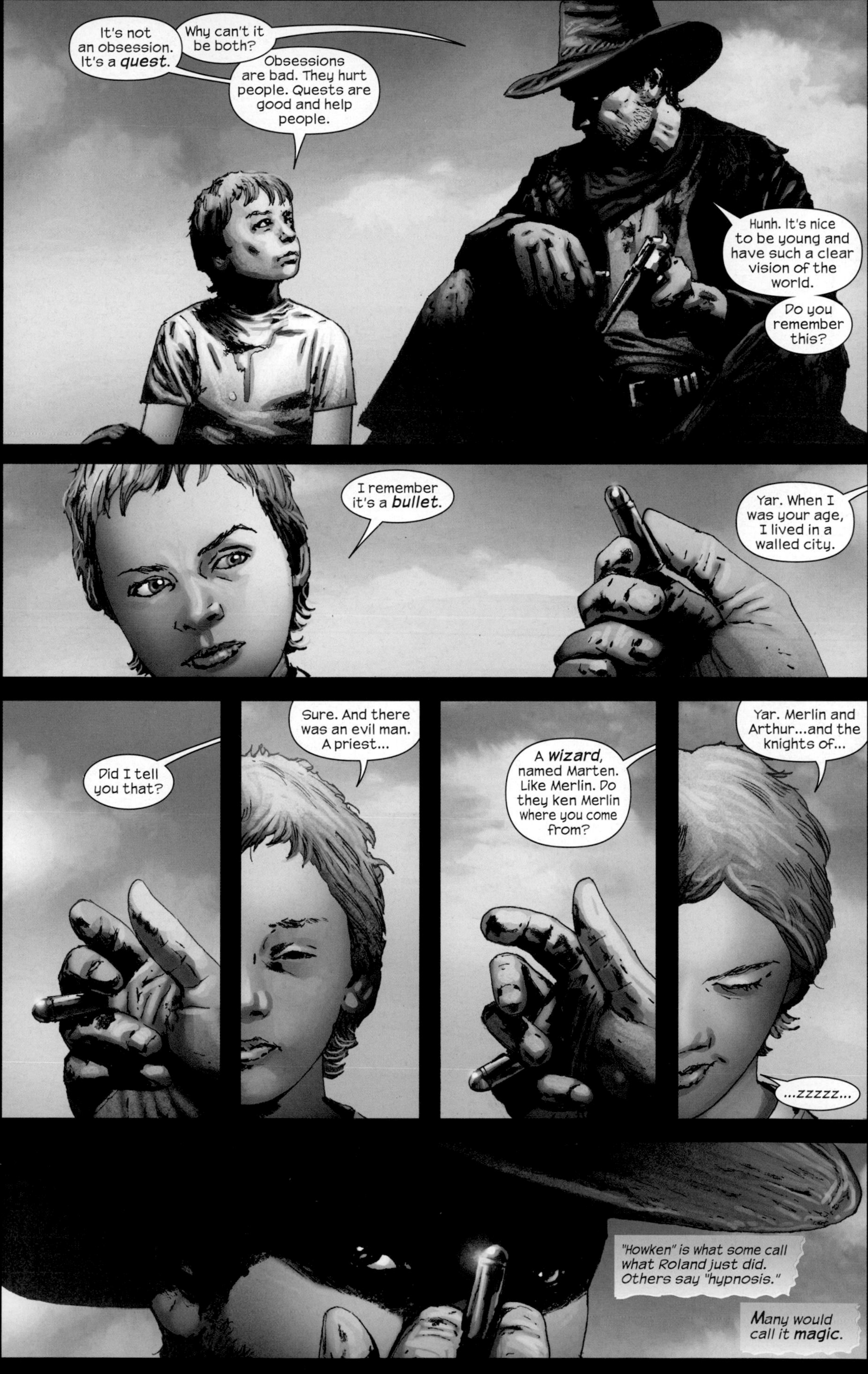
It's not an obsession. It's a *quest*.
Why can't it be both?
Obsessions are bad. They hurt people. Quests are good and help people.
Hunh. It's nice to be young and have such a clear vision of the world.
Do you remember this?
I remember it's a *bullet*.
Yar. When I was your age, I lived in a walled city.
Did I tell you that?
Sure. And there was an evil man. A priest...
A *wizard*, named Marten. Like Merlin. Do they ken Merlin where you come from?
Yar. Merlin and Arthur...and the knights of...
...zzzzz...
"Howken" is what some call what Roland just did. Others say "hypnosis."
Many would call it *magic*.

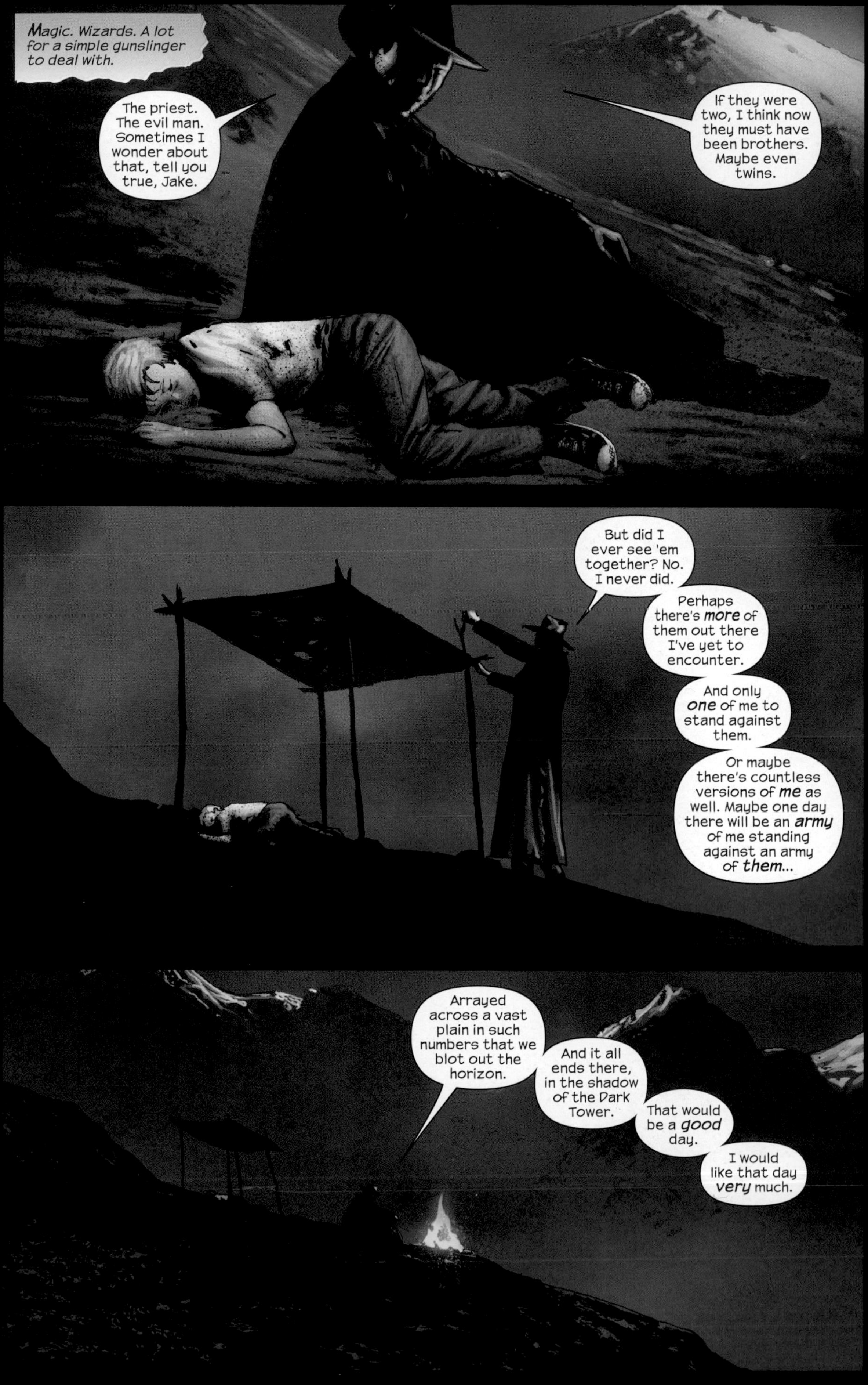
Magic. Wizards. A lot for a simple gunslinger to deal with.
The priest. The evil man. Sometimes I wonder about that, tell you true, Jake.
If they were two, I think now they must have been brothers. Maybe even twins.
But did I ever see 'em together? No. I never did.
Perhaps there's *more* of them out there I've yet to encounter.
And only *one* of me to stand against them.
Or maybe there's countless versions of *me* as well. Maybe one day there will be an *army* of me standing against an army of *them*...
Arrayed across a vast plain in such numbers that we blot out the horizon.
And it all ends there, in the shadow of the Dark Tower.
That would be a *good* day.
I would like that day *very* much.

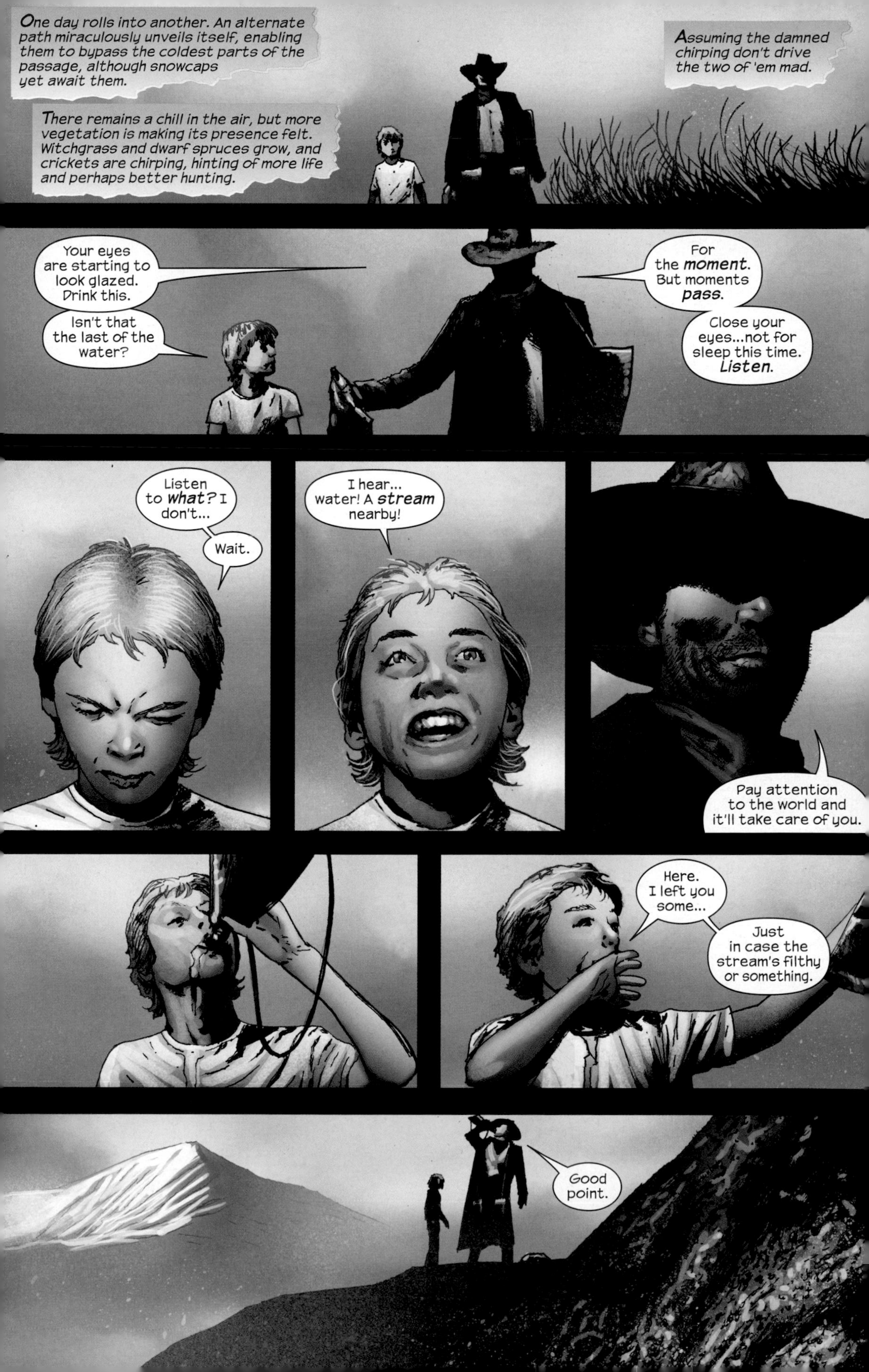
One day rolls into another. An alternate path miraculously unveils itself, enabling them to bypass the coldest parts of the passage, although snowcaps yet await them.
There remains a chill in the air, but more vegetation is making its presence felt. Witchgrass and dwarf spruces grow, and crickets are chirping, hinting of more life and perhaps better hunting.
Assuming the damned chirping don't drive the two of 'em mad.
Your eyes are starting to look glazed. Drink this.
Isn't that the last of the water?
For the *moment*. But moments *pass*.
Close your eyes...not for sleep this time. *Listen*.
Listen to *what?* I don't...
Wait.
I hear... water! A *stream* nearby!
Pay attention to the world and it'll take care of you.
Here. I left you some...
Just in case the stream's filthy or something.
Good point.

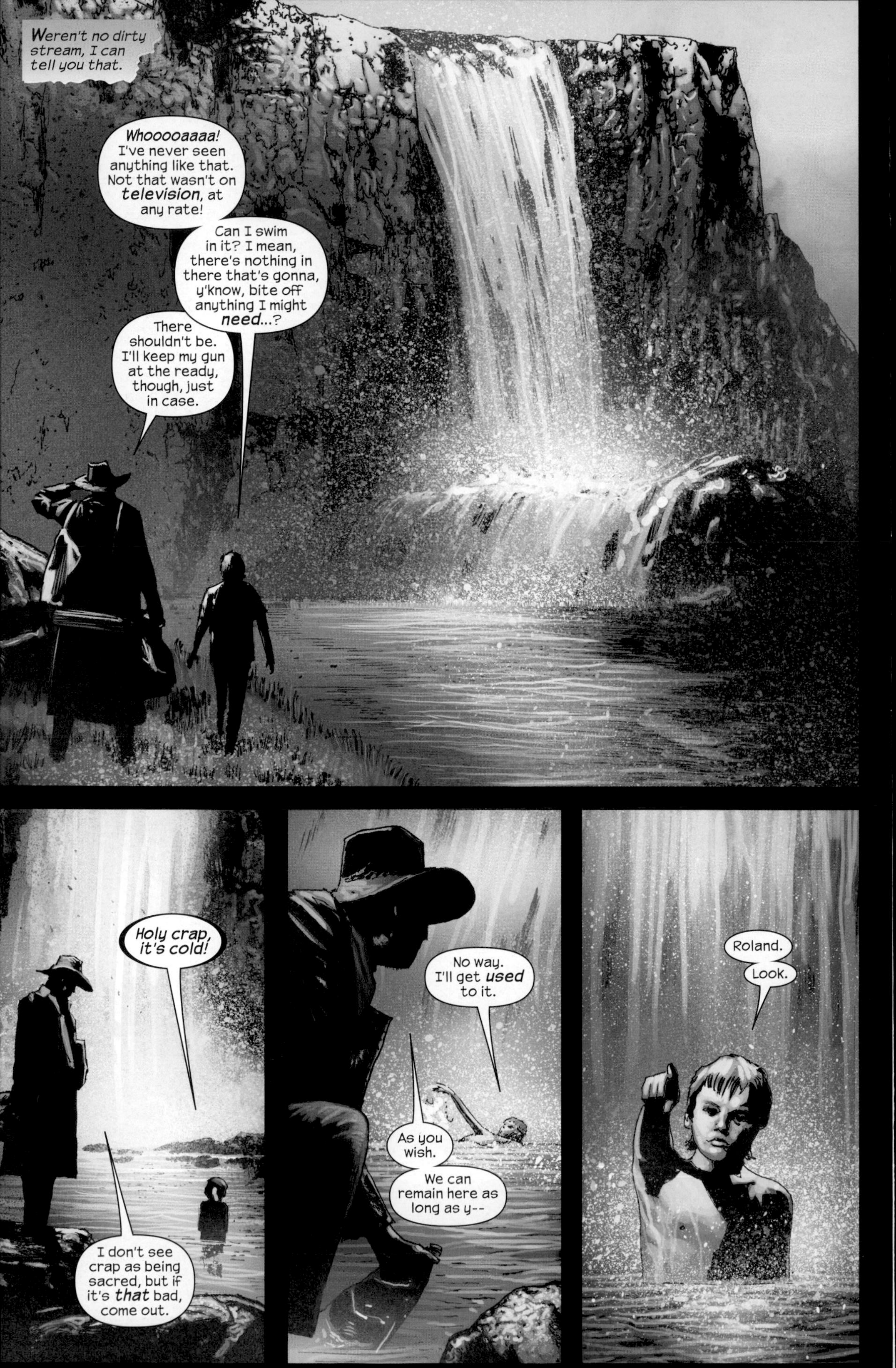
Weren't no dirty stream, I can tell you that.
Whoooooaaaa! I've never seen anything like that. Not that wasn't on television, at any rate!
Can I swim in it? I mean, there's nothing in there that's gonna, y'know, bite off anything I might need...?
There shouldn't be. I'll keep my gun at the ready, though, just in case.
Holy crap, it's cold!
I don't see crap as being sacred, but if it's that bad, come out.
No way. I'll get used to it.
As you wish.
We can remain here as long as y--
Roland.
Look.

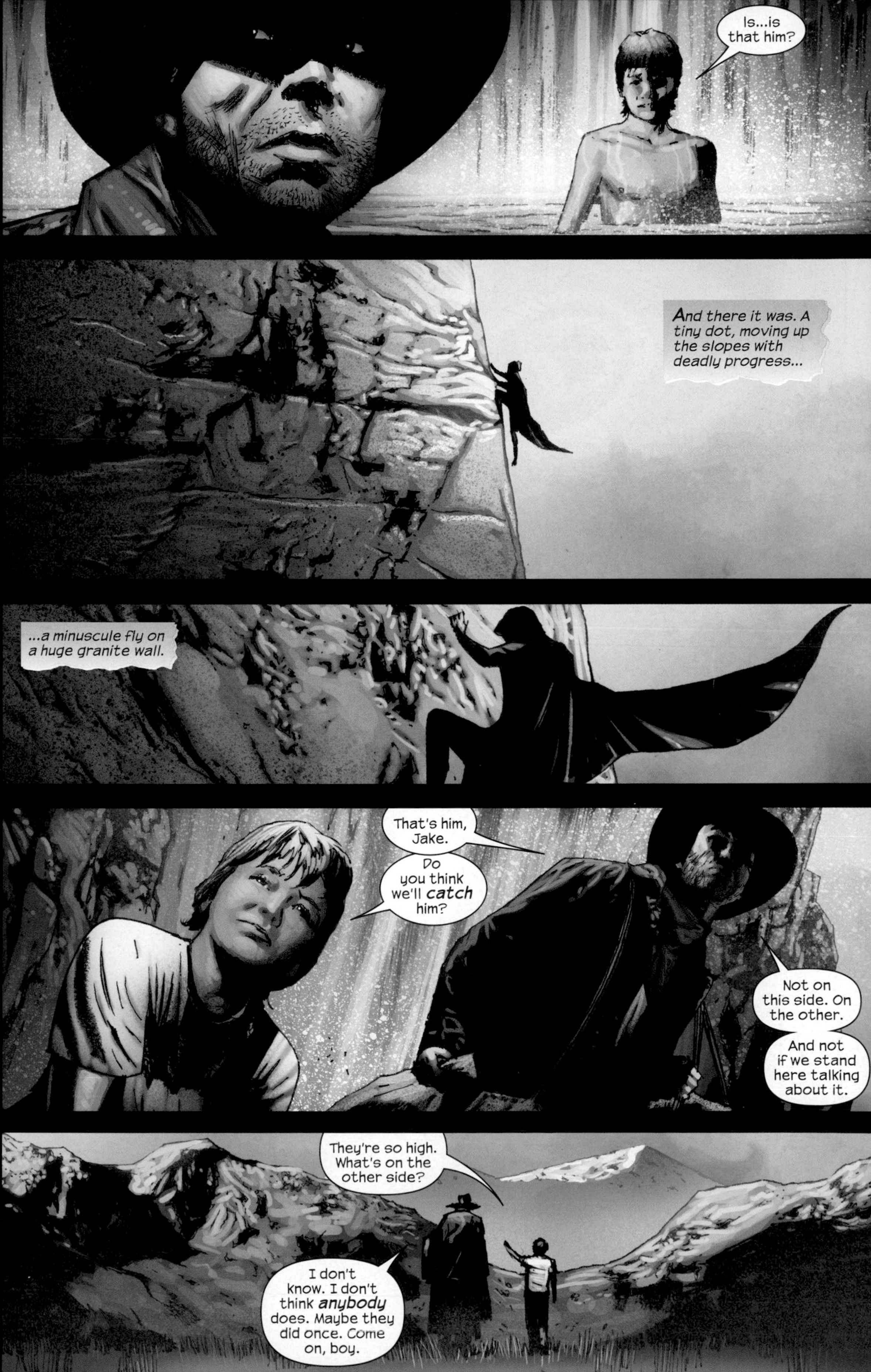
Is...is that him?
And there it was. A tiny dot, moving up the slopes with deadly progress...
...a minuscule fly on a huge granite wall.
That's him, Jake.
Do you think we'll catch him?
Not on this side. On the other.
And not if we stand here talking about it.
They're so high. What's on the other side?
I don't know. I don't think anybody does. Maybe they did once. Come on, boy.

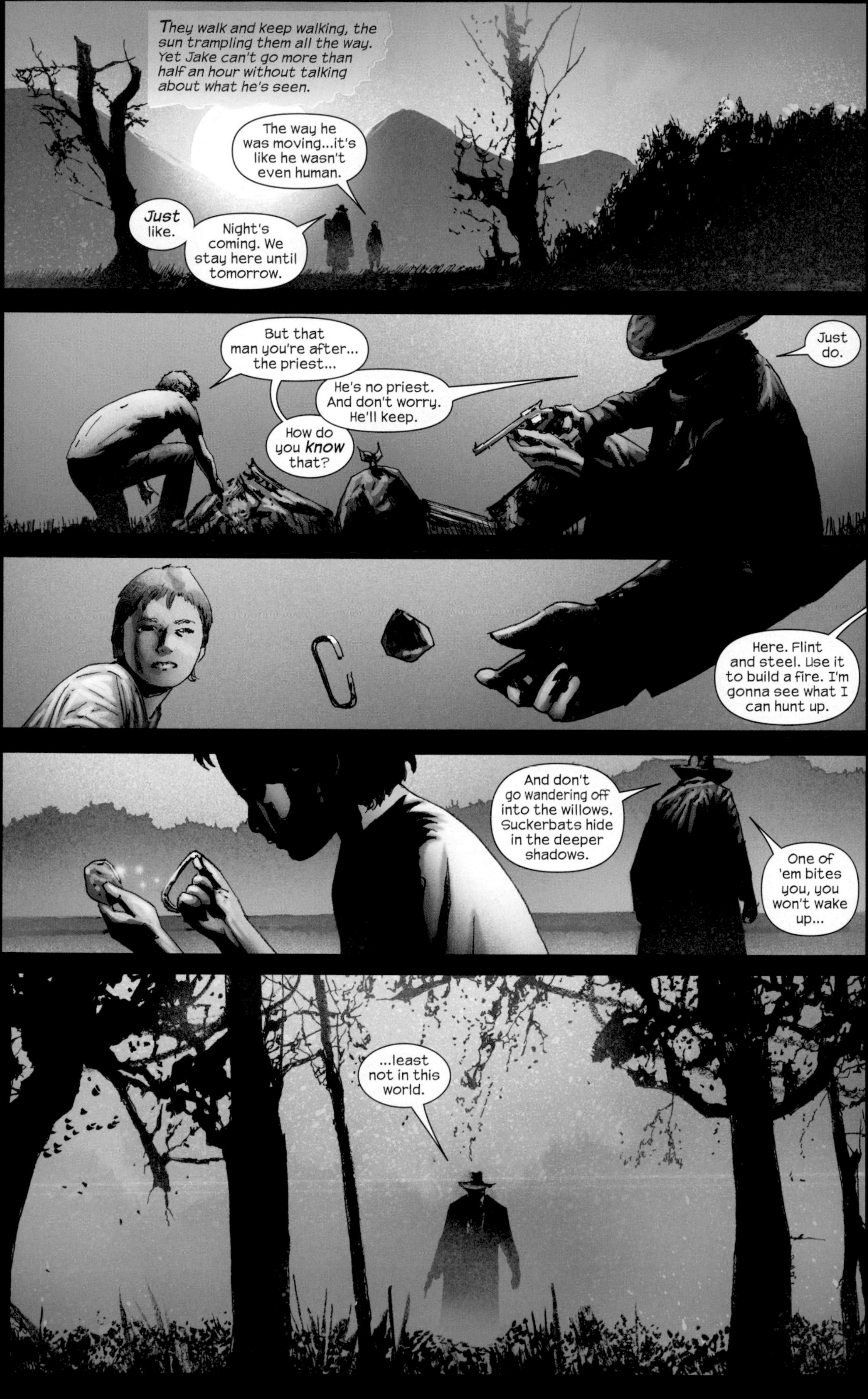
They walk and keep walking, the sun trampling them all the way. Yet Jake can't go more than half an hour without talking about what he's seen.
The way he was moving...it's like he wasn't even human.
Just like.
Night's coming. We stay here until tomorrow.
But that man you're after... the priest...
He's no priest. And don't worry. He'll keep.
How do you know that?
Just do.
Here. Flint and steel. Use it to build a fire. I'm gonna see what I can hunt up.
And don't go wandering off into the willows. Suckerbats hide in the deeper shadows.
One of 'em bites you, you won't wake up...
...least not in this world.

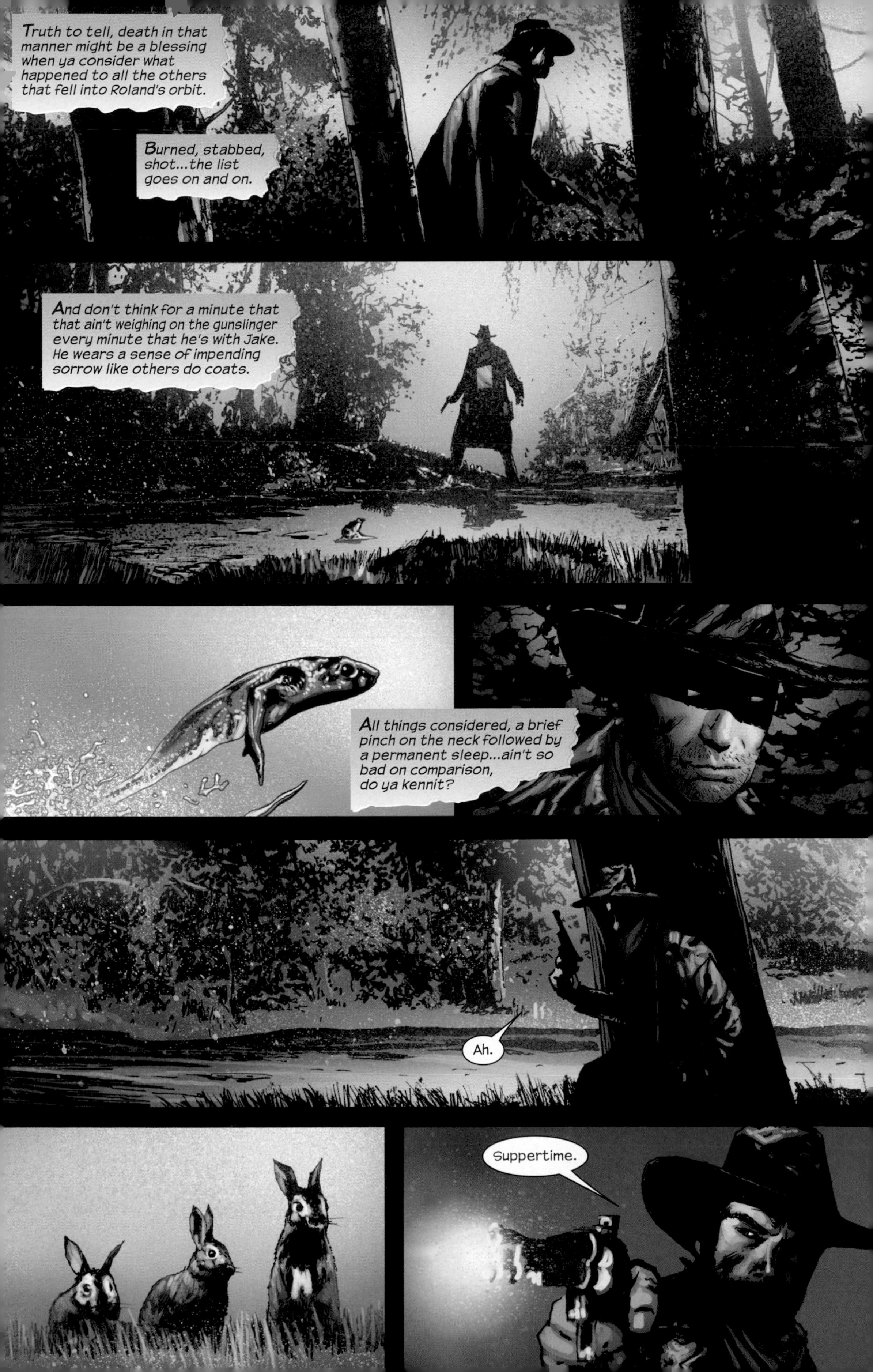
Truth to tell, death in that manner might be a blessing when ya consider what happened to all the others that fell into Roland's orbit.
Burned, stabbed, shot...the list goes on and on.
And don't think for a minute that that ain't weighing on the gunslinger every minute that he's with Jake. He wears a sense of impending sorrow like others do coats.
All things considered, a brief pinch on the neck followed by a permanent sleep...ain't so bad on comparison, do ya kennit?
Ah.
Suppertime.

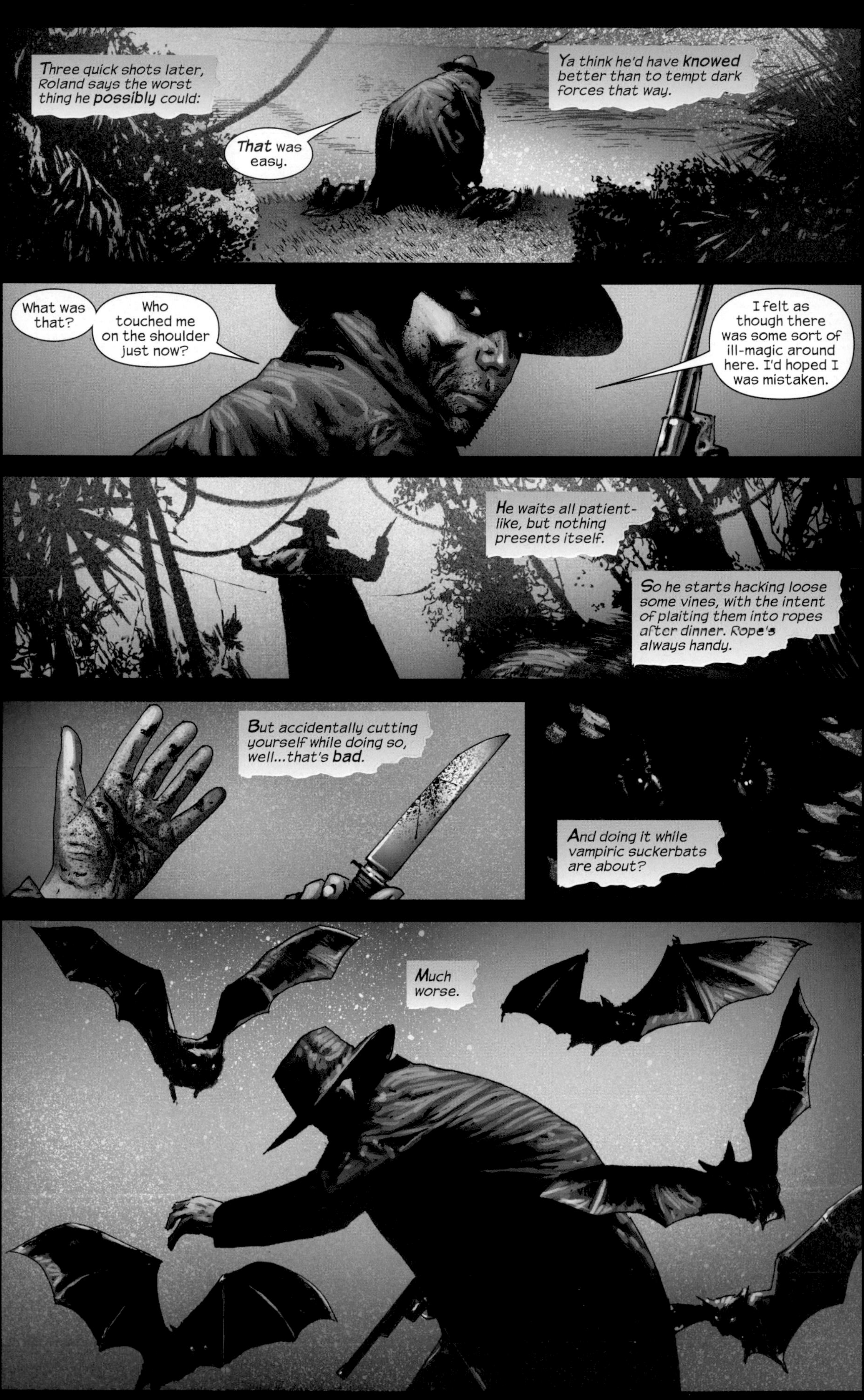

Three quick shots later, Roland says the worst thing he possibly could:
That was easy.
Ya think he'd have knowed better than to tempt dark forces that way.
What was that?
Who touched me on the shoulder just now?
I felt as though there was some sort of ill-magic around here. I'd hoped I was mistaken.
He waits all patient-like, but nothing presents itself.
So he starts hacking loose some vines, with the intent of plaiting them into ropes after dinner. Rope's always handy.
But accidentally cutting yourself while doing so, well...that's bad.
And doing it while vampiric suckerbats are about?
Much worse.

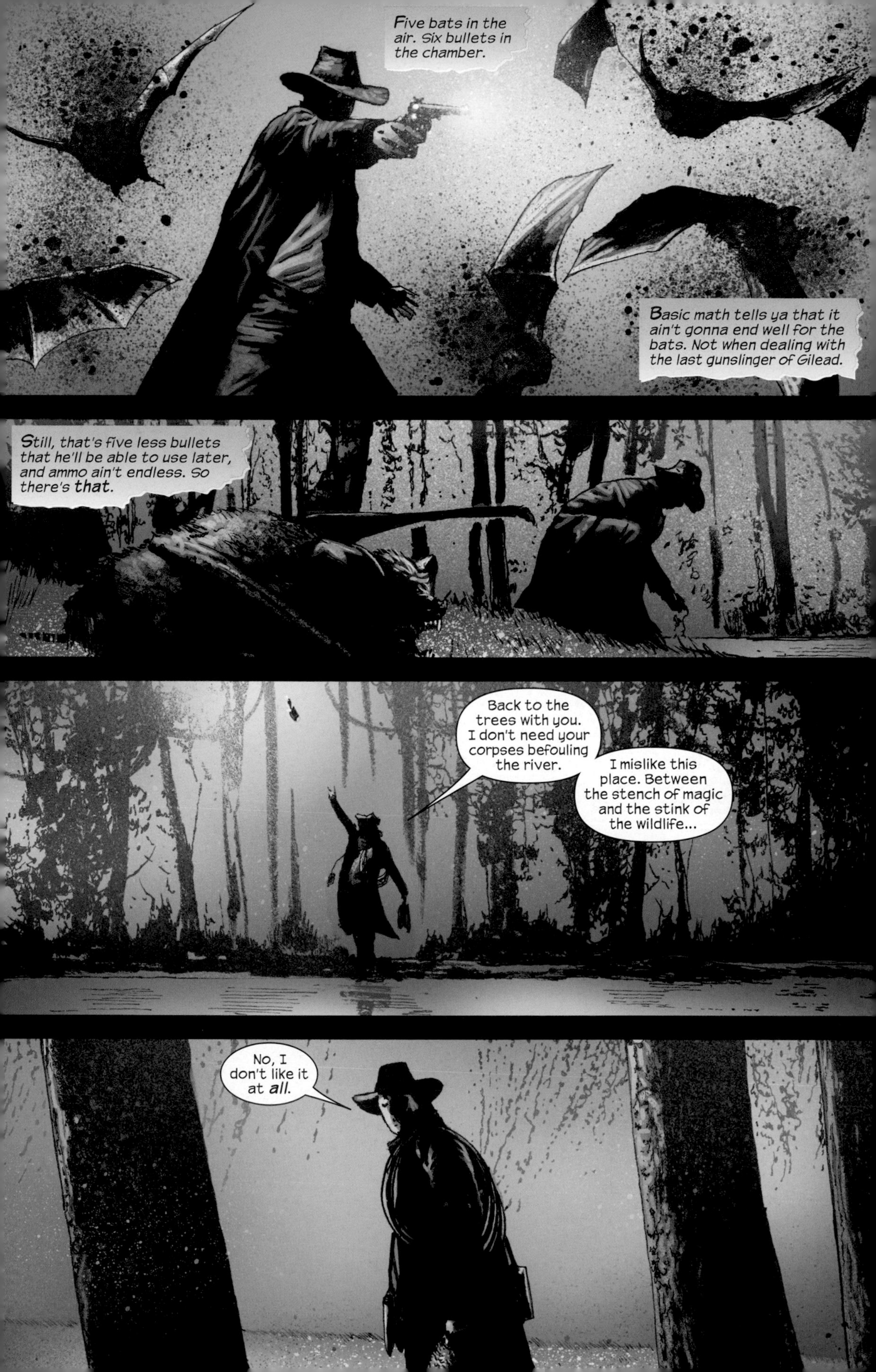
Five bats in the air. Six bullets in the chamber.
Basic math tells ya that it ain't gonna end well for the bats. Not when dealing with the last gunslinger of Gilead.
Still, that's five less bullets that he'll be able to use later, and ammo ain't endless. So there's that.
Back to the trees with you. I don't need your corpses befouling the river.
I mislike this place. Between the stench of magic and the stink of the wildlife...
No, I don't like it at all.

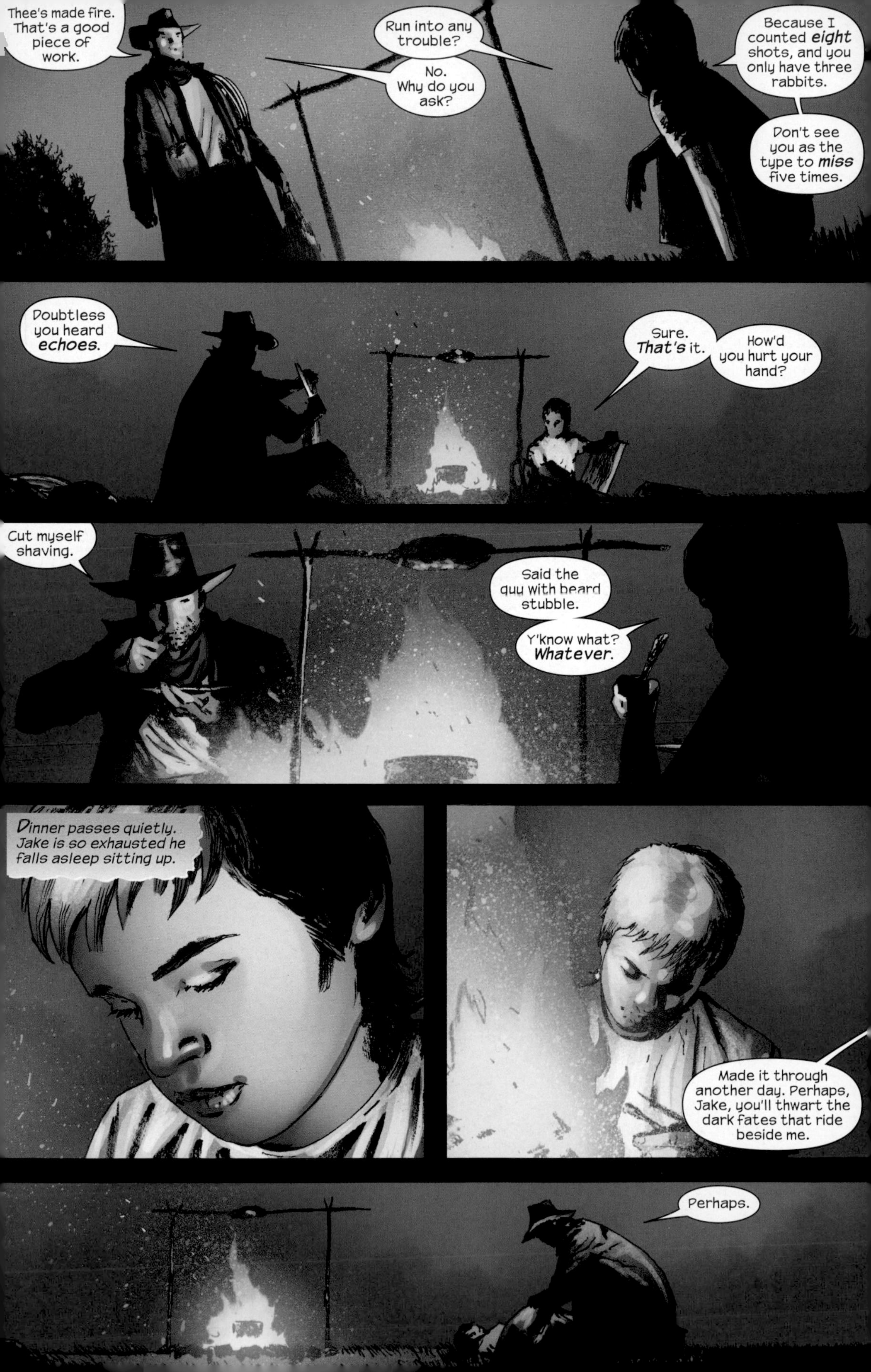

Thee's made fire. That's a good piece of work.
Run into any trouble?
No. Why do you ask?
Because I counted eight shots, and you only have three rabbits.
Don't see you as the type to miss five times.
Doubtless you heard echoes.
Sure. That's it.
How'd you hurt your hand?
Cut myself shaving.
Said the guy with beard stubble.
Y'know what? Whatever.
Dinner passes quietly. Jake is so exhausted he falls asleep sitting up.
Made it through another day. Perhaps, Jake, you'll thwart the dark fates that ride beside me.
Perhaps.

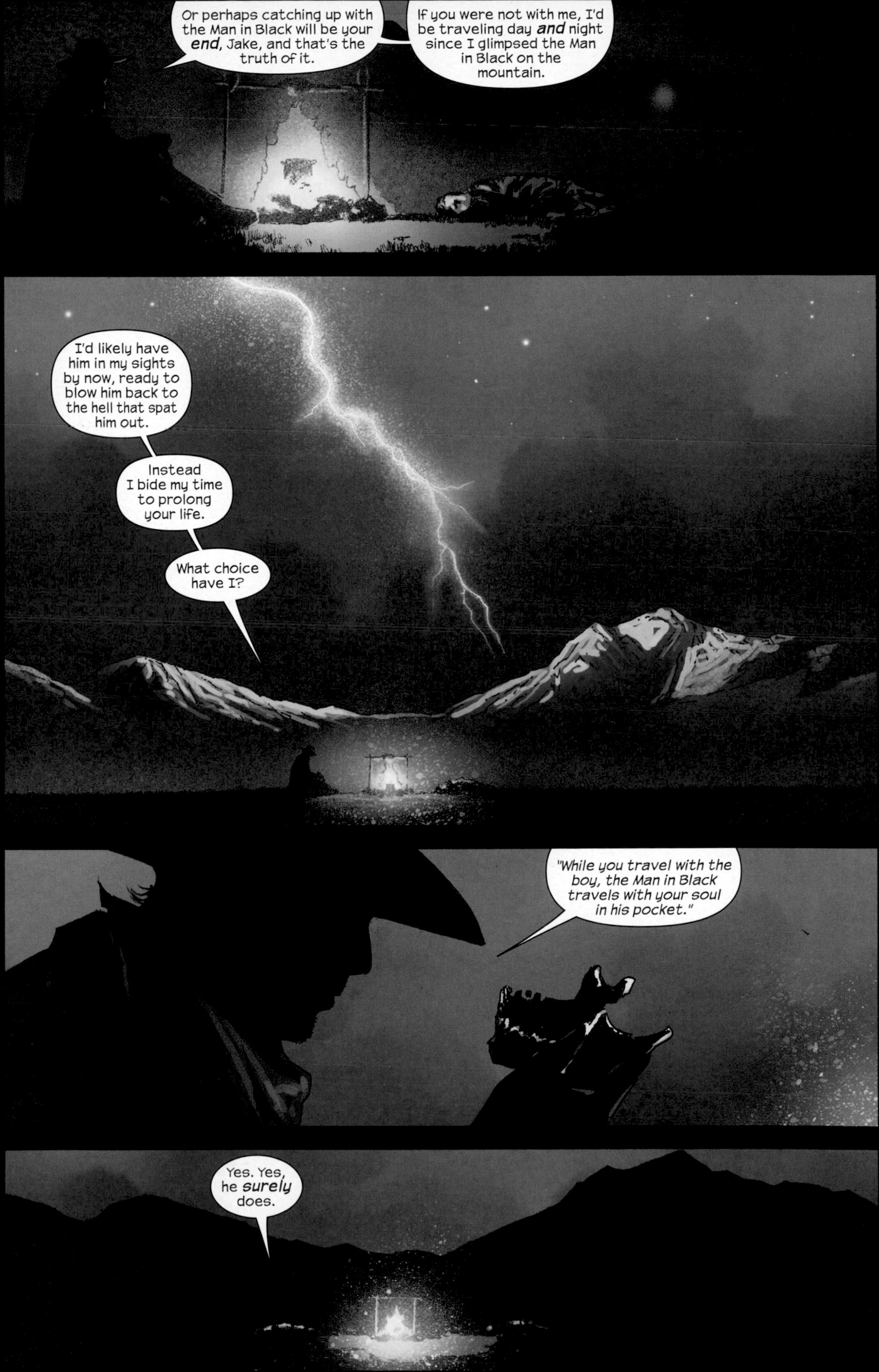
Or perhaps catching up with the Man in Black will be your *end*, Jake, and that's the truth of it.
If you were not with me, I'd be traveling day ***and*** night since I glimpsed the Man in Black on the mountain.
I'd likely have him in my sights by now, ready to blow him back to the hell that spat him out.
Instead I bide my time to prolong your life.
What choice have I?
"While you travel with the boy, the Man in Black travels with your soul in his pocket."
Yes. Yes, he ***surely*** does.

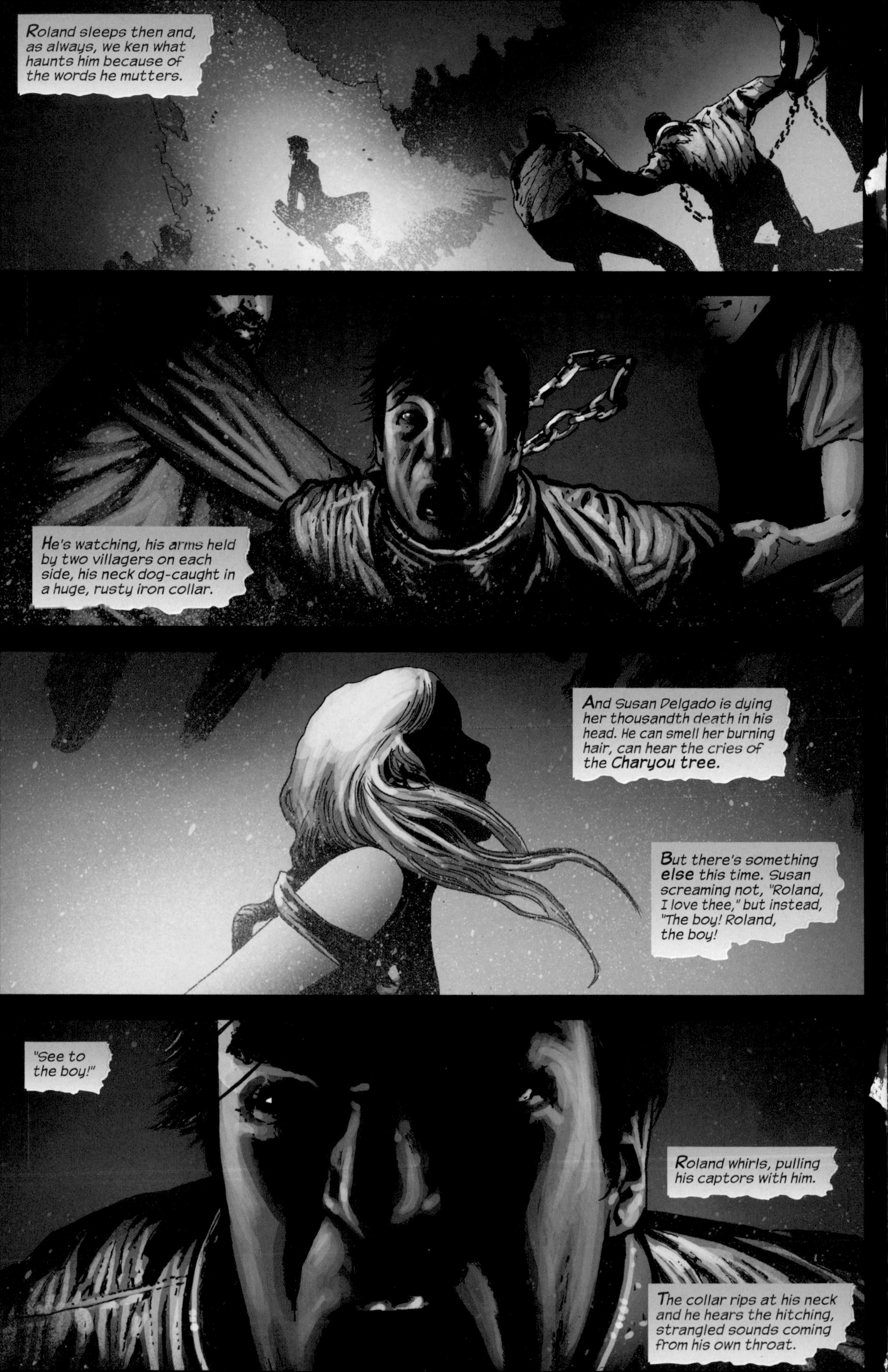
Roland sleeps then and, as always, we ken what haunts him because of the words he mutters.
He's watching, his arms held by two villagers on each side, his neck dog-caught in a huge, rusty iron collar.
And Susan Delgado is dying her thousandth death in his head. He can smell her burning hair, can hear the cries of the Charyou tree.
But there's something else this time. Susan screaming not, "Roland, I love thee," but instead, "The boy! Roland, the boy!
"See to the boy!"
Roland whirls, pulling his captors with him.
The collar rips at his neck and he hears the hitching, strangled sounds coming from his own throat.

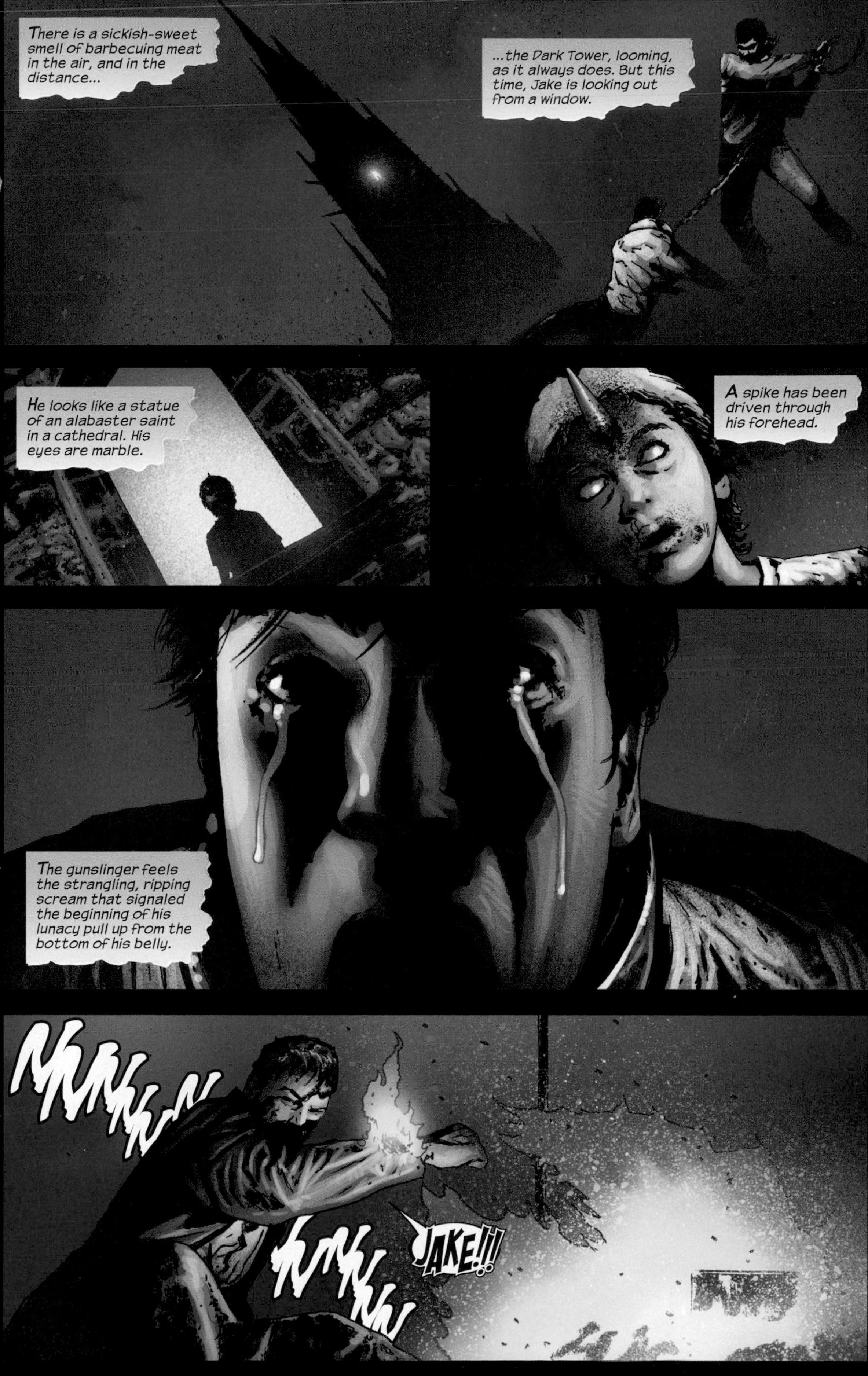
There is a sickish-sweet smell of barbecuing meat in the air, and in the distance...
...the Dark Tower, looming, as it always does. But this time, Jake is looking out from a window.
He looks like a statue of an alabaster saint in a cathedral. His eyes are marble.
A spike has been driven through his forehead.
The gunslinger feels the strangling, ripping scream that signaled the beginning of his lunacy pull up from the bottom of his belly.
NNNNNN
NNNNNN
JAKE!!!

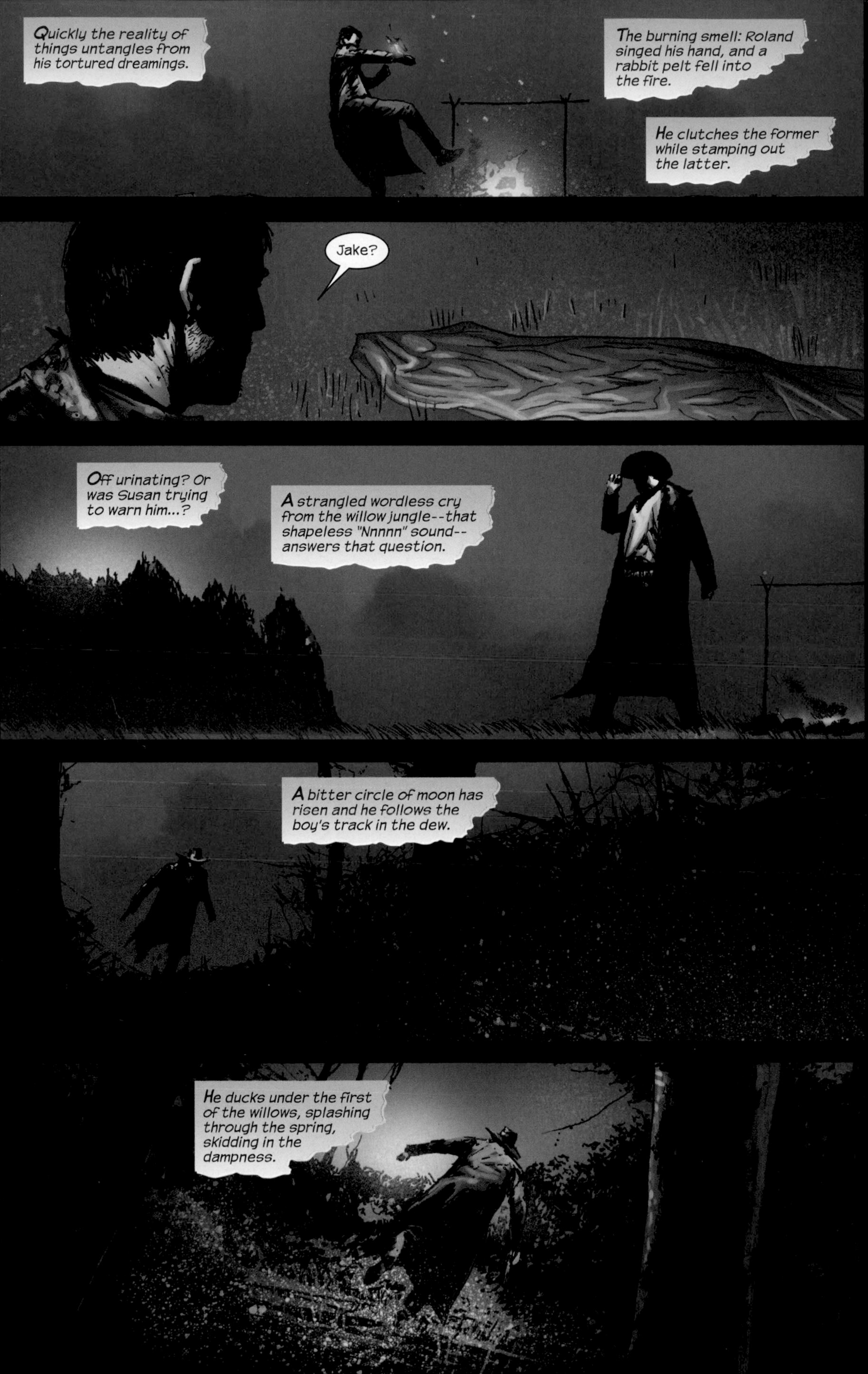
Quickly the reality of things untangles from his tortured dreamings.
The burning smell: Roland singed his hand, and a rabbit pelt fell into the fire.
He clutches the former while stamping out the latter.
Jake?
Off urinating? Or was Susan trying to warn him...?
A strangled wordless cry from the willow jungle--that shapeless "Nnnnn" sound--answers that question.
A bitter circle of moon has risen and he follows the boy's track in the dew.
He ducks under the first of the willows, splashing through the spring, skidding in the dampness.

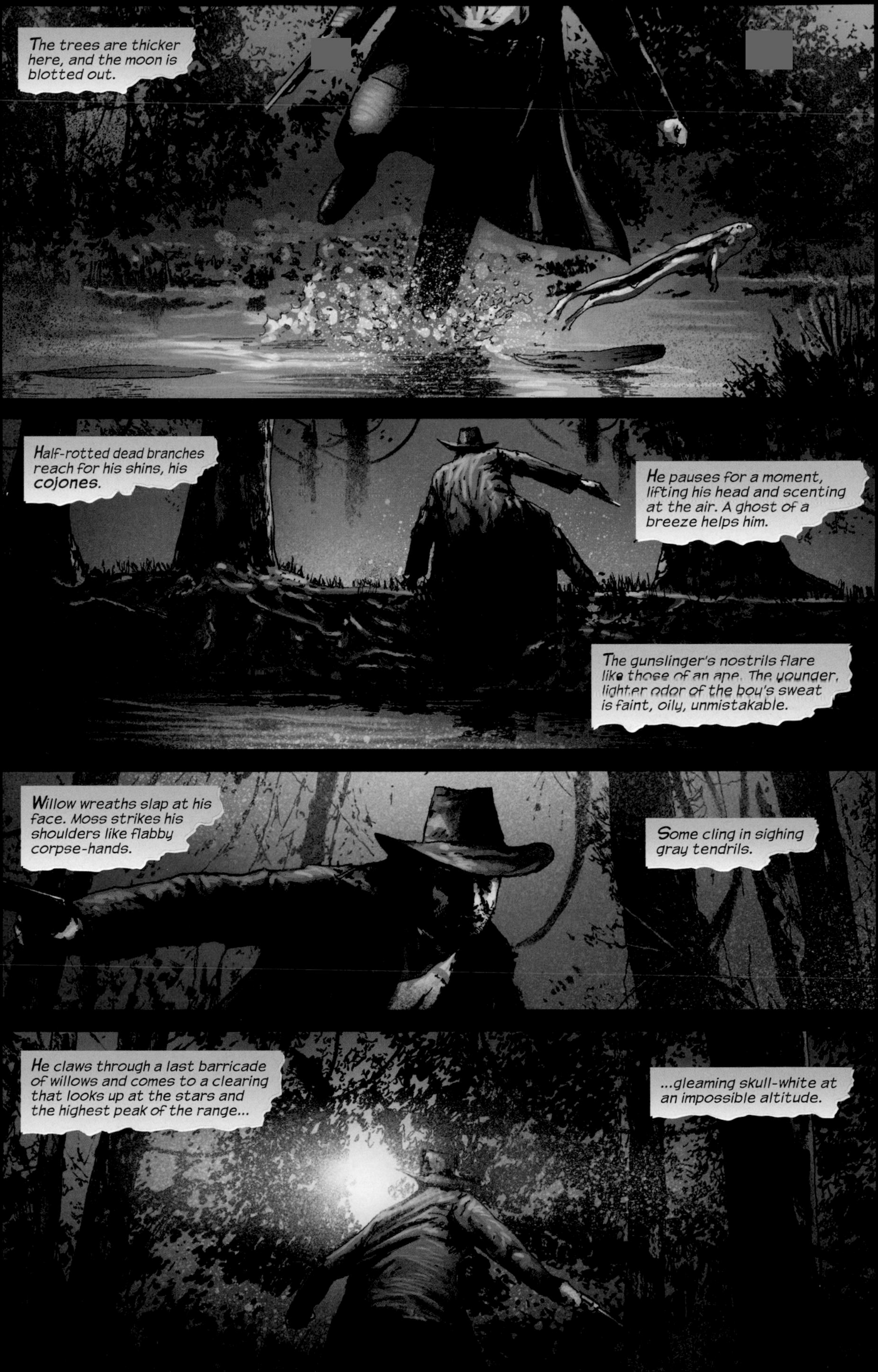
The trees are thicker here, and the moon is blotted out.
Half-rotted dead branches reach for his shins, his cojones.
He pauses for a moment, lifting his head and scenting at the air. A ghost of a breeze helps him.
The gunslinger's nostrils flare like those of an ape. The younger, lighter odor of the boy's sweat is faint, oily, unmistakable.
Willow wreaths slap at his face. Moss strikes his shoulders like flabby corpse-hands.
Some cling in sighing gray tendrils.
He claws through a last barricade of willows and comes to a clearing that looks up at the stars and the highest peak of the range...
...gleaming skull-white at an impossible altitude.

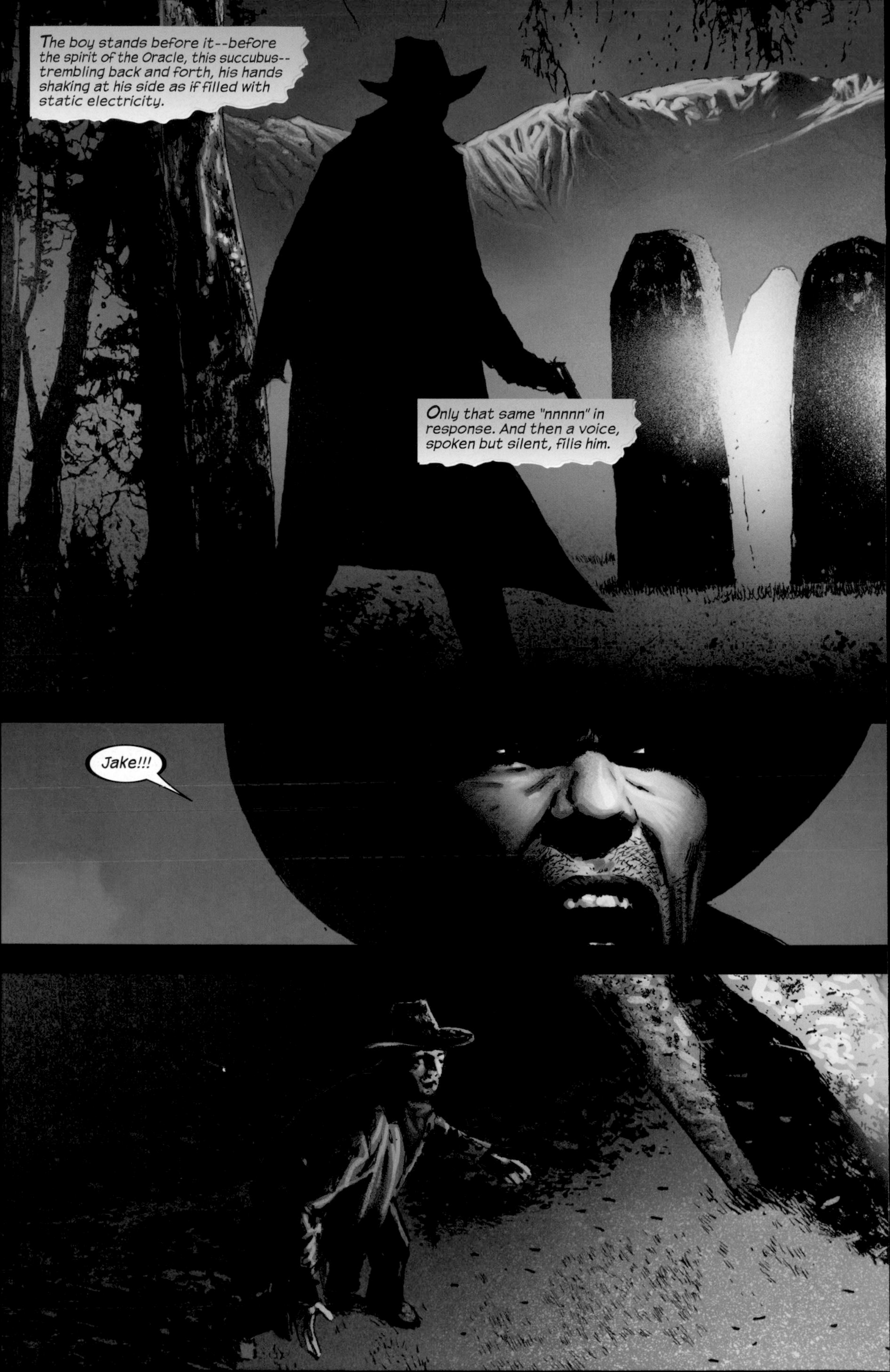
The boy stands before it--before the spirit of the Oracle, this succubus--trembling back and forth, his hands shaking at his side as if filled with static electricity.
Only that same "nnnnn" in response. And then a voice, spoken but silent, fills him.
Jake!!!

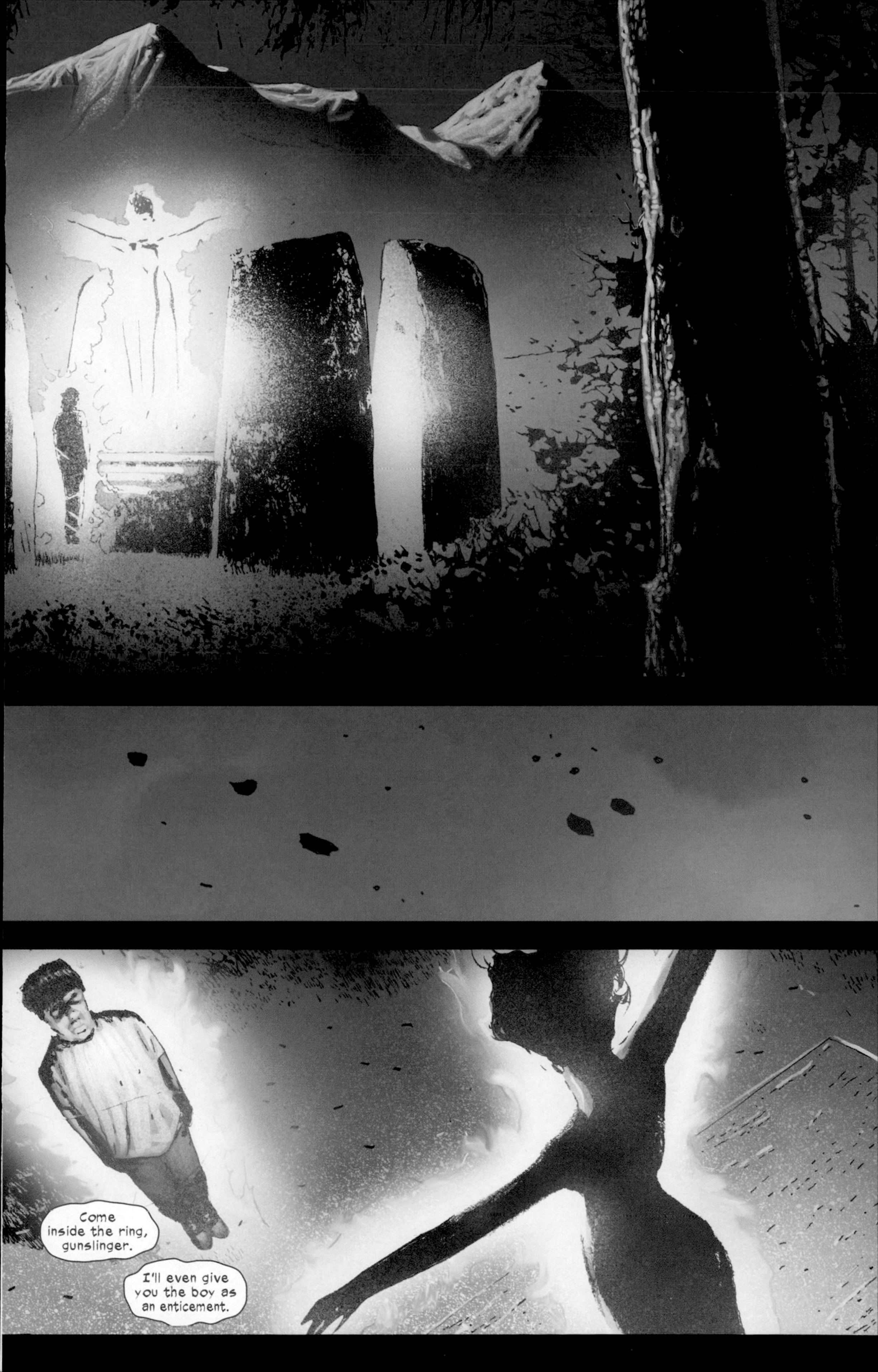
Come inside the ring, gunslinger.
I'll even give you the boy as an enticement.

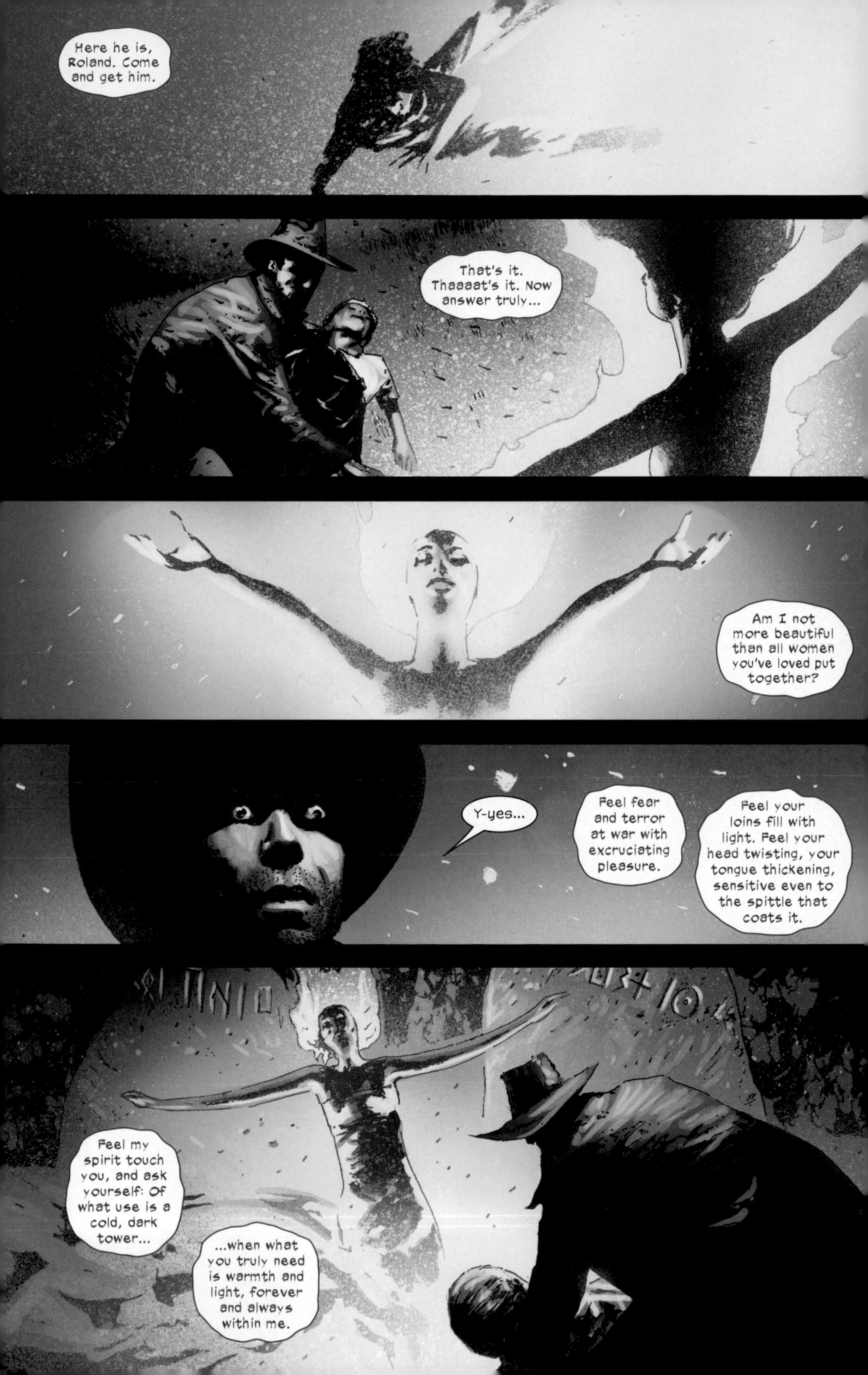
Here he is, Roland. Come and get him.
That's it. Thaaaat's it. Now answer truly...
Am I not more beautiful than all women you've loved put together?
Y-yes...
Feel fear and terror at war with excruciating pleasure.
Feel your loins fill with light. Feel your head twisting, your tongue thickening, sensitive even to the spittle that coats it.
Feel my spirit touch you, and ask yourself: Of what use is a cold, dark tower...
...when what you truly need is warmth and light, forever and always within me.

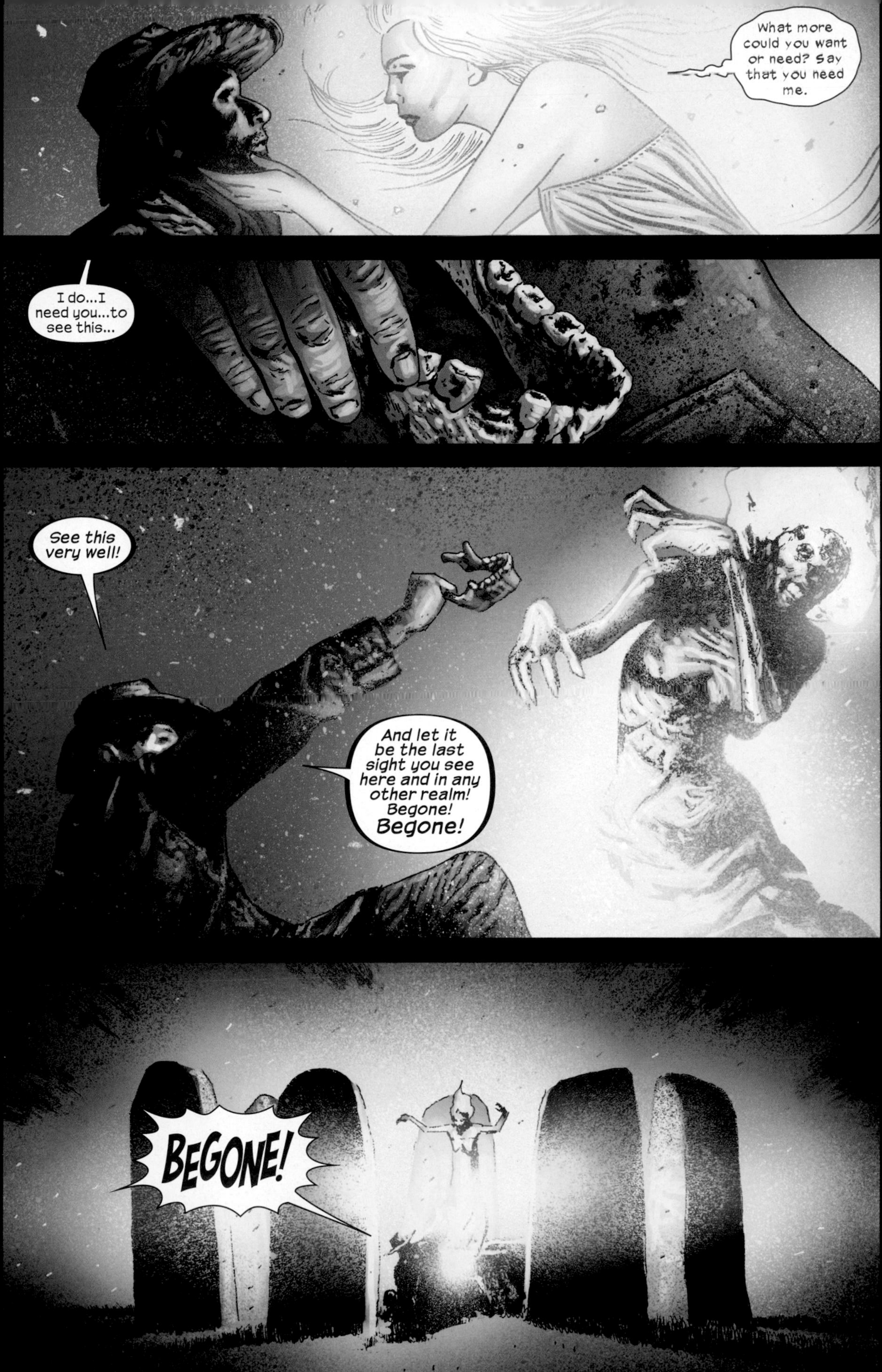
What more could you want or need? Say that you need me.
I do...I need you...to see this...
See this very well!
And let it be the last sight you see here and in any other realm! Begone! Begone!
BEGONE!

STEPHEN KING

THE DARK TOWER
~THE GUNSLINGER~

THE WAY STATION

CHAPTER FIVE

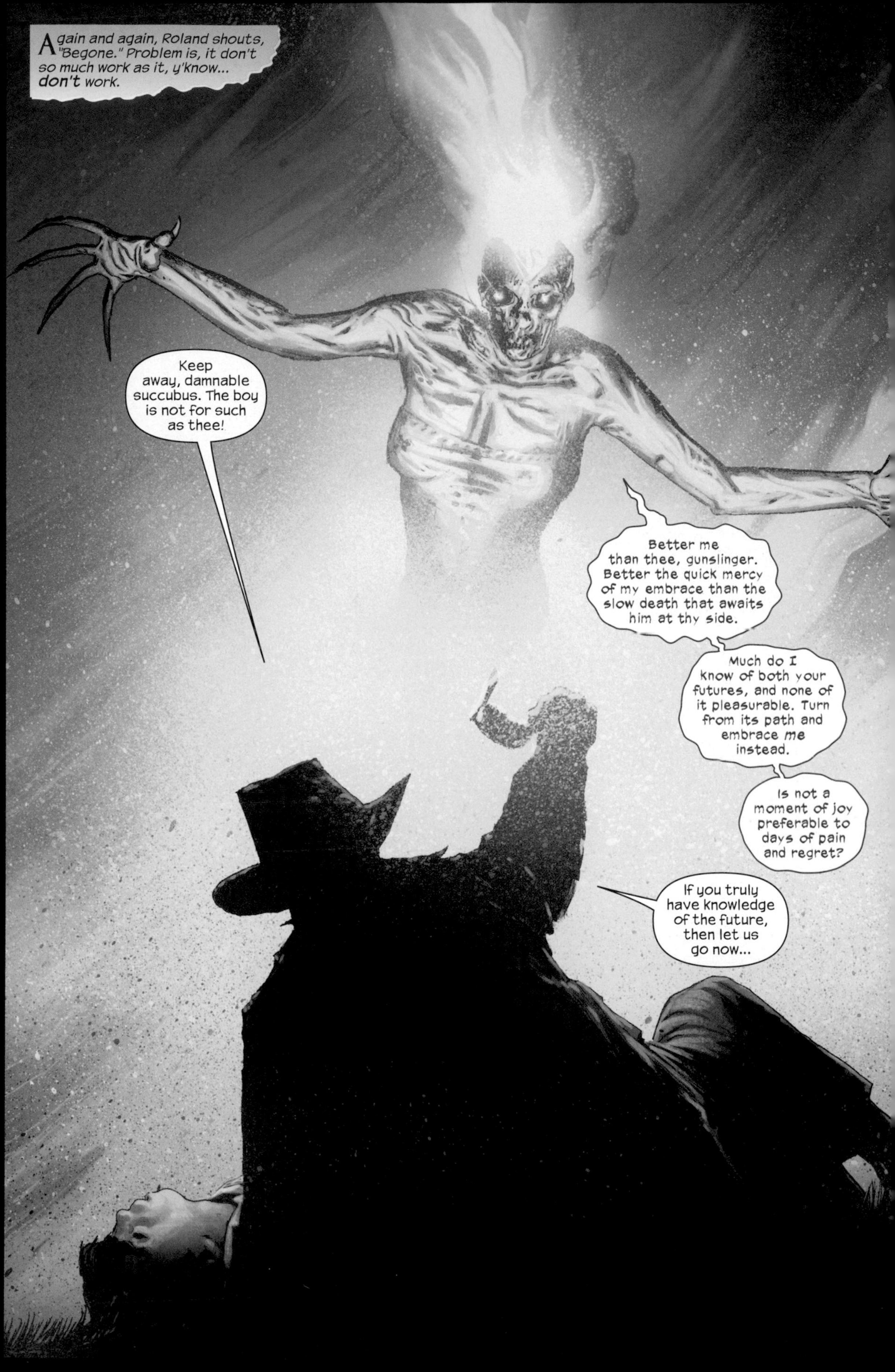
Again and again, Roland shouts, "Begone." Problem is, it don't so much work as it, y'know... **don't** work.
Keep away, damnable succubus. The boy is not for such as thee!
Better me than thee, gunslinger. Better the quick mercy of my embrace than the slow death that awaits him at thy side.
Much do I know of both your futures, and none of it pleasurable. Turn from its path and embrace *me* instead.
Is not a moment of joy preferable to days of pain and regret?
If you truly have knowledge of the future, then let us go now...

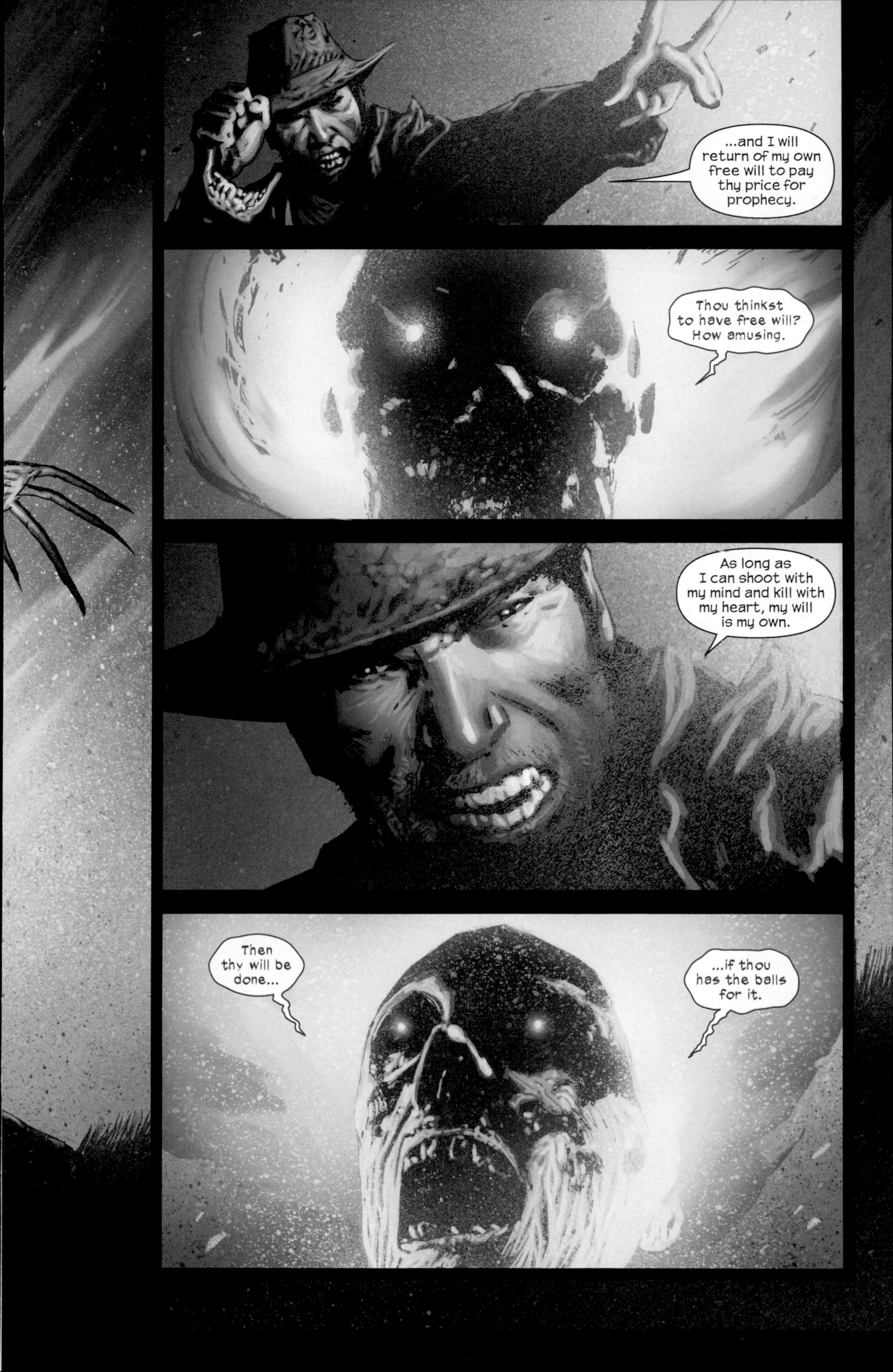
...and I will return of my own free will to pay thy price for prophecy.
Thou thinkst to have free will? How amusing.
As long as I can shoot with my mind and kill with my heart, my will is my own.
Then thy will be done...
...if thou has the balls for it.

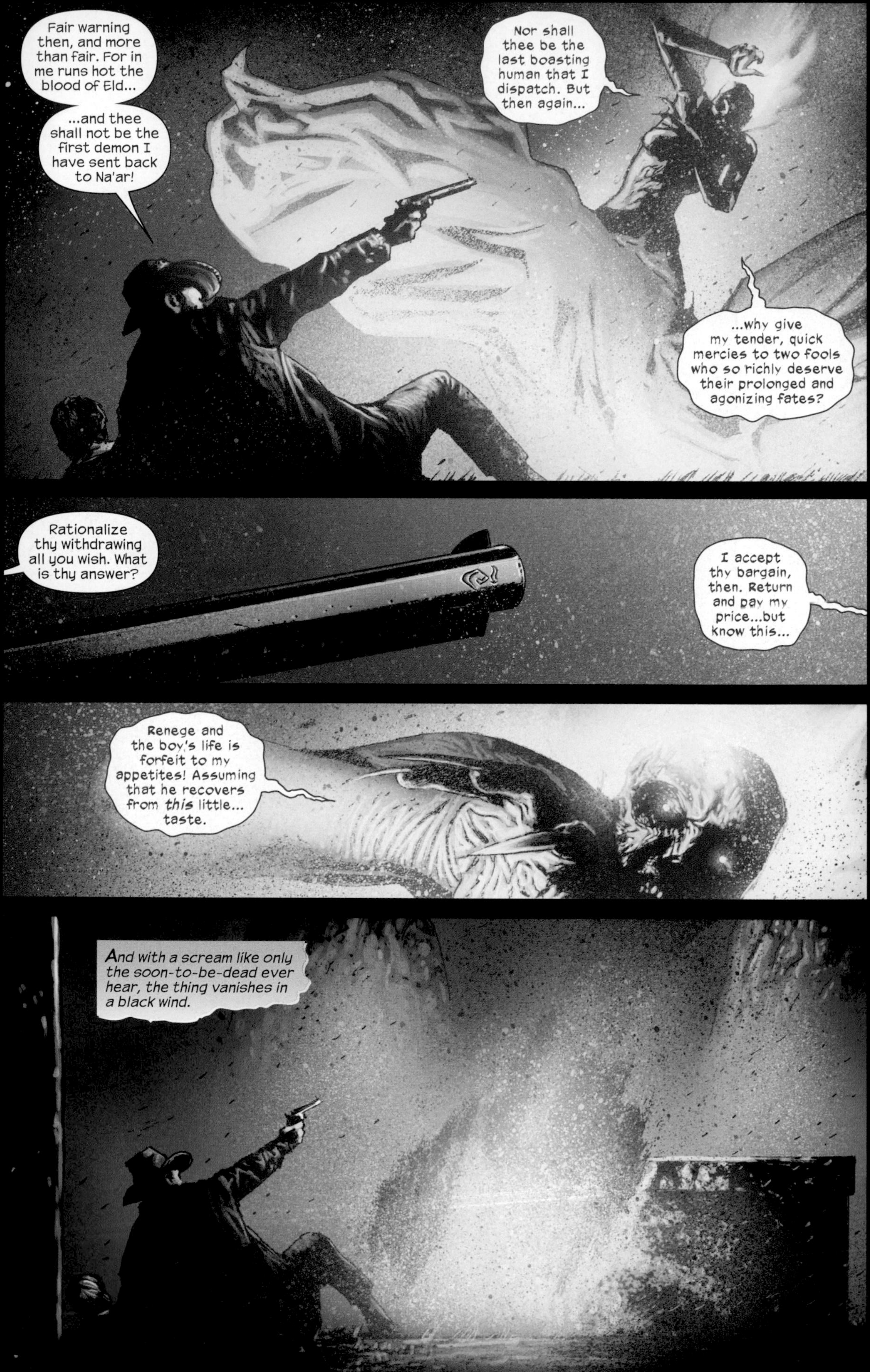
Fair warning then, and more than fair. For in me runs hot the blood of Eld...
...and thee shall not be the first demon I have sent back to Na'ar!
Nor shall thee be the last boasting human that I dispatch. But then again...
...why give my tender, quick mercies to two fools who so richly deserve their prolonged and agonizing fates?
Rationalize thy withdrawing all you wish. What is thy answer?
I accept thy bargain, then. Return and pay my price...but know this...
Renege and the boy's life is forfeit to my appetites! Assuming that he recovers from this little... taste.
And with a scream like only the soon-to-be-dead ever hear, the thing vanishes in a black wind.

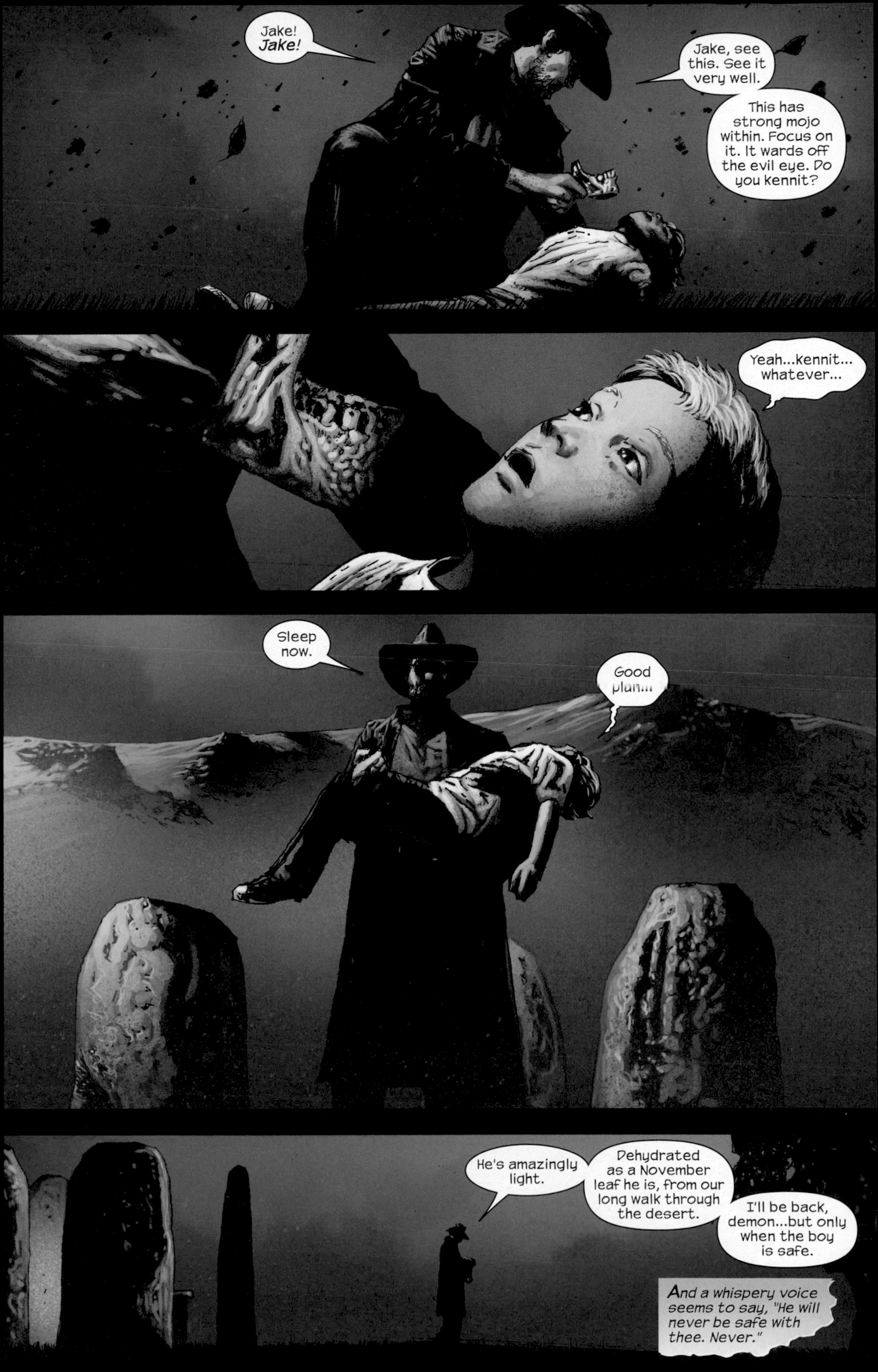

Jake! *Jake!*
Jake, see this. See it very well.
This has strong mojo within. Focus on it. It wards off the evil eye. Do you kennit?
Yeah...kennit... whatever...
Sleep now.
Good plan...
He's amazingly light.
Dehydrated as a November leaf he is, from our long walk through the desert.
I'll be back, demon...but only when the boy is safe.
And a whispery voice seems to say, "He will never be safe with thee. Never."

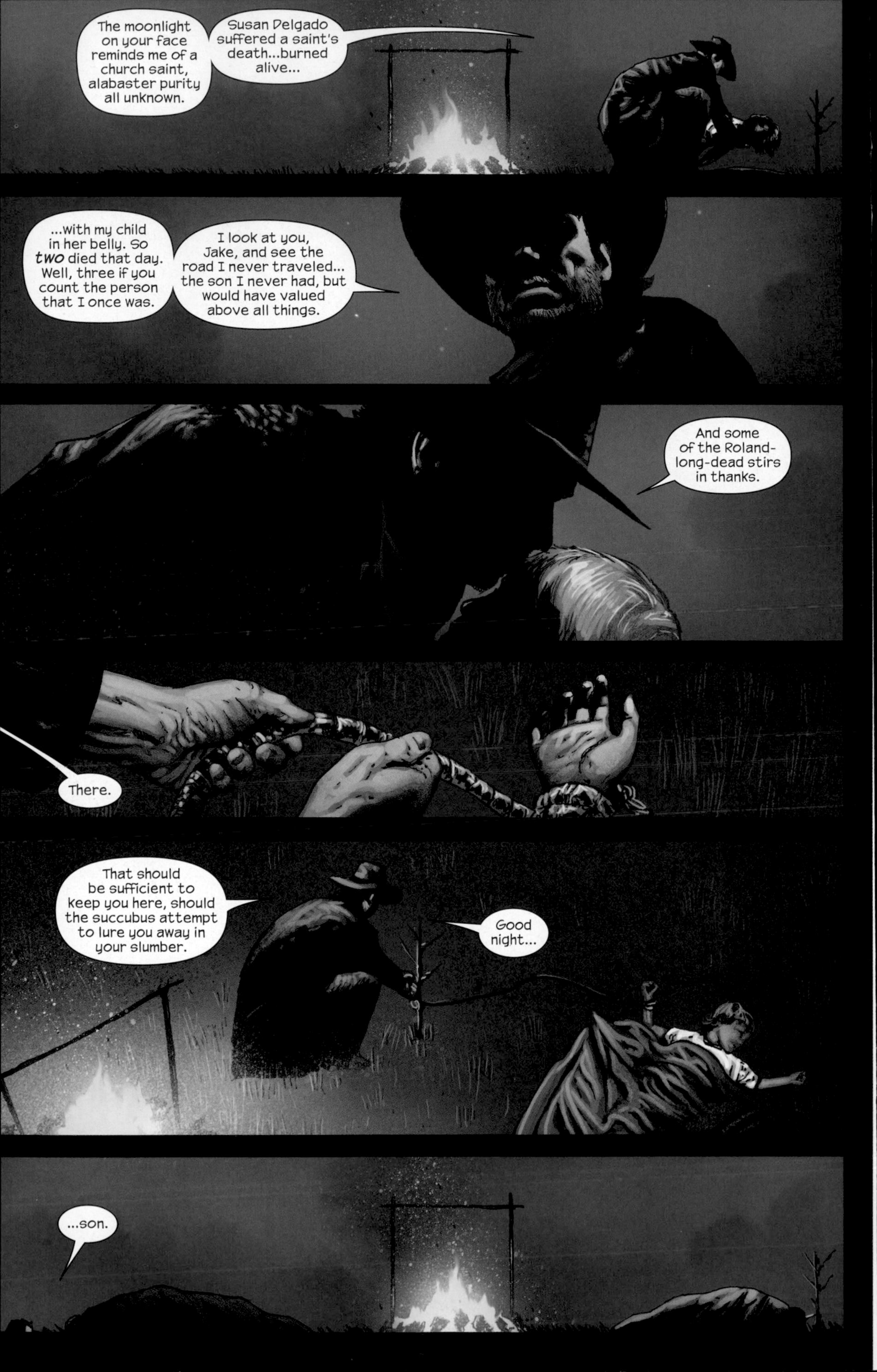
The moonlight on your face reminds me of a church saint, alabaster purity all unknown.
Susan Delgado suffered a saint's death...burned alive...
...with my child in her belly. So two died that day. Well, three if you count the person that I once was.
I look at you, Jake, and see the road I never traveled... the son I never had, but would have valued above all things.
And some of the Roland-long-dead stirs in thanks.
There.
That should be sufficient to keep you here, should the succubus attempt to lure you away in your slumber.
Good night...
...son.

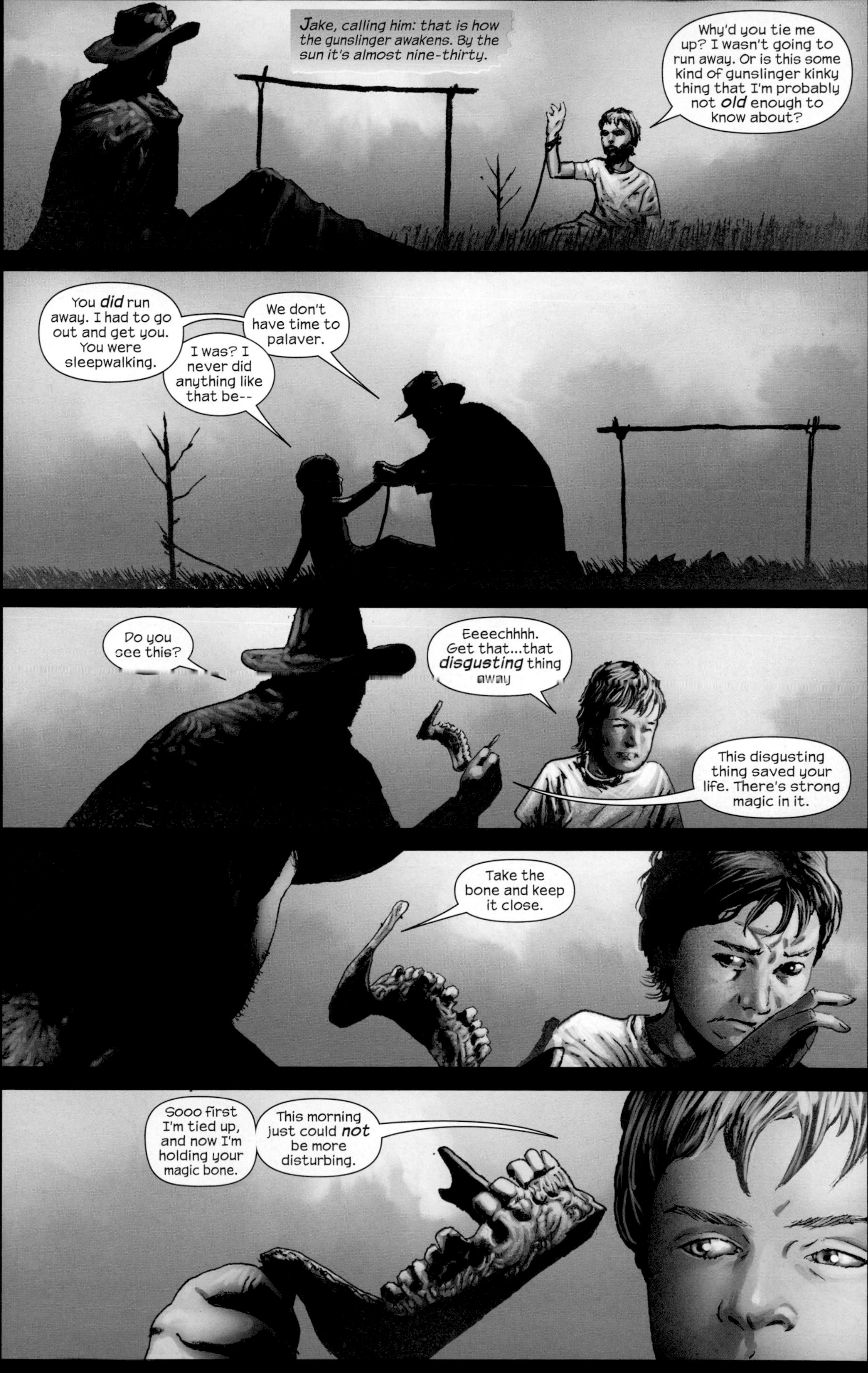
Jake, calling him: that is how the gunslinger awakens. By the sun it's almost nine-thirty.
Why'd you tie me up? I wasn't going to run away. Or is this some kind of gunslinger kinky thing that I'm probably not old enough to know about?
You did run away. I had to go out and get you. You were sleepwalking.
I was? I never did anything like that be--
We don't have time to palaver.
Do you see this?
Eeeechhhh. Get that...that disgusting thing away
This disgusting thing saved your life. There's strong magic in it.
Take the bone and keep it close.
Sooo first I'm tied up, and now I'm holding your magic bone.
This morning just could not be more disturbing.

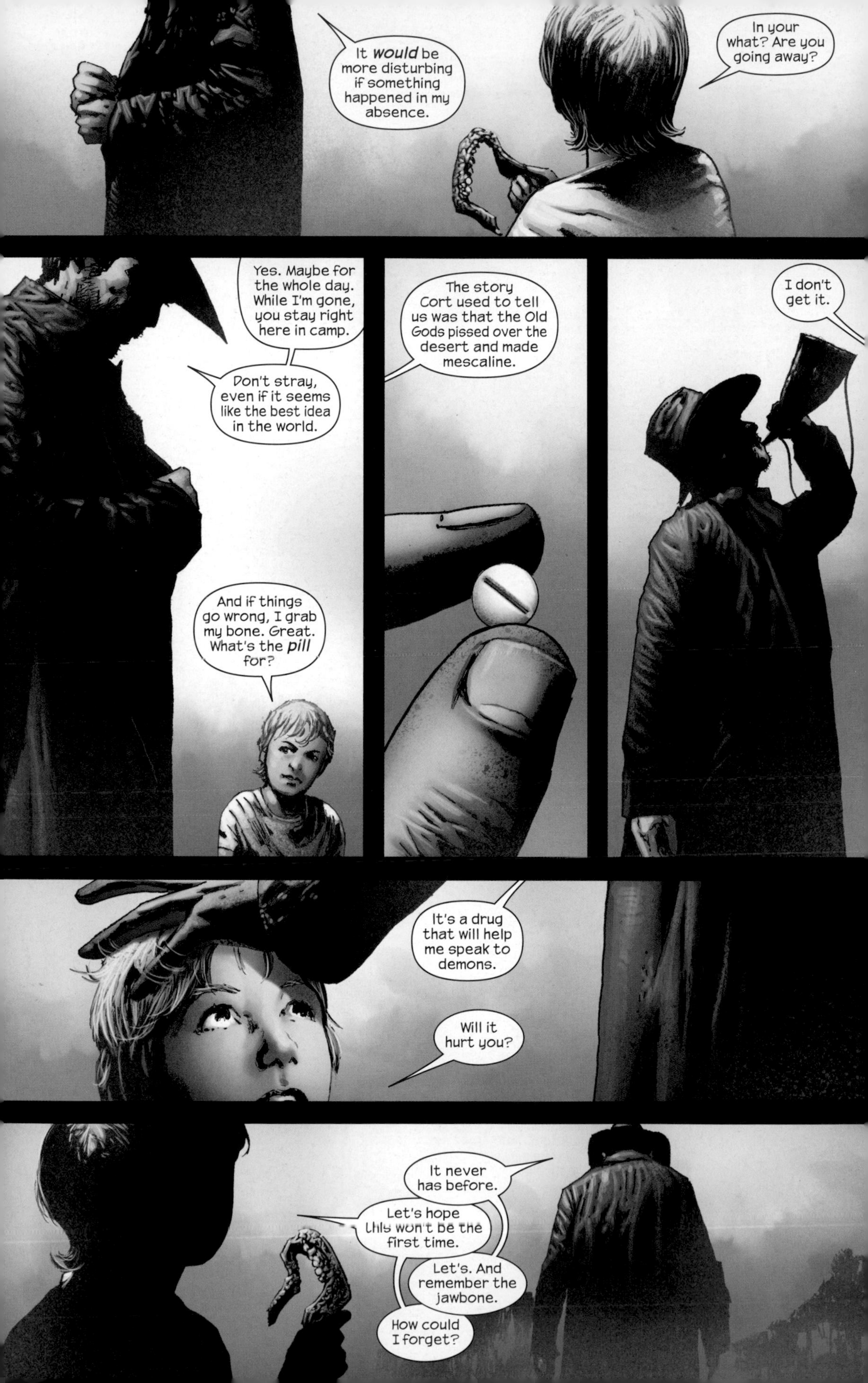
It *would* be more disturbing if something happened in my absence.
In your what? Are you going away?
Yes. Maybe for the whole day. While I'm gone, you stay right here in camp.
Don't stray, even if it seems like the best idea in the world.
And if things go wrong, I grab my bone. Great. What's the *pill* for?
The story Cort used to tell us was that the Old Gods pissed over the desert and made mescaline.
I don't get it.
It's a drug that will help me speak to demons.
Will it hurt you?
It never has before.
Let's hope this won't be the first time.
Let's. And remember the jawbone.
How could I forget?

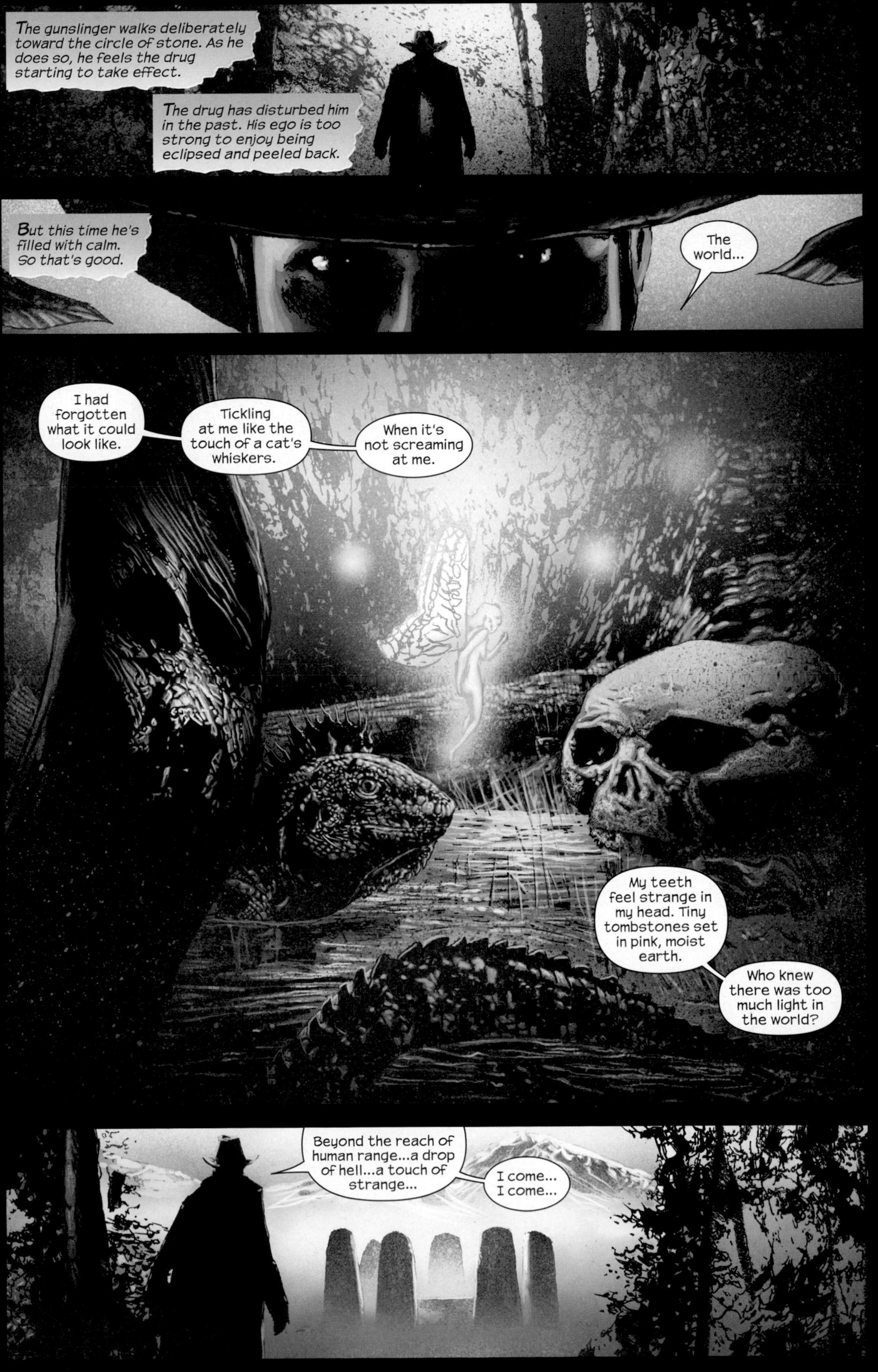
The gunslinger walks deliberately toward the circle of stone. As he does so, he feels the drug starting to take effect.
The drug has disturbed him in the past. His ego is too strong to enjoy being eclipsed and peeled back.
But this time he's filled with calm. So that's good.
The world...
I had forgotten what it could look like.
Tickling at me like the touch of a cat's whiskers.
When it's not screaming at me.
My teeth feel strange in my head. Tiny tombstones set in pink, moist earth.
Who knew there was too much light in the world?
Beyond the reach of human range...a drop of hell...a touch of strange...
I come... I come...

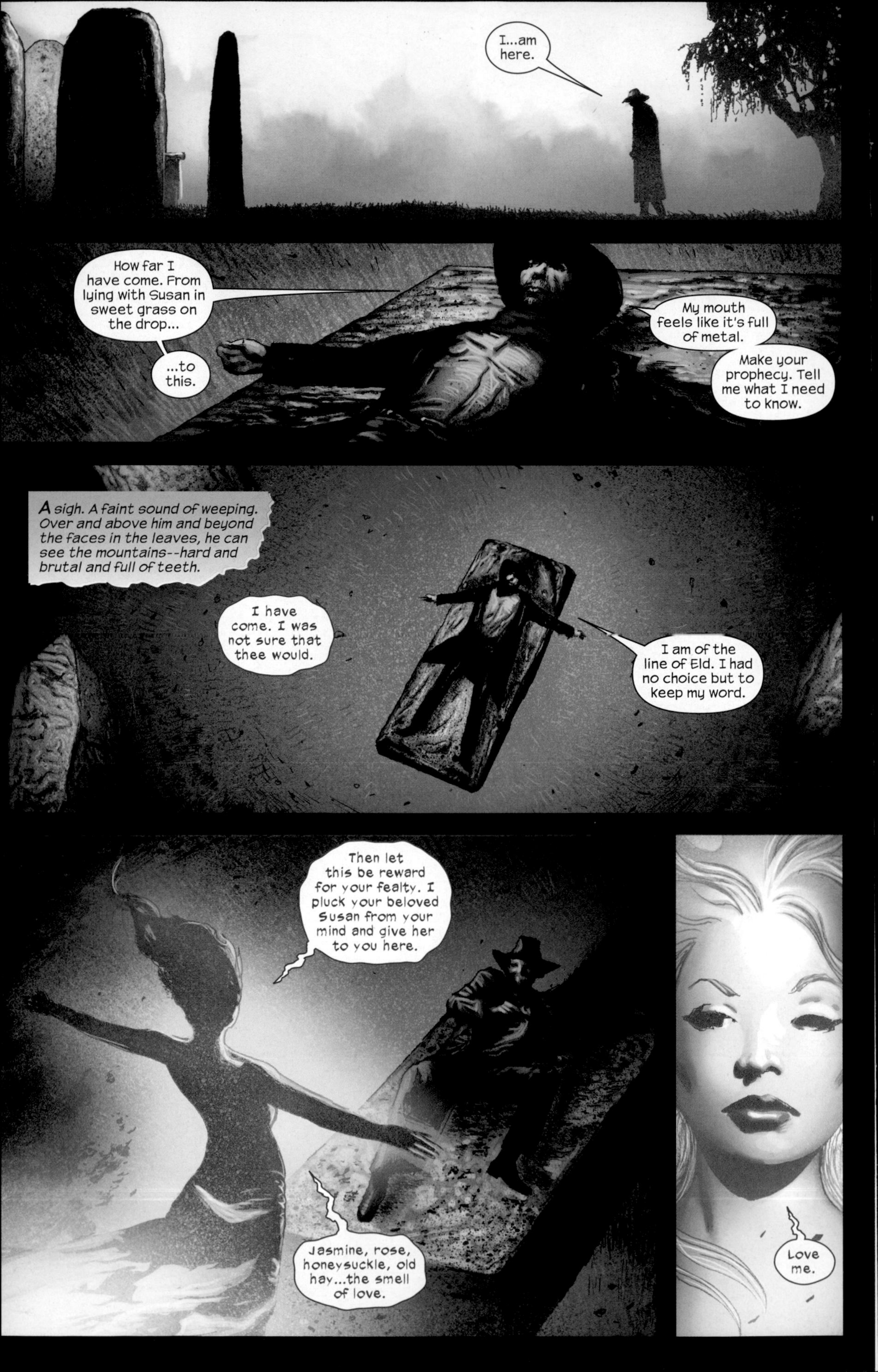
I...am here.
How far I have come. From lying with Susan in sweet grass on the drop...
...to this.
My mouth feels like it's full of metal.
Make your prophecy. Tell me what I need to know.
A sigh. A faint sound of weeping. Over and above him and beyond the faces in the leaves, he can see the mountains--hard and brutal and full of teeth.
I have come. I was not sure that thee would.
I am of the line of Eld. I had no choice but to keep my word.
Then let this be reward for your fealty. I pluck your beloved Susan from your mind and give her to you here.
Jasmine, rose, honeysuckle, old hay...the smell of love.
Love me.

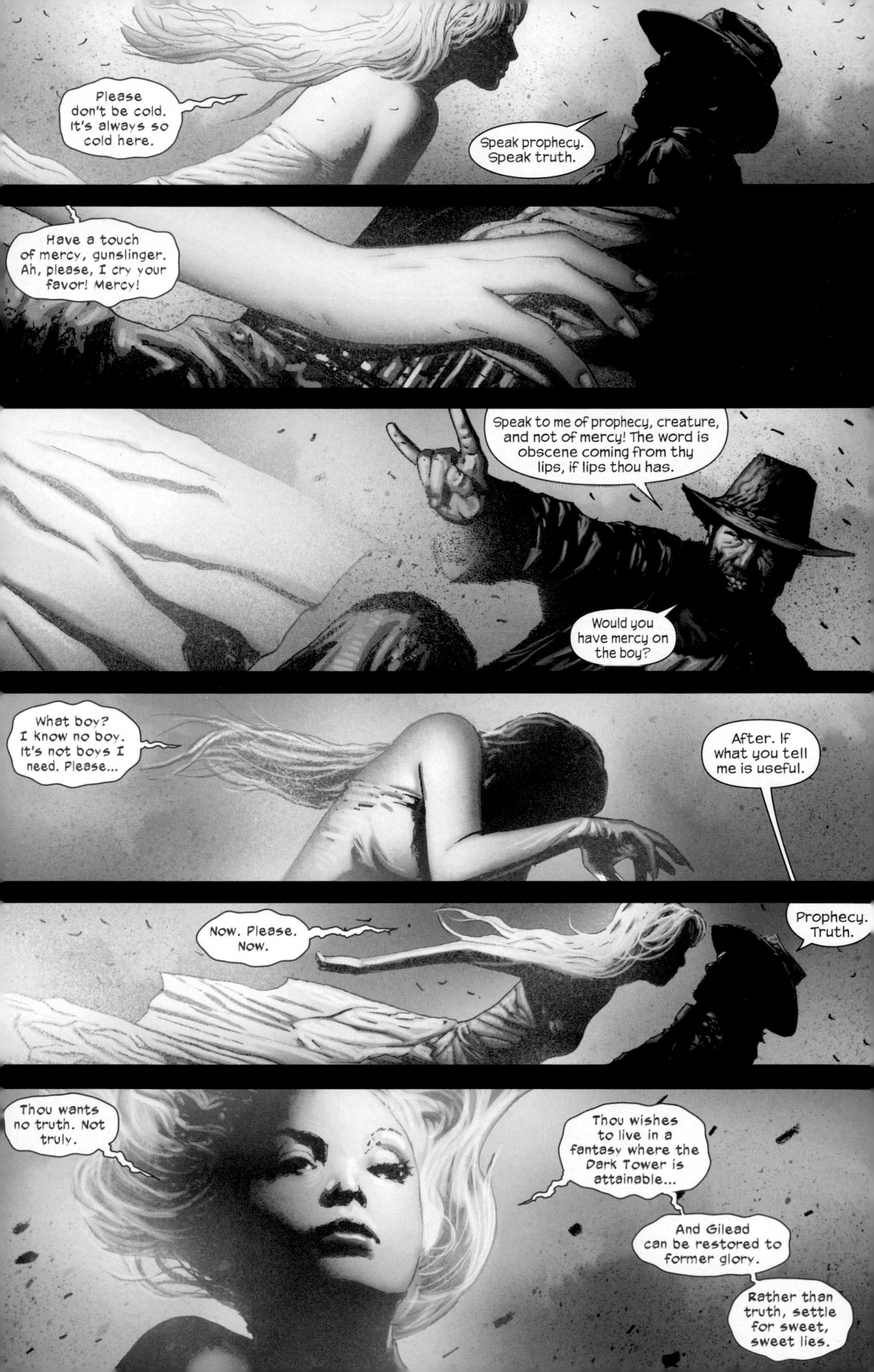
Please don't be cold. It's always so cold here.
Speak prophecy. Speak truth.
Have a touch of mercy, gunslinger. Ah, please, I cry your favor! Mercy!
Speak to me of prophecy, creature, and not of mercy! The word is obscene coming from thy lips, if lips thou has.
Would you have mercy on the boy?
What boy? I know no boy. It's not boys I need. Please...
After. If what you tell me is useful.
Now. Please. Now.
Prophecy. Truth.
Thou wants no truth. Not truly.
Thou wishes to live in a fantasy where the Dark Tower is attainable...
And Gilead can be restored to former glory.
Rather than truth, settle for sweet, sweet lies.

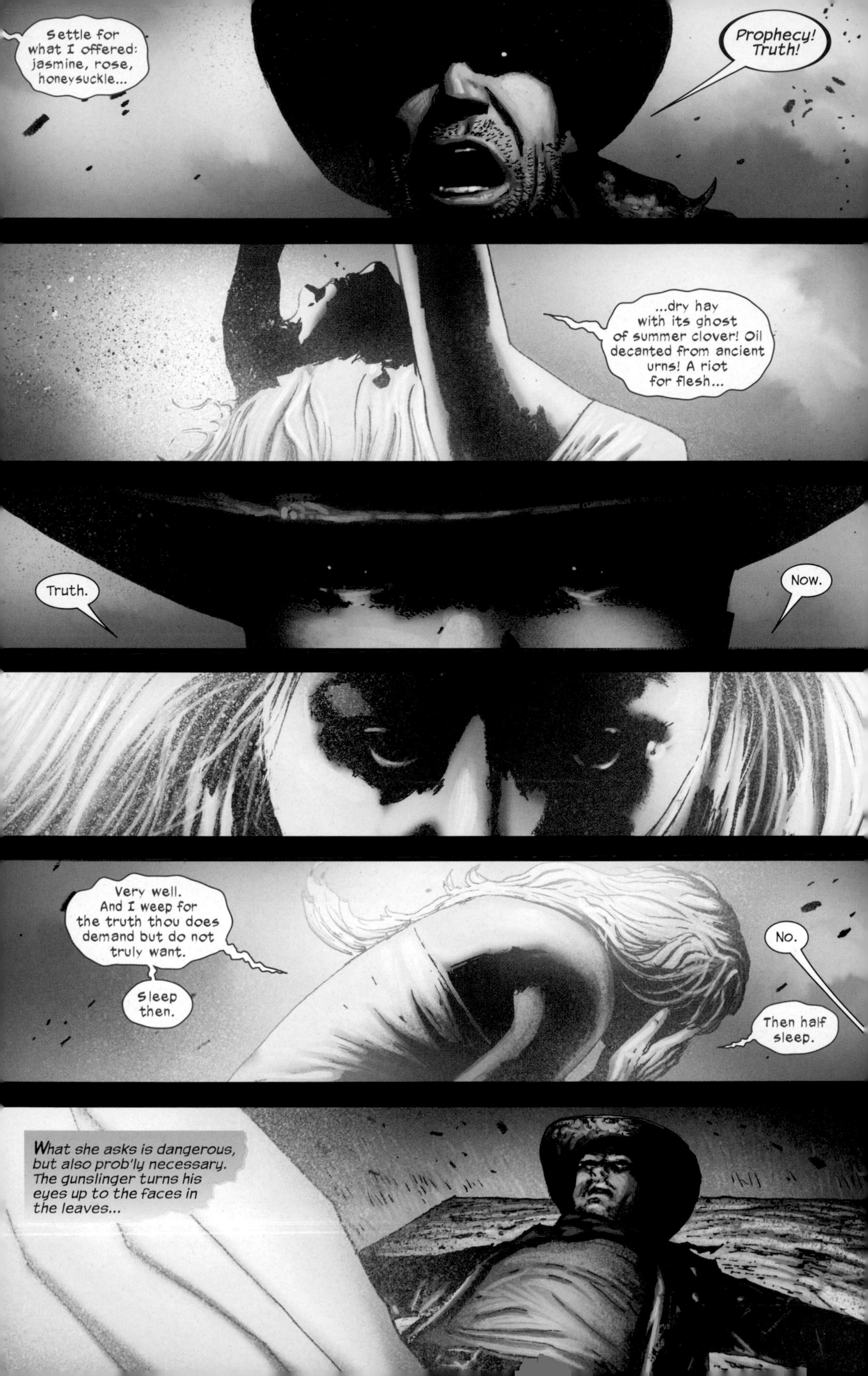
Settle for what I offered: jasmine, rose, honeysuckle...
Prophecy! Truth!
...dry hay with its ghost of summer clover! Oil decanted from ancient urns! A riot for flesh...
Truth.
Now.
Very well. And I weep for the truth thou does demand but do not truly want.
Sleep then.
No.
Then half sleep.
What she asks is dangerous, but also prob'ly necessary. The gunslinger turns his eyes up to the faces in the leaves...

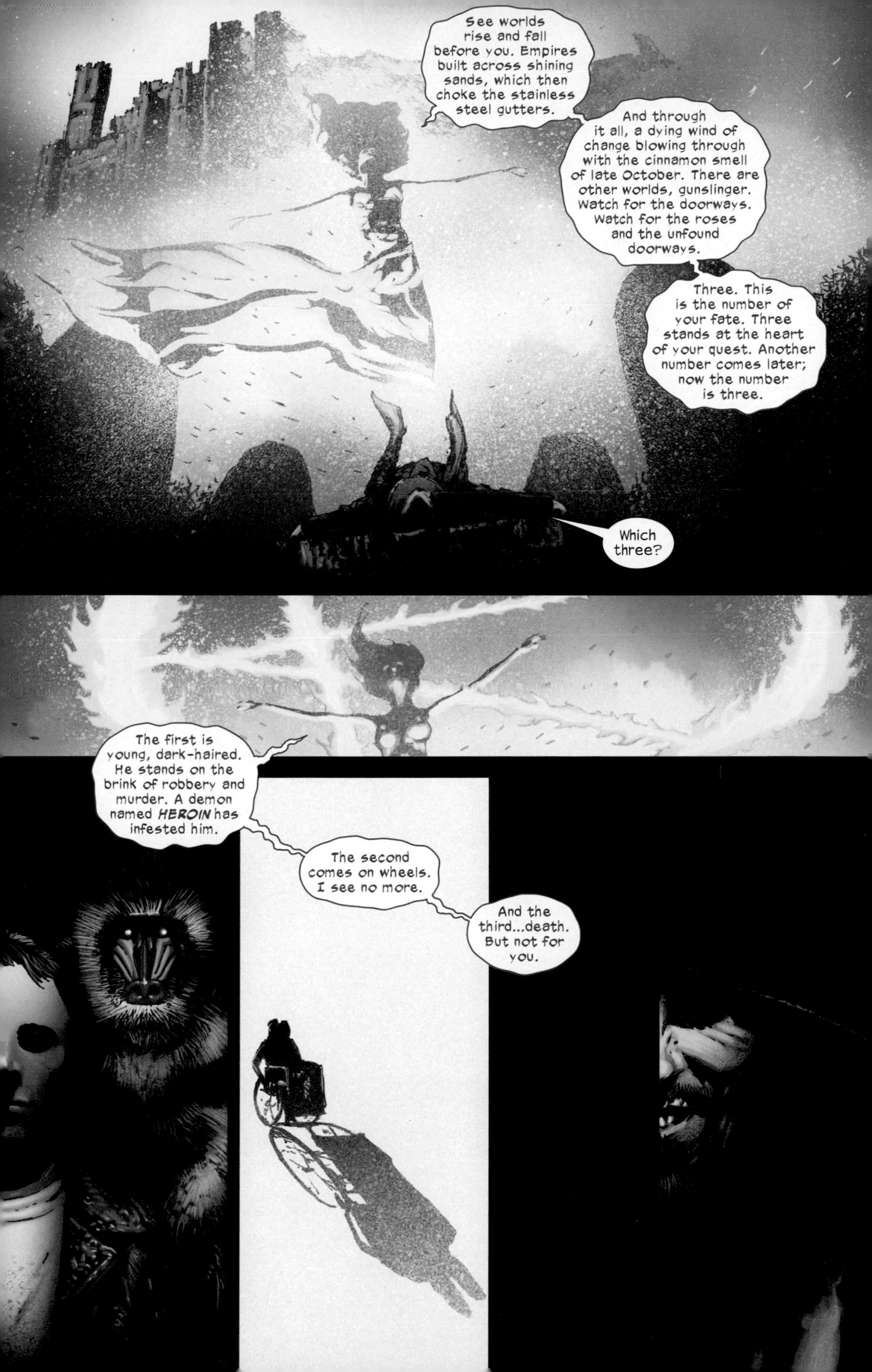
See worlds rise and fall before you. Empires built across shining sands, which then choke the stainless steel gutters.
And through it all, a dying wind of change blowing through with the cinnamon smell of late October. There are other worlds, gunslinger. Watch for the doorways. Watch for the roses and the unfound doorways.
Three. This is the number of your fate. Three stands at the heart of your quest. Another number comes later; now the number is three.
Which three?
The first is young, dark-haired. He stands on the brink of robbery and murder. A demon named HEROIN has infested him.
The second comes on wheels. I see no more.
And the third...death. But not for you.

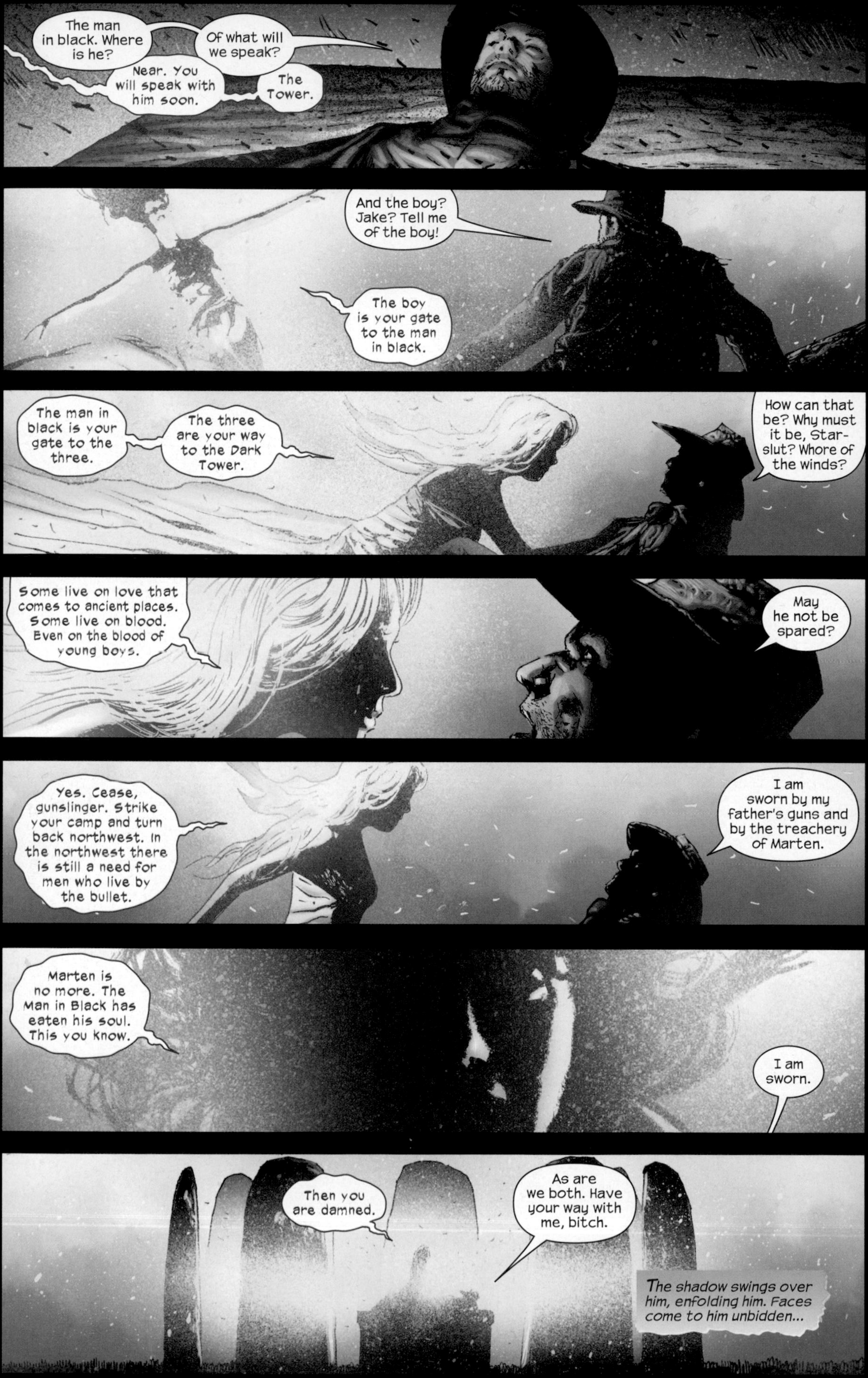

The man in black. Where is he?
Of what will we speak?
Near. You will speak with him soon.
The Tower.
And the boy? Jake? Tell me of the boy!
The boy is your gate to the man in black.
The man in black is your gate to the three.
The three are your way to the Dark Tower.
How can that be? Why must it be, Star-slut? Whore of the winds?
Some live on love that comes to ancient places. Some live on blood. Even on the blood of young boys.
May he not be spared?
Yes. Cease, gunslinger. Strike your camp and turn back northwest. In the northwest there is still a need for men who live by the bullet.
I am sworn by my father's guns and by the treachery of Marten.
Marten is no more. The Man in Black has eaten his soul. This you know.
I am sworn.
Then you are damned.
As are we both. Have your way with me, bitch.
The shadow swings over him, enfolding him. Faces come to him unbidden...

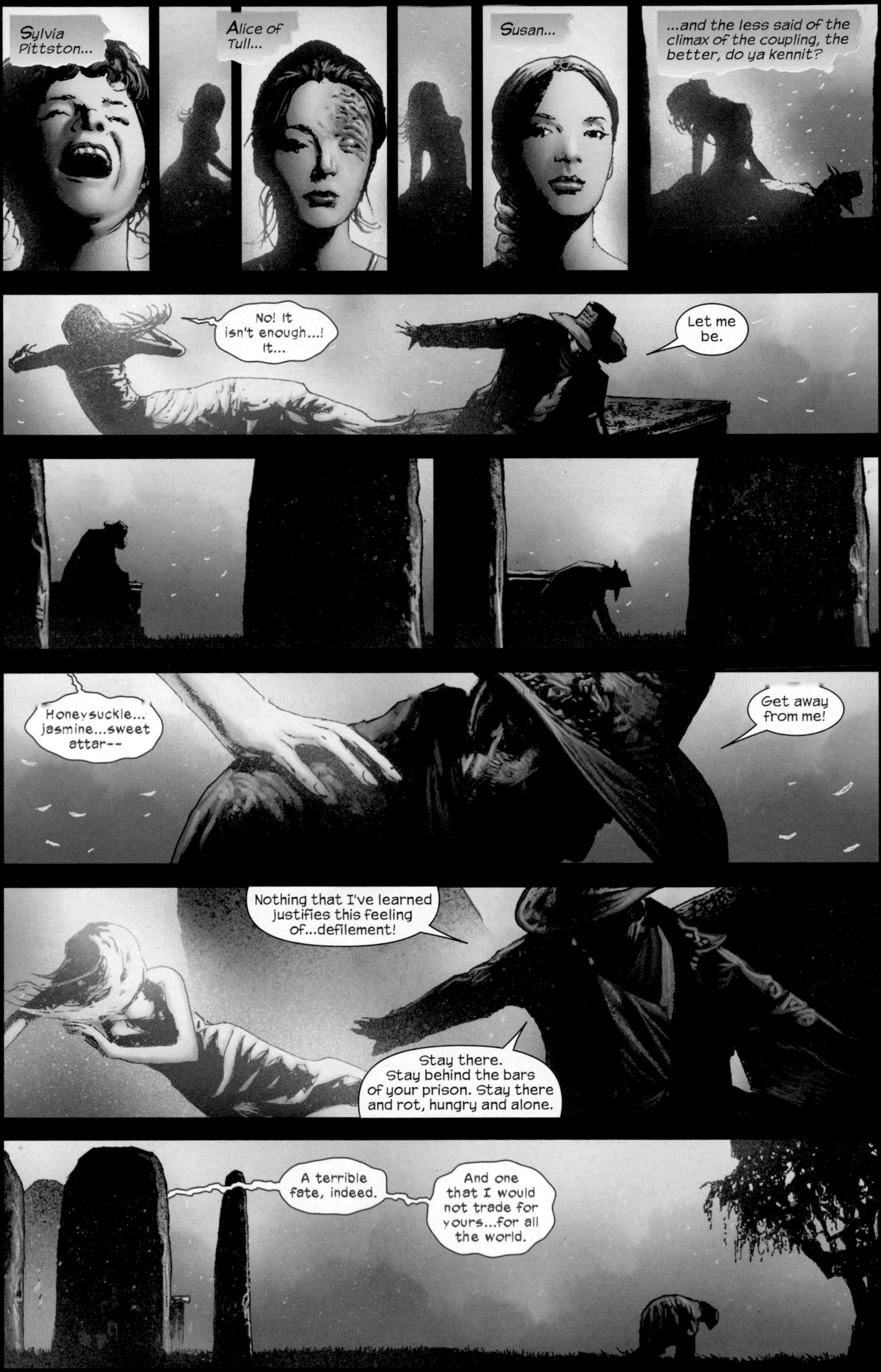
Sylvia Pittston...
Alice of Tull...
Susan...
...and the less said of the climax of the coupling, the better, do ya kennit?
No! It isn't enough...! It...
Let me be.
Honeysuckle... jasmine...sweet attar--
Get away from me!
Nothing that I've learned justifies this feeling of...defilement!
Stay there. Stay behind the bars of your prison. Stay there and rot, hungry and alone.
A terrible fate, indeed.
And one that I would not trade for yours...for all the world.

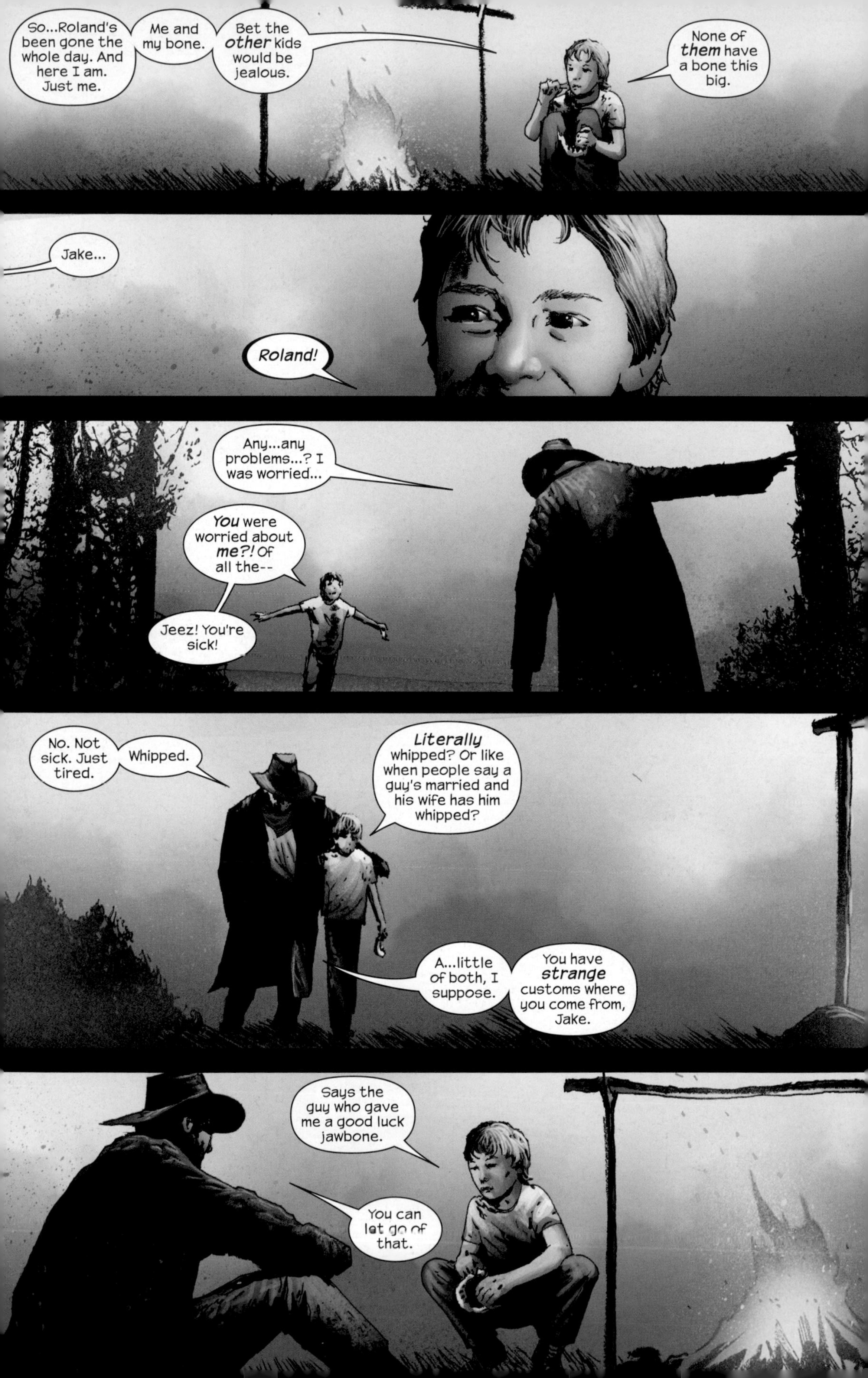
So...Roland's been gone the whole day. And here I am. Just me.
Me and my bone.
Bet the *other* kids would be jealous.
None of *them* have a bone this big.
Jake...
Roland!
Any...any problems...? I was worried...
You were worried about *me?!* Of all the--
Jeez! You're sick!
No. Not sick. Just tired.
Whipped.
Literally whipped? Or like when people say a guy's married and his wife has him whipped?
A...little of both, I suppose.
You have *strange* customs where you come from, Jake.
Says the guy who gave me a good luck jawbone.
You can let go of that.

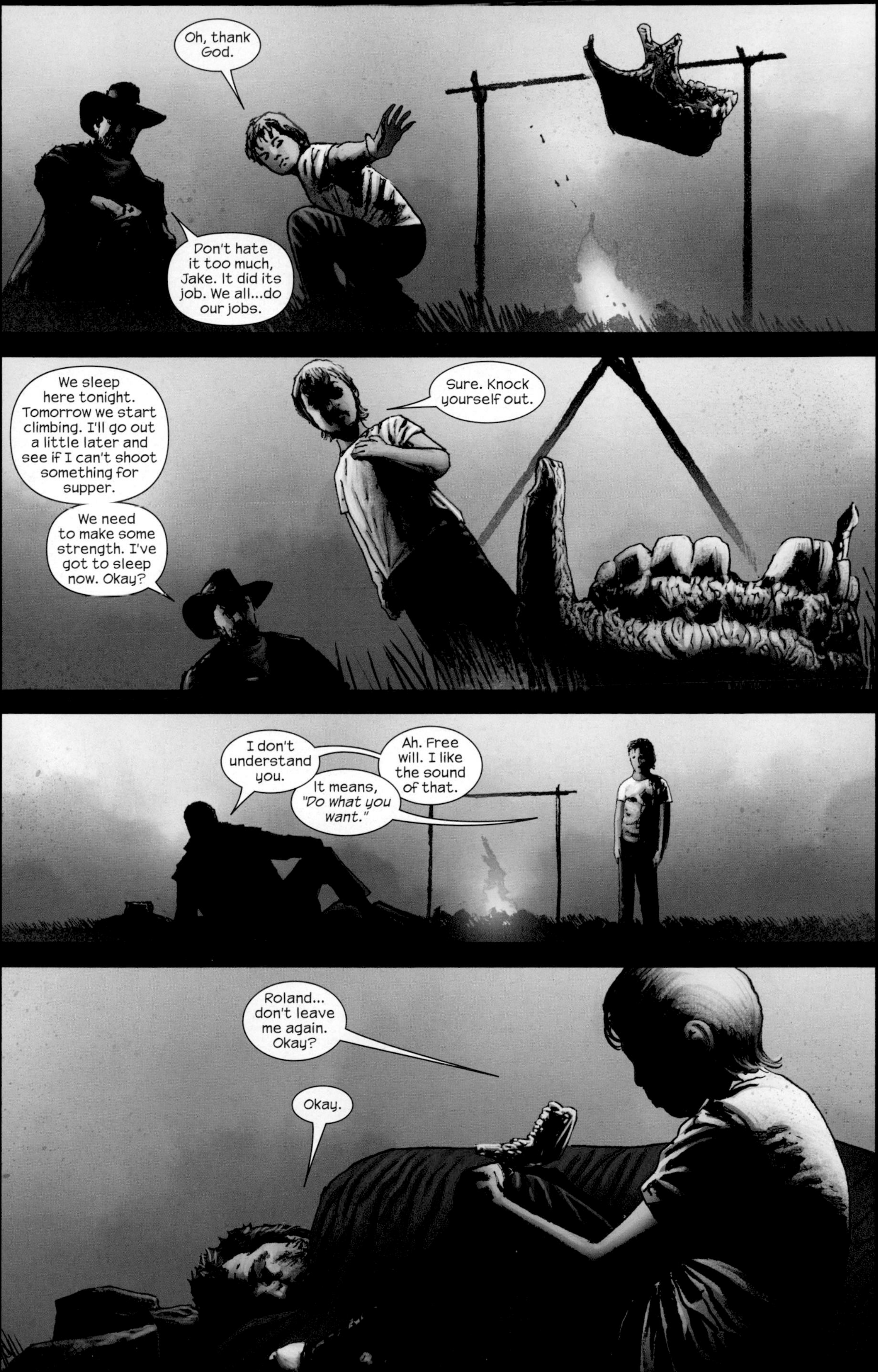
Oh, thank God.
Don't hate it too much, Jake. It did its job. We all...do our jobs.
We sleep here tonight. Tomorrow we start climbing. I'll go out a little later and see if I can't shoot something for supper.
We need to make some strength. I've got to sleep now. Okay?
Sure. Knock yourself out.
I don't understand you.
It means, "Do what you want."
Ah. Free will. I like the sound of that.
Roland... don't leave me again. Okay?
Okay.

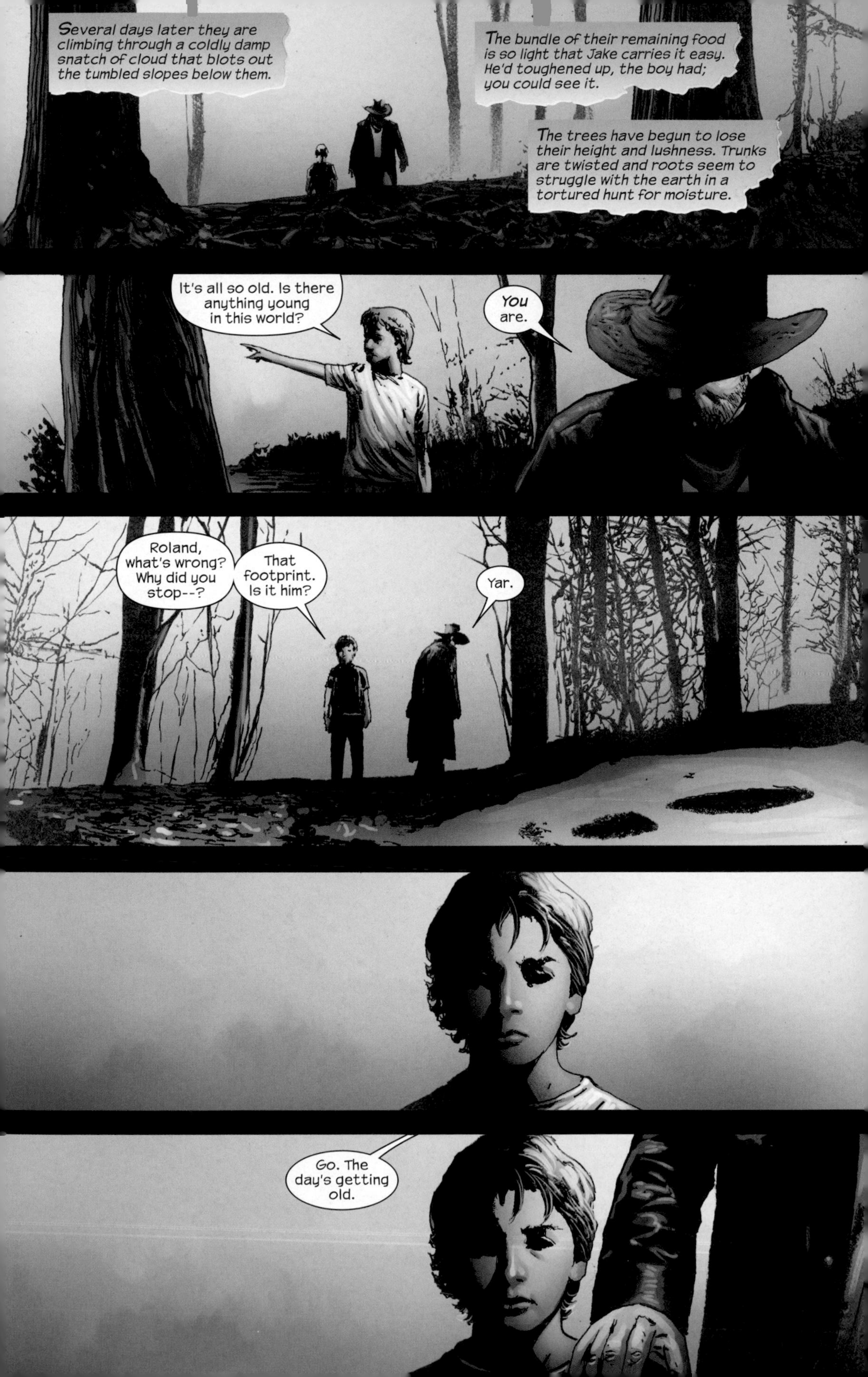
Several days later they are climbing through a coldly damp snatch of cloud that blots out the tumbled slopes below them.
The bundle of their remaining food is so light that Jake carries it easy. He'd toughened up, the boy had; you could see it.
The trees have begun to lose their height and lushness. Trunks are twisted and roots seem to struggle with the earth in a tortured hunt for moisture.
It's all so old. Is there anything young in this world?
You are.
Roland, what's wrong? Why did you stop--?
That footprint. Is it him?
Yar.
Go. The day's getting old.

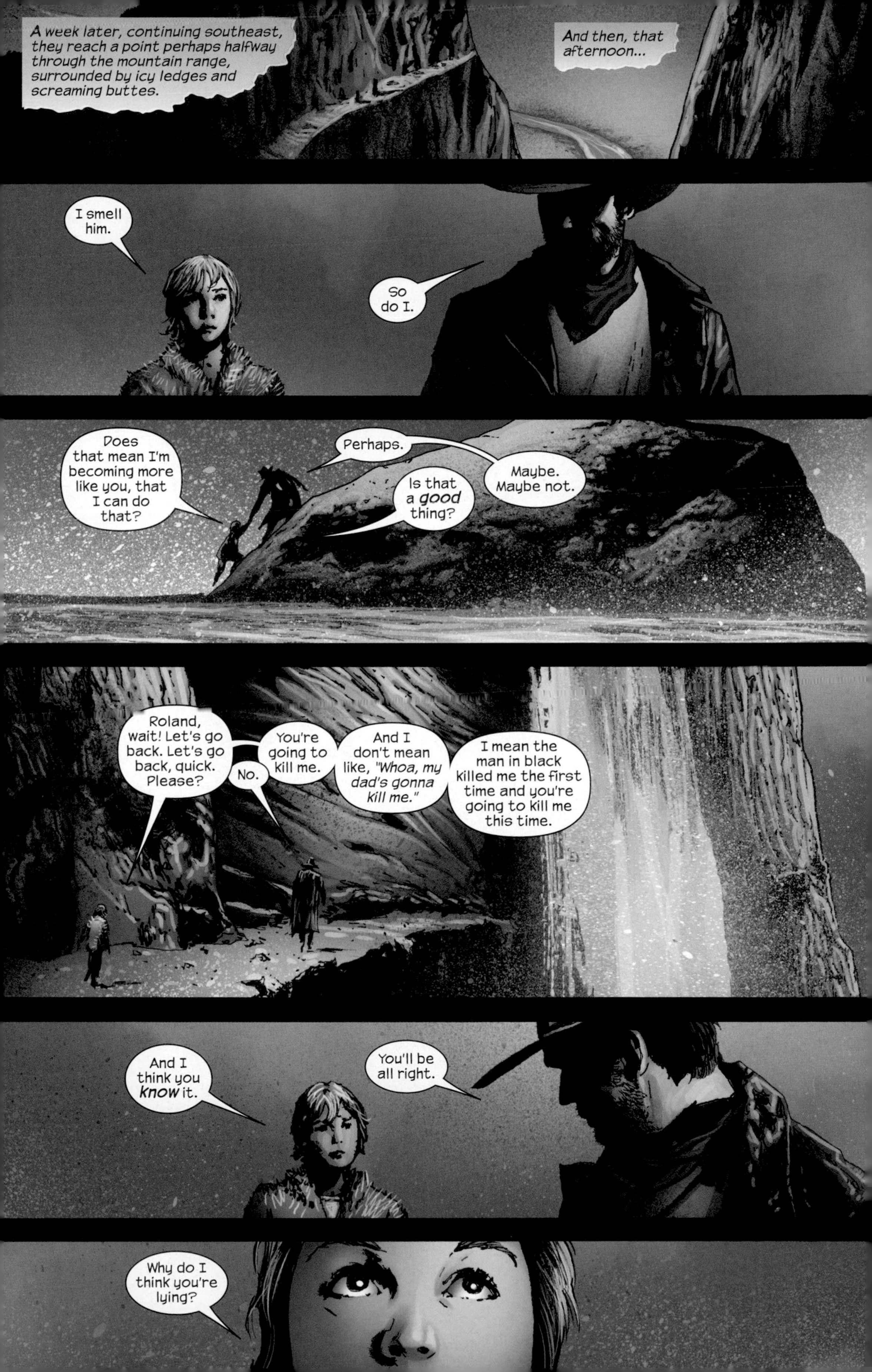
A week later, continuing southeast, they reach a point perhaps halfway through the mountain range, surrounded by icy ledges and screaming buttes.
And then, that afternoon...
I smell him.
So do I.
Does that mean I'm becoming more like you, that I can do that?
Perhaps.
Is that a *good* thing?
Maybe. Maybe not.
Roland, wait! Let's go back. Let's go back, quick. Please?
No.
You're going to kill me.
And I don't mean like, *"Whoa, my dad's gonna kill me."*
I mean the man in black killed me the first time and you're going to kill me this time.
And I think you ***know*** it.
You'll be all right.
Why do I think you're lying?

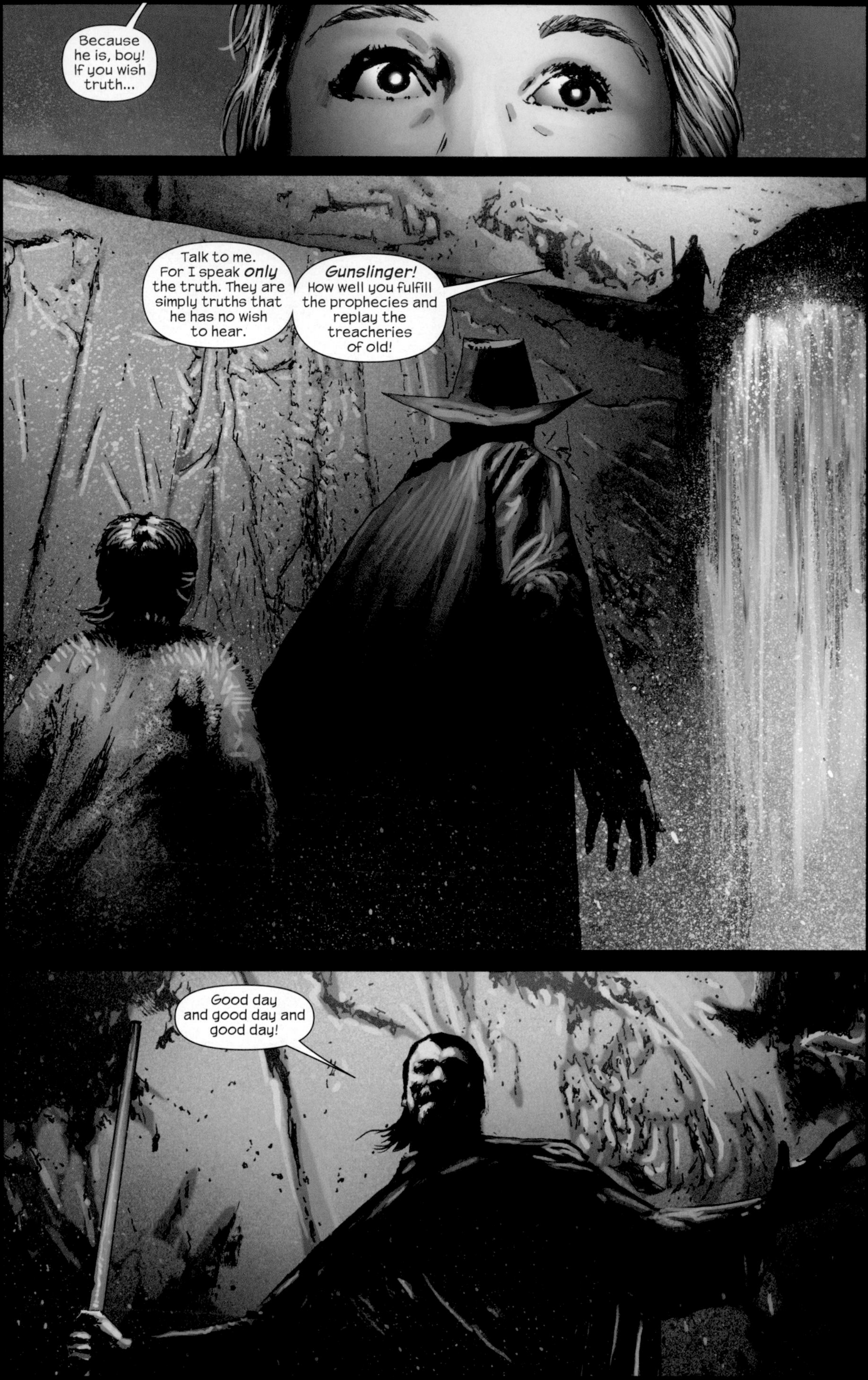
Because he is, boy! If you wish truth...
Talk to me. For I speak *only* the truth. They are simply truths that he has no wish to hear.
Gunslinger! How well you fulfill the prophecies and replay the treacheries of old!
Good day and good day and good day!

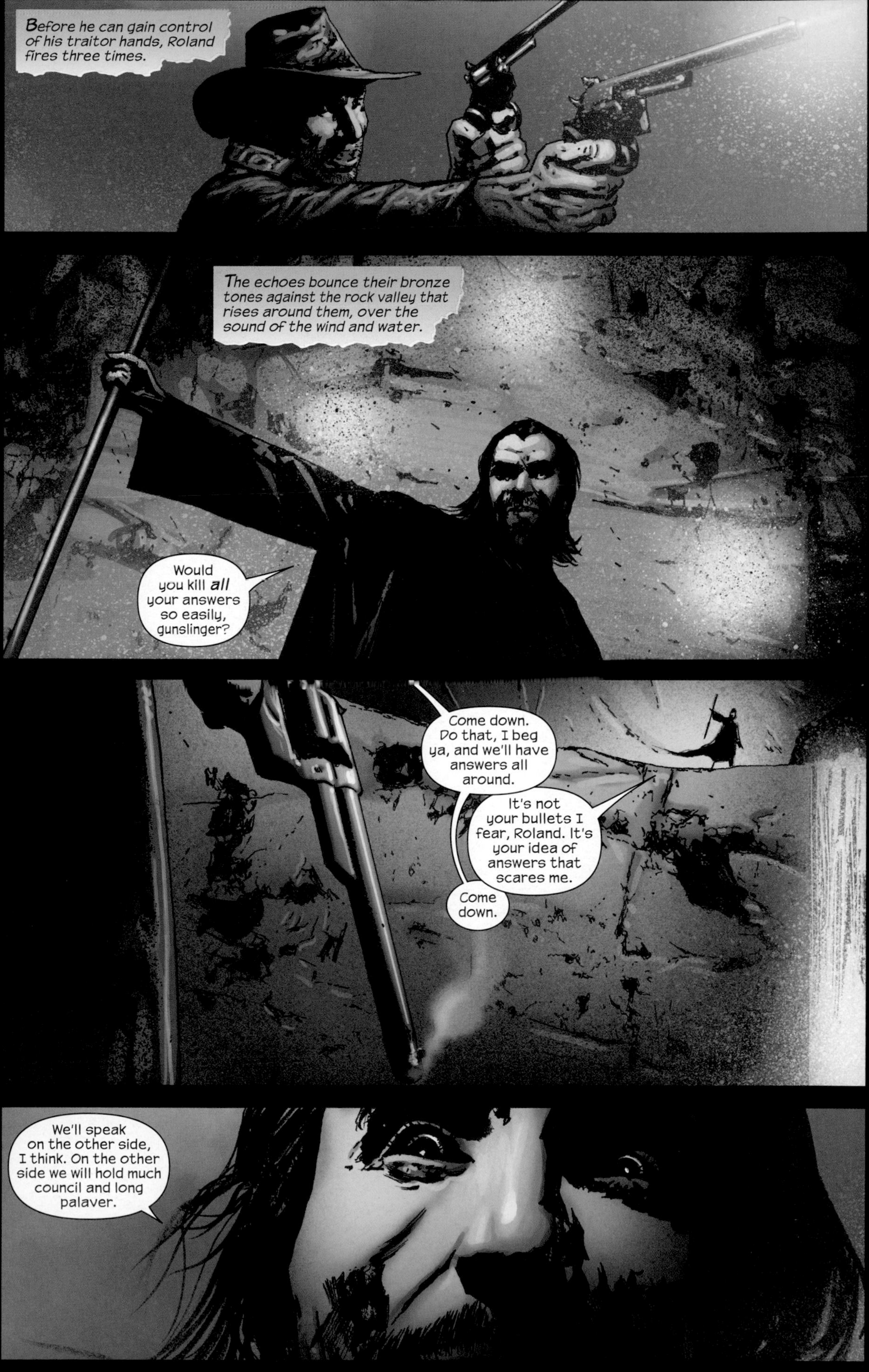
Before he can gain control of his traitor hands, Roland fires three times.
The echoes bounce their bronze tones against the rock valley that rises around them, over the sound of the wind and water.
Would you kill *all* your answers so easily, gunslinger?
Come down. Do that, I beg ya, and we'll have answers all around.
It's not your bullets I fear, Roland. It's your idea of answers that scares me.
Come down.
We'll speak on the other side, I think. On the other side we will hold much council and long palaver.

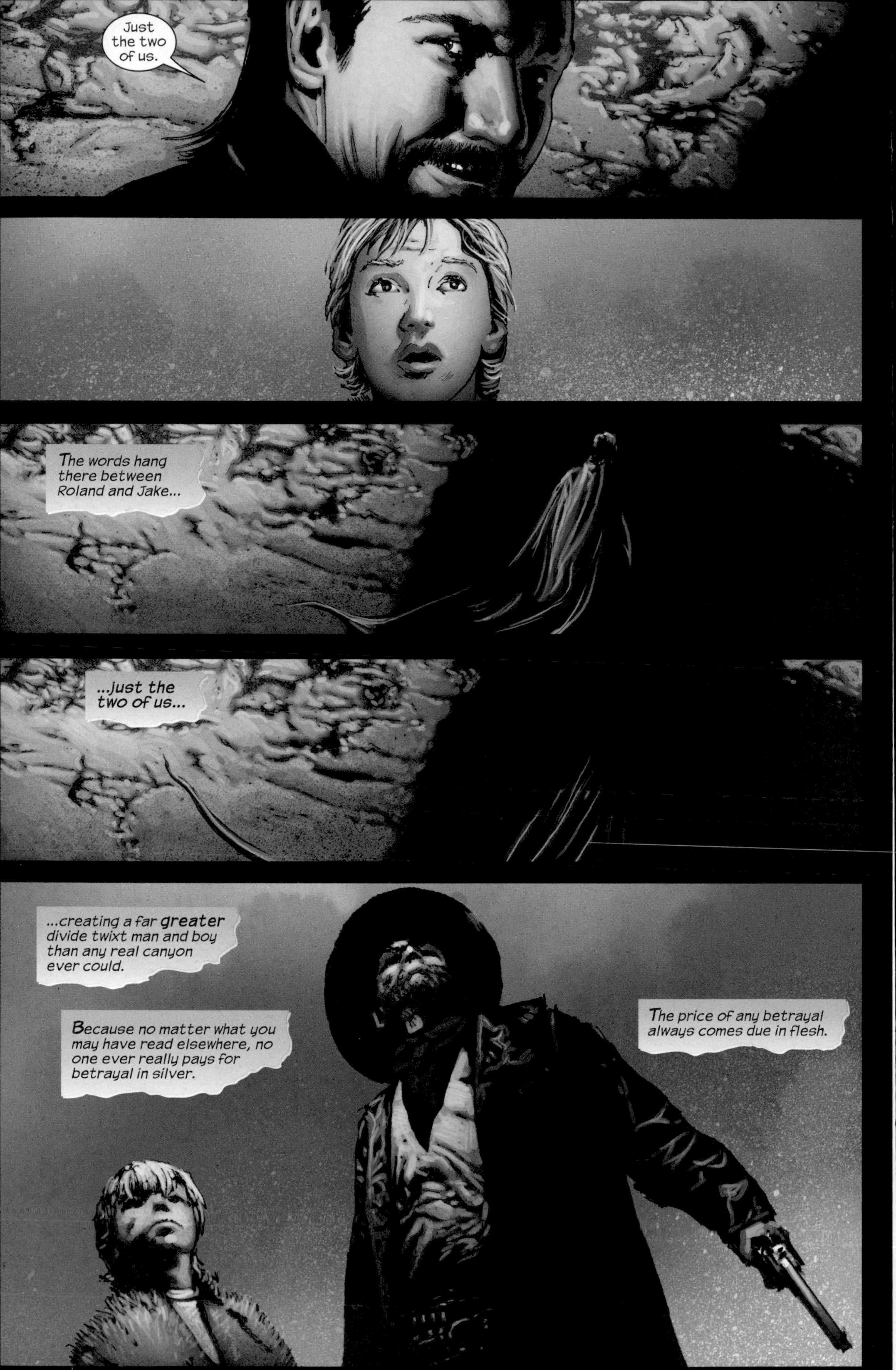
Just the two of us.
The words hang there between Roland and Jake...
...just the two of us...
...creating a far greater divide twixt man and boy than any real canyon ever could.
Because no matter what you may have read elsewhere, no one ever really pays for betrayal in silver.
The price of any betrayal always comes due in flesh.

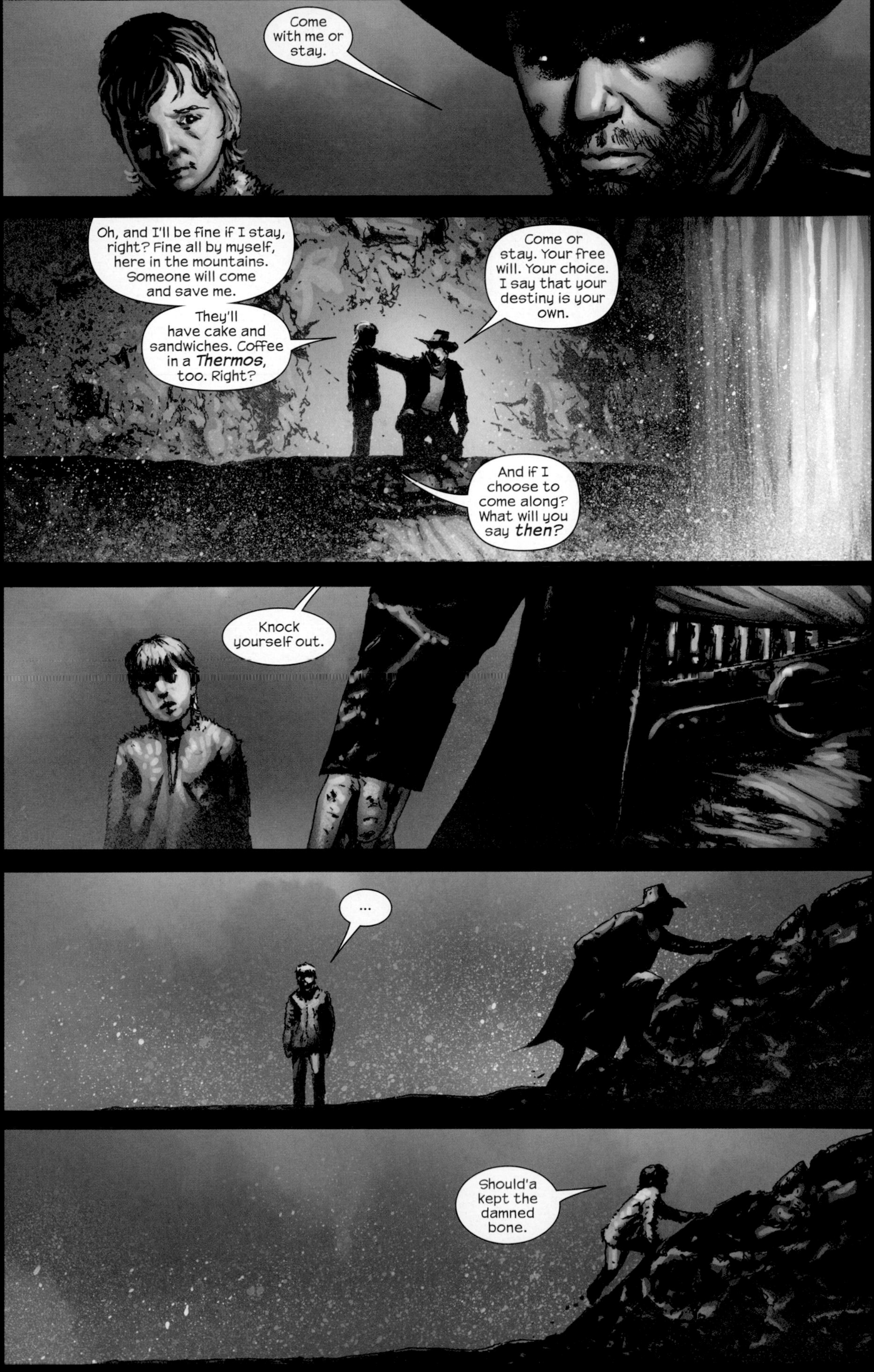
Come with me or stay.
Oh, and I'll be fine if I stay, right? Fine all by myself, here in the mountains. Someone will come and save me.
They'll have cake and sandwiches. Coffee in a *Thermos*, too. Right?
Come or stay. Your free will. Your choice. I say that your destiny is your own.
And if I choose to come along? What will you say *then*?
Knock yourself out.
...
Should'a kept the damned bone.

The story continues in *Dark Tower: The Gunslinger — The Man In Black*

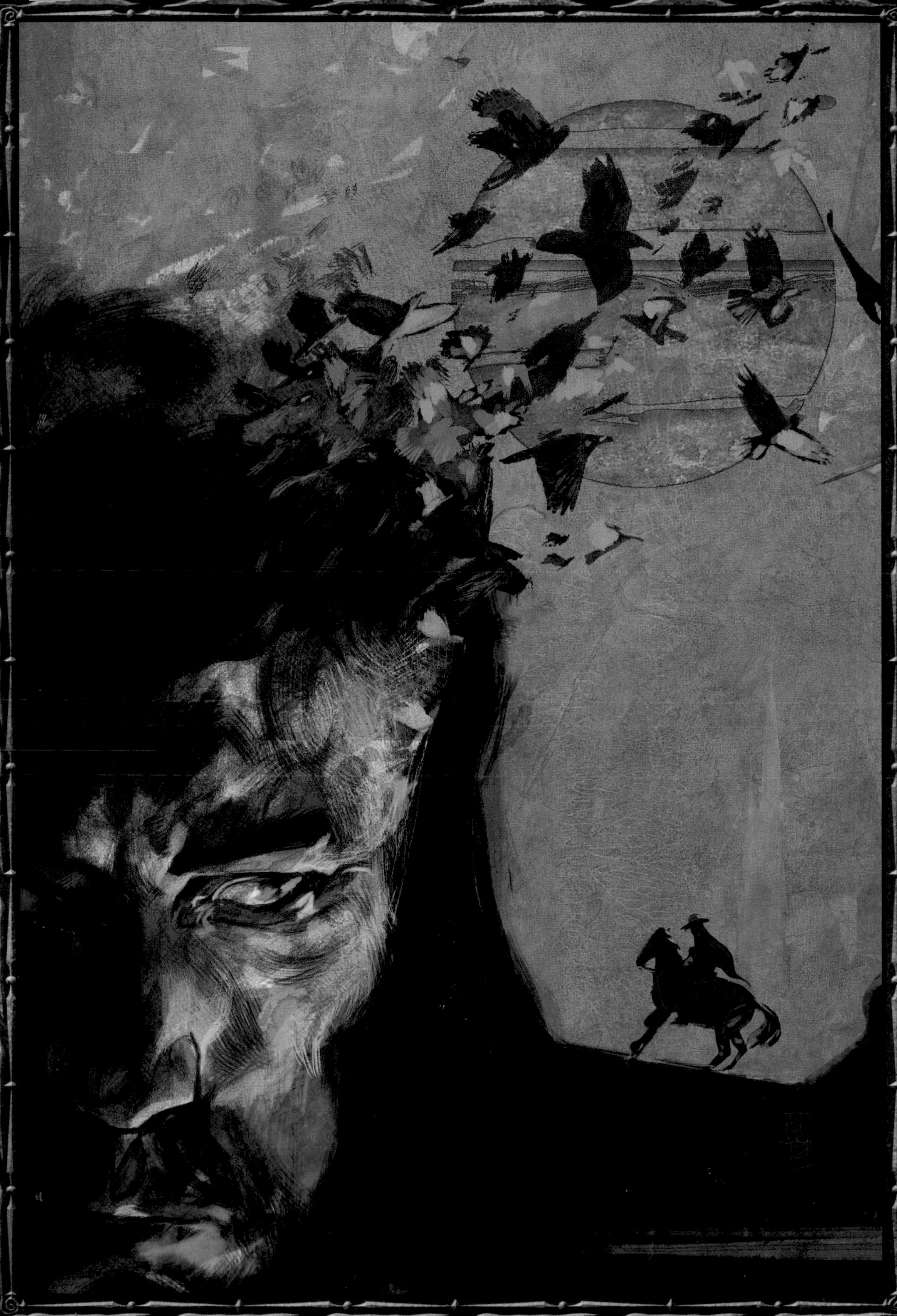

The Dark Tower: The Gunslinger — The Way Station #1 **Cover by Laurence Campbell & Richard Isanove**

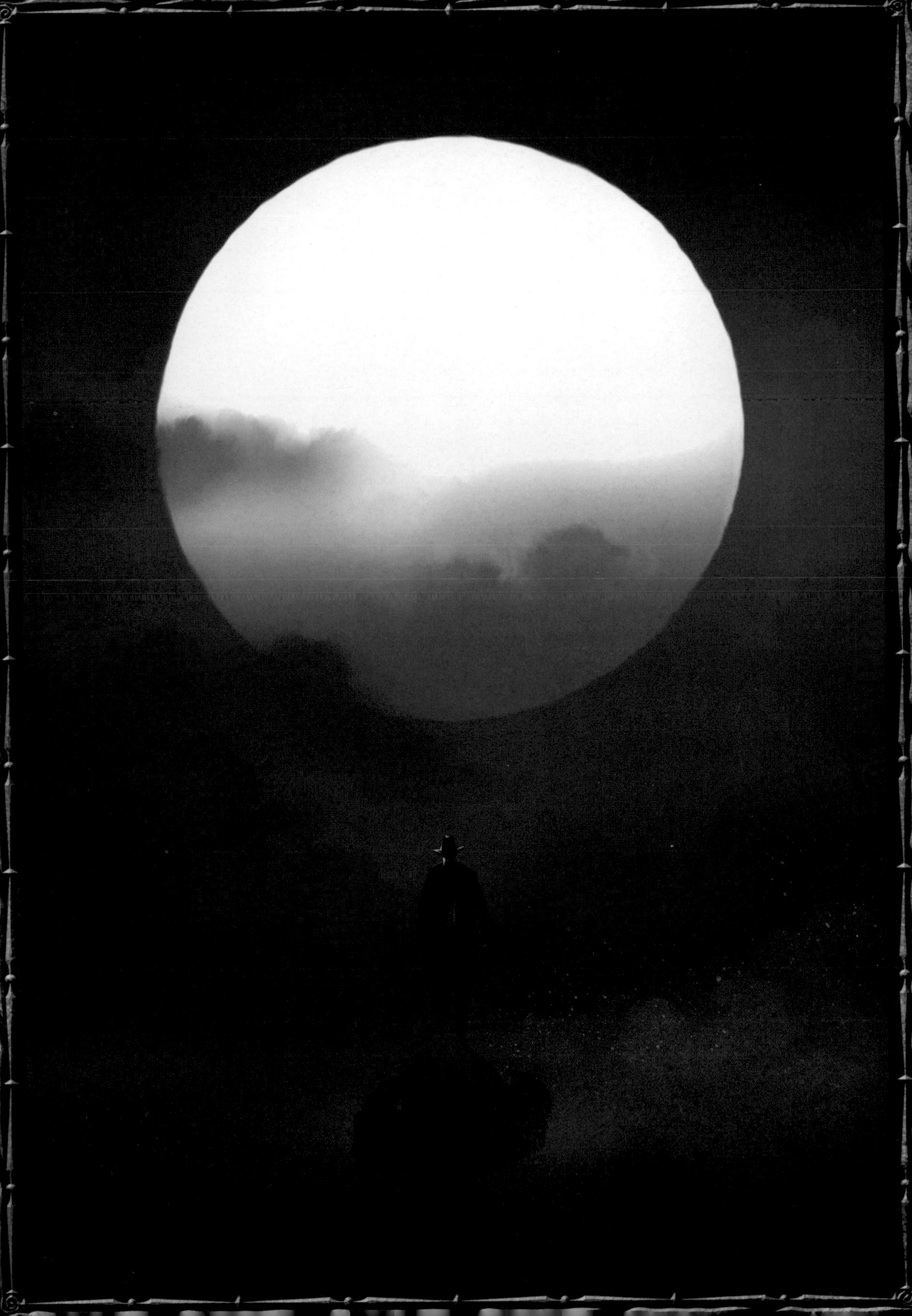

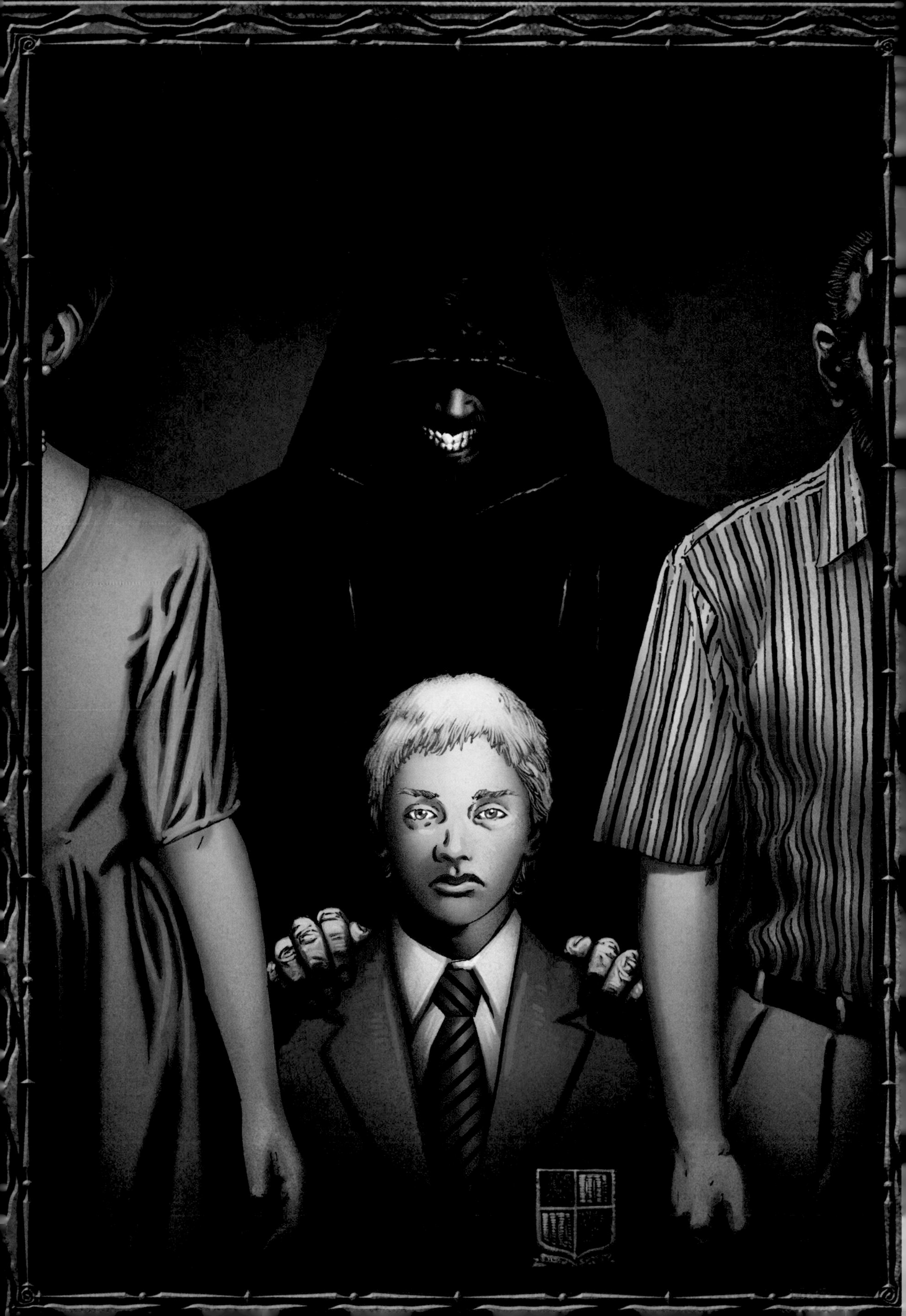

The Dark Tower: The Gunslinger — The Way Station #2 **Cover by Laurence Campbell & Richard Isanove**

The Dark Tower: The Gunslinger — The Way Station #3 **Cover by Laurence Campbell & Richard Isanove**

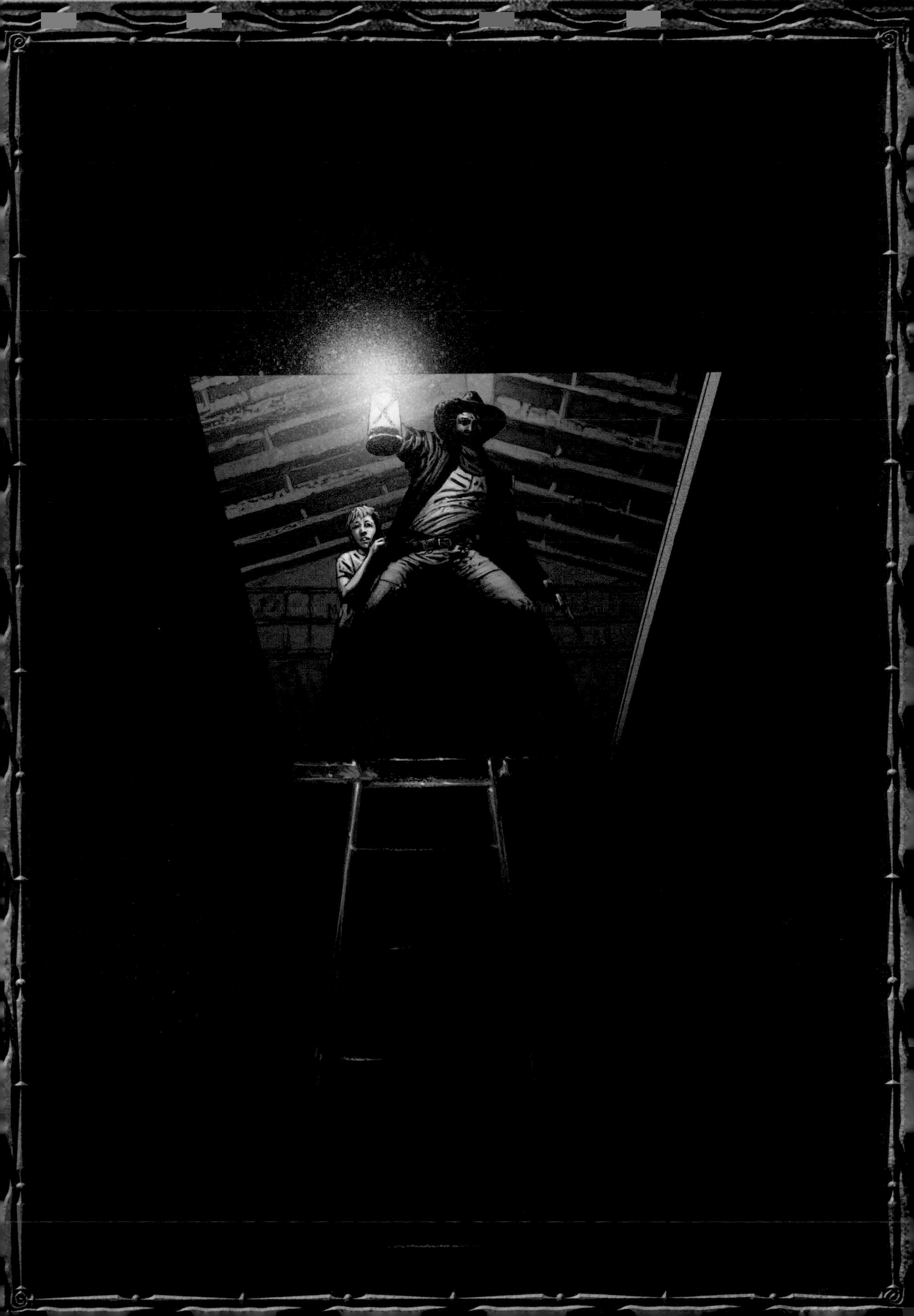

The Dark Tower: The Gunslinger — The Way Station #4 **Cover by Laurence Campbell & Richard Isanove**

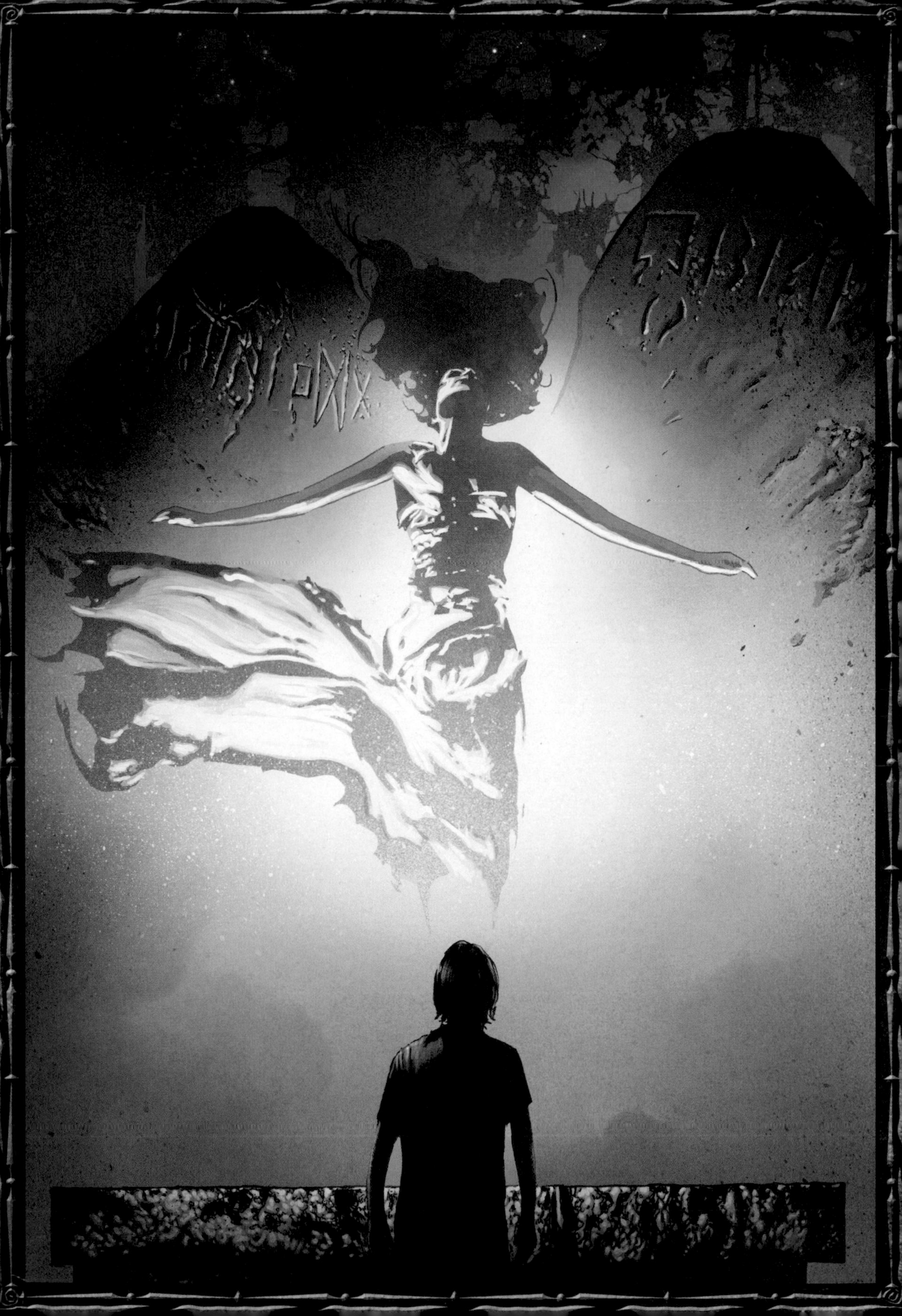

The Dark Tower: The Gunslinger — The Way Station #5 **Cover by Laurence Campbell & Richard Isanove**

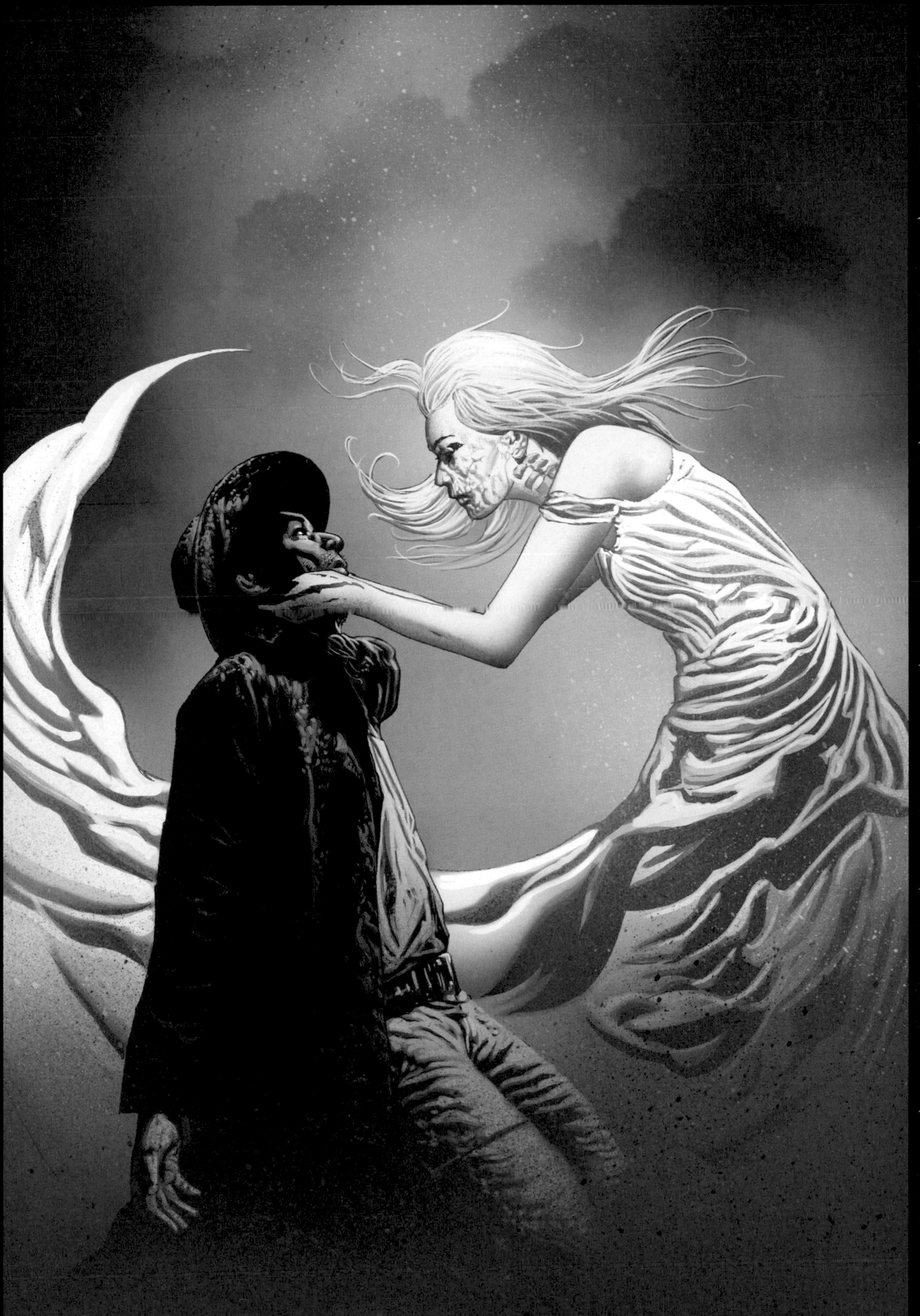

THE DARK TOWER READING CHRONOLOGY

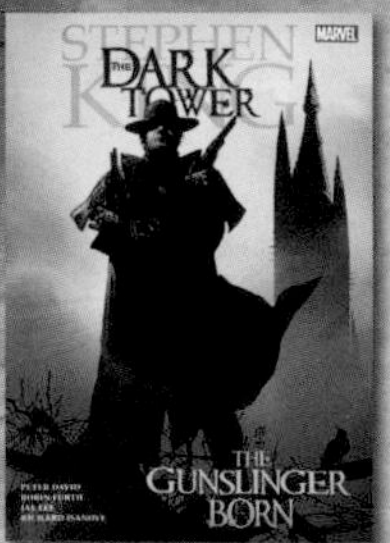
STEPHEN KING
DARK TOWER
THE GUNSLINGER BORN

THE DARK TOWER
THE GUNSLINGER BORN

BOOK 1

ISBN: 978 0 7851 2144 2

A man's quest begins with a boy's test. The world of Roland Deschain — the world of the Dark Tower — has been a thirty-year obsession for Stephen King. And now, King carries his masterwork of fantasy to Marvel, bringing stunning new textures to his epic story! *The Gunslinger Born* seamlessly integrates the wonder of Mid-World and the story of its hard-bitten cast of characters into the finest Marvel Comics storytelling tradition.

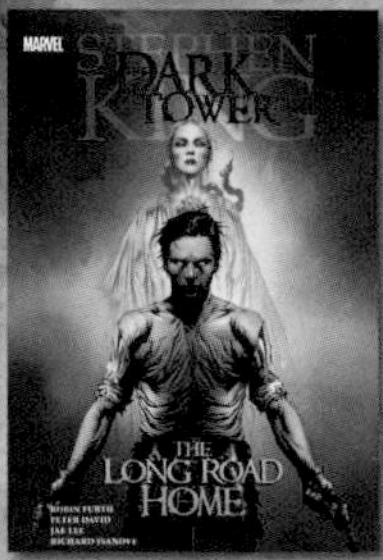
STEPHEN KING
DARK TOWER
THE LONG ROAD HOME

THE DARK TOWER
THE LONG ROAD HOME

BOOK 2

ISBN: 978 0 7851 2709 3

The gunslinger is born into a harsh world of mystery and violence. Susan Delgado is dead. Clay Reynolds and the vestiges of the Big Coffin Hunters are in pursuit. The ka-tet fragments as evil abounds. It will be a long road home. With Roland seemingly lost inside the haunted world of Maerlyn's Grapefruit, and the dark forces therein tugging at his soul, it will take all the courage of his ka-tet to get him out of Hambry and back home. But as the Dogan stirs, portending an evil of which Roland and his ka-tet have no ken, it may very well be that the gunslinger born walks a long road home to death.

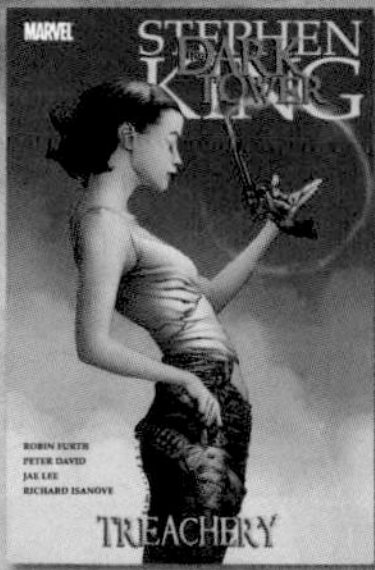
STEPHEN KING
TREACHERY

THE DARK TOWER
TREACHERY

BOOK 3

ISBN: 978 0 7851 3574 6

From the creative team that brought Roland's early adventures to life in *Dark Tower: The Gunslinger Born* and *Dark Tower: The Long Road Home* comes the third chapter of this dark saga of friendship, betrayal and a cosmic quest as conceived by master storyteller Stephen King.

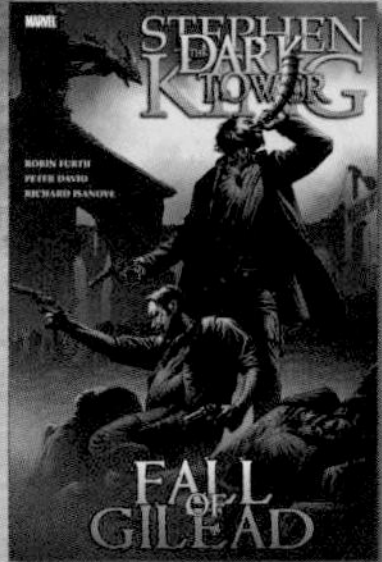
STEPHEN KING
DARK TOWER
FALL OF GILEAD

THE DARK TOWER
FALL OF GILEAD

BOOK 4

ISBN: 978 0 7851 2951 6

How could you have done it, Roland? How could you have killed your own mother? That's what everyone in Gilead's asking — even your grieving father. But you know the answer: Marten Broadcloak and one of them evil grapefruits. That's how. And while you rot in jail, the plot your matricide was only one small part of is wrapping its bloody and black tendrils around Gilead. Your town — the home of the Gunslingers — is the prize possession of the great enemy of the land, John Farson. And he means to have it. Gilead will fall, it will. And it will fall to the death of a thousand cuts. It started with your mother, yes, but it won't end there.

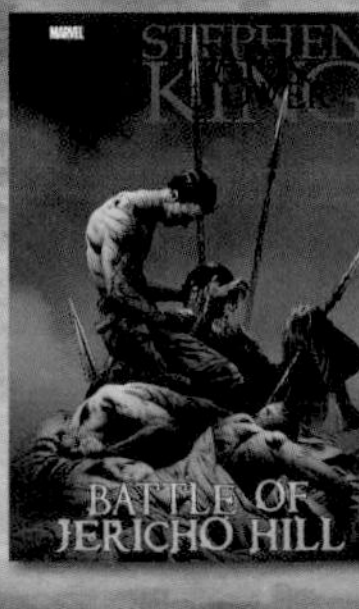
STEPHEN KING
BATTLE OF JERICHO HILL

THE DARK TOWER
BATTLE OF JERICHO HILL

BOOK 5

ISBN: 978 0 7851 2953 0

A brand-new story featuring Roland Deschain and his beleaguered ka-tet as they go on the run following the complete destruction of their beloved city of Gilead! And when such as Gilead falls, the pillars of reality itself — the six beams holding all of existence together — begins to crumble. The satanic plan of the Crimson King to return all of existence to the primal state of chaos is nigh.

THE DARK TOWER READING CHRONOLOGY

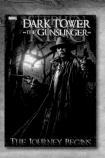

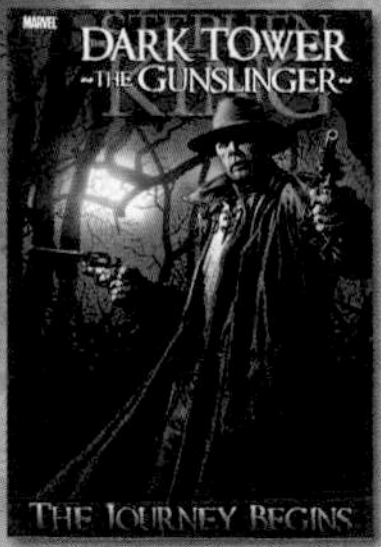
MARVEL
DARK TOWER
THE GUNSLINGER
THE JOURNEY BEGINS

THE DARK TOWER THE GUNSLINGER
THE JOURNEY BEGINS

ISBN: 978 0 7851 4709 1

The Barony of Gilead has fallen to the forces of the evil John Farson, as the Gunslingers are massacred at the Battle of Jericho Hill. But one Gunslinger rises from the ashes: Roland Deschain. As Deschain's limp body is tossed onto a funeral pyre...he's not dead yet. Roland escapes; as the last of the Gunslingers, he sets out in search of the mysterious Dark Tower — the one place where he can set the events of his out-of-synch world right. Along the way, Roland will battle the Not-Men, the Slow Mutants and more as he trails the Man in Black, the sorcerer who holds the key to Roland's finding the Dark Tower.

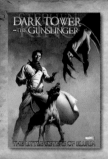

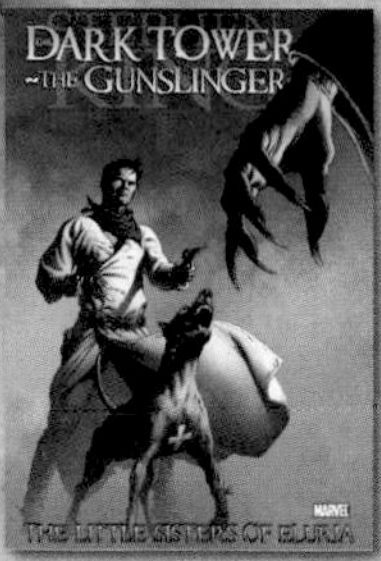
DARK TOWER
THE GUNSLINGER
MARVEL
THE LITTLE SISTERS OF ELURIA

THE DARK TOWER THE GUNSLINGER
THE LITTLE SISTERS OF ELURIA

ISBN: 978 0 7851 4931 6

Near death from an attack by slow mutants, Roland Deschain is taken in by a group of nuns who specialize in anything but the healing arts. These hideous, corpse-like creatures — the Little Sisters of Eluria — have murder on their twisted minds. And in his current condition, there's almost nothing the last Gunslinger can do to prevent their tender mercies from taking hold

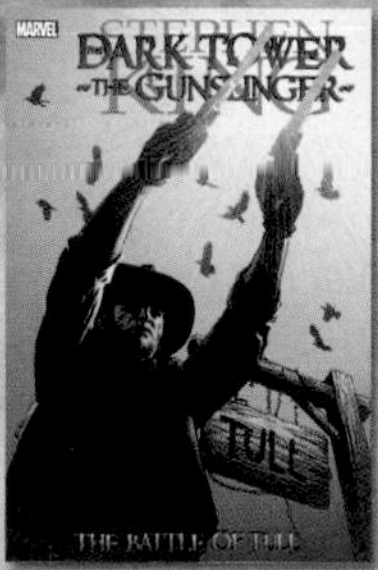
MARVEL
DARK TOWER
THE GUNSLINGER
TULL
THE BATTLE OF TULL

THE DARK TOWER THE GUNSLINGER
THE BATTLE OF TULL

ISBN: 978 0 7851 4933 0

Roland Deschain continues his epic search for the Man in Black. Instead, he finds Tull, the last stop of civilization. A town of devil grass, desert sand and despair It may seem Tull is on the very edge of the world, with nothing past the horizon but a steep fall to oblivion. But Roland believes otherwise: that beyond the limits of Tull lies a hidden truth that means everything to the fate of Mid-World. The Man in Black holds the key to that mystery, and Roland is going to keep following him — even through a trap set in Tull — to unlock it.

COLLECTING THE FIRST FIVE VOLUMES OF THE *NEW YORK TIMES* BEST-SELLING SERIES IN ONE OMNIBUS HARDCOVER

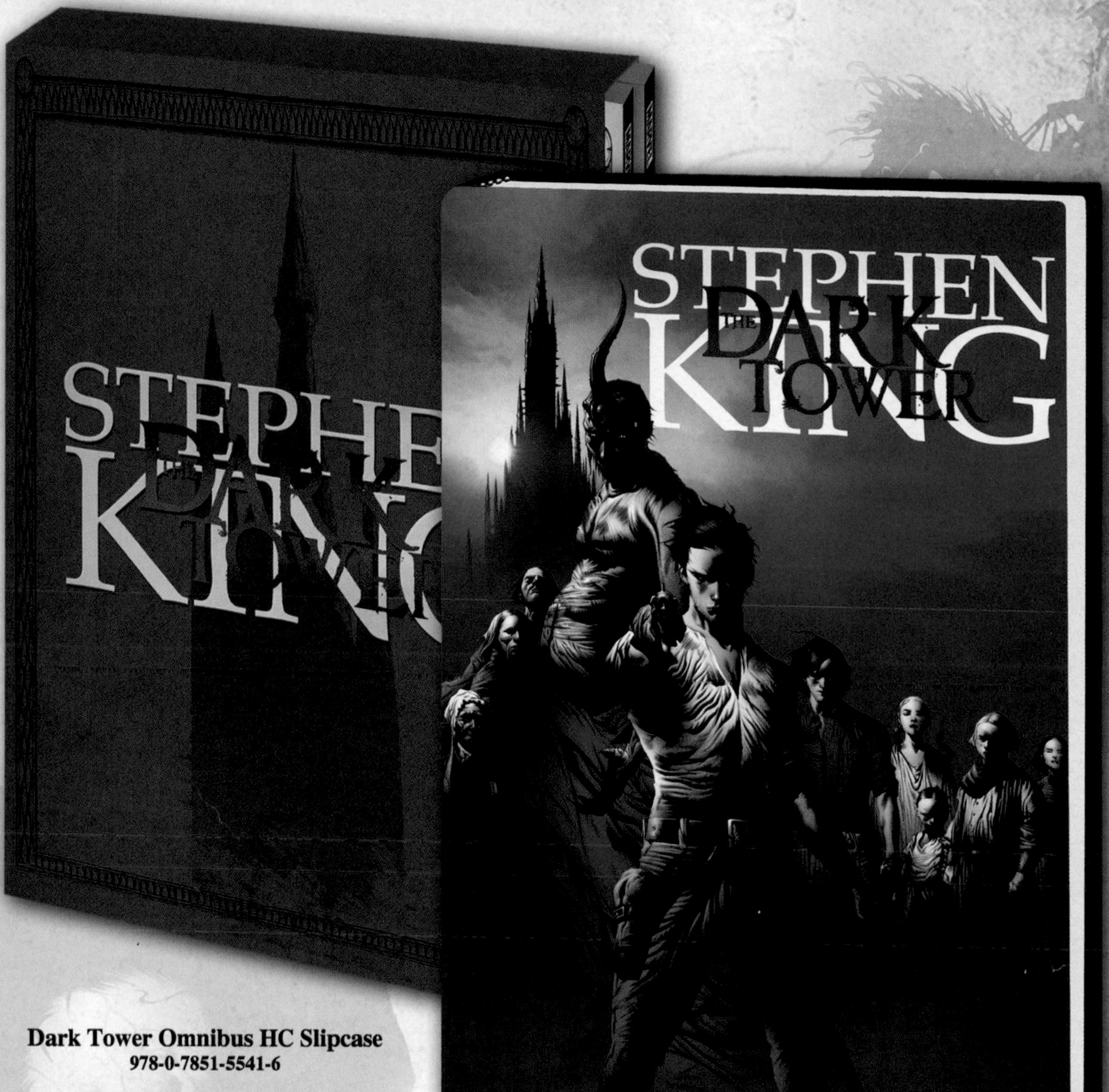
STEPHEN KING
THE DARK TOWER
STEPHEN KING
THE DARK TOWER

Dark Tower Omnibus HC Slipcase
978-0-7851-5541-6

"Marvel's Dark Tower series, with Robin Furth and Peter David and a team of exceptional artists travelling a path that is more than I imagined, ends here with this book of wonders. It's terrific!" – ***Stephen King***

Includes a Companion HC featuring material never before collected!

On Sale Now

MARVEL